THE LITTLE WHITE BOAT

THE LITTLE WHITE BOAT

MY SEARCH FOR THE JOY BEYOND TIME

HOWARD MARTIN

For Barclay and Doozie,
and Jenny Wren, too.

Contents

A Word or Two to Begin

I have walked through many lives,
some of them my own,
and I am not who I was,
though some principle of being
abides, from which I struggle
not to stray.
—Stanley Kunitz, "The Layers"

I'm writing this book for an audience of two. It's for my two beloved sons, Barclay, and Alexander, always and forever known as "Doozie." Now that I can enjoy the restful days of retirement, I want to tell them my story and try to explain, if I can, why their dad was like he was.

I want them to know about the formative years of my childhood, their deepest sorrows and sweetest joys, and introduce them to some of the colorful people from generations past whose blood still runs in their own and whose DNA is implanted in the very marrow of their bones.

I want them to know why I left one of the most scenic and welcoming countries on earth to come to the United States, where I met their beautiful mother and where—to my eternal gratitude—they were born. Along the way, I want to disclose what I learned from the shock of immersion in the vast cauldron of American culture, and why I decided to stay.

I also want them to know how the dark storms I encountered in my early years help set the course of my journey toward a harbor called Joy and how the peace I felt in a small white boat on the still waters of a New Zealand lake became the compass for a lifetime of exhilarating search and discovery.

There is, of course, a time for everything, and this is the time for me to write this story. If I had told it five years ago, it would have been too soon; I'd have had neither the perspective I needed to bring it near its conclusion nor the stillness I needed to say what is so difficult to say. If I had waited another five years, well, who knows?

While I have written these pages for an audience of two, I trust that, if they have fallen into your hands, they are also for you. As you read them, I ask only this—that you receive them in the spirit with which they are given: with kindness, compassion, and openness of heart.

Sit beside me now in the little white boat. Let's row together through the storms into the still waters. Beauty below us. Beauty above us. Beauty all around.

Howard Martin
Westwood Hills
Spring, 2021

CHAPTER 1

A Quiet Tender Joy

"It's the great mystery of human life that old grief passes gradually into a quiet tender joy."
—*Fyodor Dostoevsky,* The Brothers Karamazov

There were fearful ghosts in the house where I grew up, and they cried at night. Long, loud wails in the darkness, with a cold moon staring down like a blindman's eye. Unearthly yet familiar, they lingered in the half-light for years, until one by one, they faded into the hazy distance of time. I hear them still.

I have a clear memory of my young mother, barely 25 years old, weeping in the arms of a kindly neighbor. She is sitting on the sharp-edged wooden steps of our Bayswater home, with a kind lady cradling her head, wiping away her tears, and whispering sweet words of comfort. "You just go on and cry, girl," I hear the kind lady say. "It's too sad for words . . . you know it is." Moments pass, and my mother looks up into a watery sun, her face trembling. She takes the kind lady's hand in hers and pats it: "We'll get through it," she says. "We surely will," says the kind lady. "You bet."

I look on, as a child does, from a distance. I sense a dark shadow across my mother's world, till now bathed in undiminished sunshine.

I see her tears, but, protected by the merciful oblivion of childhood, I have no idea what her tears are for. Nor do I have any premonition that her tears would some day be my own. It was to be some time before I knew what had broken my mother's heart that day. My sister, Olive, had been born with a debilitating genetic disorder that would remain a mystery for years and would never be cured: Hurler Syndrome.

Mother and son, 1942

Hurler Syndrome is a severe form of mucopolysaccharide disorder (MPS) a genetically inherited abnormality (a missing enzyme) that interferes with the body's ability to metabolize sugars at the cellular level. Without this enzyme, sugars build up in the body's cells, causing irreversible damage to vital internal organs including the liver, spleen, and heart. It is extremely rare, occurring in about one in 100,000 births, and its symptoms vary widely in their severity. If both parents are carriers of the genetic markers connected to this condition, they have a one in four chance of having a child with Hurler Syndrome. My parents, Torrey and Rene, had three such children. Especially distressing for them, as with all such parents, is the fact that Hurler babies appear to be developing perfectly normally in their first few months of life. The changes come later and get progressively more severe.

When they carried Olive home from the hospital in 1945, cozily wrapped in a lambswool blanket, Torrey and Rene had no idea that what terrible forces were already at work in every cell of their baby's tiny body. With her bright hazel eyes, their little Olive was, to all appearances, a vibrant, thriving child. Even as a toddler she was full of life. She skipped and tumbled around the house, babbling and laughing, as if joining in the playfulness at the heart of the world. She sang with a sweet, true voice that rang high like the sound of a tui bird among the punga ferns. She wandered from room to room proudly displaying her pretty smock dresses, running her hands down her sides, making sure the fit was just right, checking the mirror to admire her reflected image. We called her "Ollie." There was an air of grace about her, a loveliness, like a dew-splashed daisy in the early morning sun.

Then, slowly, ominously, everything began to change. Not yet five years old, she would be running tip-toe in a game of hide and seek, then abruptly, stumble and fall. Crying softly, she would pick herself up, run a hand through her golden hair, then stumble again. And again. There were often bruise marks on her arms and legs, and painful knots on her head. Increasingly she suffered from earaches and colds. There were times when she struggled for breath, her lungs

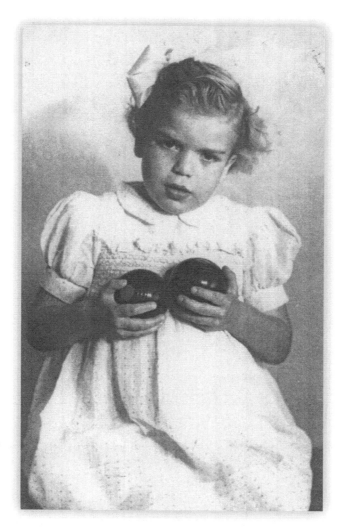

Olive,
"Ollie," age 3

rattling with congestion, her nose blocked with mucous, her tongue
hanging out to one side as if to clear a space for the vital passage of air.

It got worse. As seasons passed, Ollie's joints stiffened, her
facial features changed, her hair grew thick and coarse, and very
hard to brush, and her tummy ballooned like a tiny and unnatural
pregnancy—the result, we would later discover, of a grossly enlarged
liver and spleen. At some point, she stopped learning new words and,
more distressing, began losing the words she already knew. She got
thinner and weaker, unable to tell us where she was hurting, unable

to get out of bed, unable to feed herself, unable to swallow anything but oatmeal, pureed vegetables, and crushed bananas. We took turns scooping mush into her bird-like mouth with a teaspoon, hiding her medications in a small mound of mashed peas or soft-boiled carrots.

Long months turned into long years until it became clear that little Ollie would inevitably lose her battle for life. Day after day, night after night, with inexhaustible tenderness, my mother—not yet thirty years old—would touch the face of her dying child, dabbing her brow with a cool, wet cloth, and whisper comforting words: "Precious little one," she would say. "Mummy's beautiful girl. Go to sleep now. Go to sleep." Under the spell of her mother's presence, Ollie would finally close her eyes and surrender to her dreams. We would hear the creak of footsteps on the carpeted floor, a rustle of bedcovers, and then, at last, an uneasy quiet.

In those death-haunted days, the quiet was always uneasy. There were nights I lay awake listening as Ollie cried out in pain, fighting back the desire for sleep lest, upon awaking, I would find her gone. In the long hours of night, when the silence and the darkness merged into a void of nervy apprehension, I would pray that somehow there might be a miracle restoring her to us beautiful and whole. It was not to be.

Through all this, the kind lady was there. Her name was Vera Duncan. Once a week we'd hear the call of her sweet voice at the door and welcome her inside. She was there, as she had promised, to lend a loving hand. With quick, efficient energy, she shared the burdens of a growing household—sloshing through mounds of washing, pegging clothes on outdoor clotheslines, ironing and folding bed linens, wiping windows, scrubbing floors, and attending to the needs of a severely diminished little girl, now confined to bed in an upstairs sun-room. That, however, was not the half of it. With her bright laughing spirit, her winsome storytelling, and her resilient can-do attitude, Vera

Duncan became my mother's closest confidant and her heart's dearest companion. Ollie called her "Dunty" and so did we all.

Vera Duncan,
"Dunty,"
The kind lady

Through all the days of our anguish and laughter, Dunty offered herself to us in faithful, self-sacrificing love. From my earliest memory of her, when she sat beside my weeping mother on the wooden steps of our Bayswater home, to the last, when she welcomed me at the door of her cozy retirement flat in Epsom, she was the purest essence of kindliness. I shall never forget that last day I saw her. Radiant with spontaneous delight, she reached out and touched my face with her strong, warm hands: "Is it really my Howard?" she asked. "Oh, true! True!"

At the very heart of Dunty's deep humanity lay her unrehearsed spirit of gratefulness. She once said that life had offered her the opportunity to be happy or sad, and she had chosen to be happy. In every circumstance of life, she found a reason to give praise. She was grateful for the sun. She was grateful for the rain. She was grateful for the heat of summer. She was grateful for the cold of winter. She was grateful for work. She was grateful for her daily five-minute nap. She was grateful for a ride with a friend to work ("less time on the bus"). She was grateful for an hour-long commute by ferryboat and tram ("more time to watch the world waking up"). She was grateful for her home and garden. She was grateful for her five adoring daughters. She was grateful for her two sons. After her younger son, David, was gone—too soon, of cancer—she was grateful for his life and for the fact she'd had him living nearby as long as she did.

In 1974, Dunty drove with us to New Hampshire in "Buttercup," our vintage yellow VW bug. She was grateful for the coziness of the tiny back seat. She snuggled in as if she were a princess in a golden carriage. We stopped for a break at a city park in Illinois where we found a playground with a swing. She was grateful for the swing. She said the swing made her feel like a little girl again. She was grateful for feeling like a little girl again.

On another trip, she traveled with us to New Orleans, similarly grateful for every new turn in the road and for this new exotic destination. When we checked her into her room at a high-rise hotel with sweeping views of the Mississippi River, she was grateful for the light sparkling off the slow, wide waters below her. "Is my name Vera Duncan?" she asked, as if the sight before her could be nothing but a dream. "Someone pinch me. Please." Her sense of wonder was so irresistibly contagious, I felt amazement awakening within me, breaking like sunrise into my own tired, distracted brain. I've rarely been more surprised by wonder than I was in Vera Duncan's company that late afternoon above the great river.

Was Vera Duncan protected from the harsh winds of life so
that she could see only blessing? No one who knew her would have
said so. Her scarred hands and deep-lined face bore witness to great
sorrows and years of hard physical work. In difficult times, when
the Depression years cut especially deep, she made an art out of
necessity. She dug up homegrown potatoes. She collected eggs from
the backyard chicken coop and carried them to the kitchen in the folds
of her apron. She baked fat loaves of bread and puffy scones in the
wood-burning stove. After scrubbing and polishing her own home in
Bayswater, she scrubbed and polished the homes of others. She never
owned a car, rarely took a holiday, and hardly even stopped for lunch.
Yet, with an elegant balance of tough love, kindly forbearance, and
an uncomplicated faith in a loving God, she nurtured the lives of her
accomplished daughters and fine sons, and for her lovely guardianship
over their lives, earned their undying love.

If it was helpful to someone else, no effort was too much for Vera
Duncan, no journey too far. She ran—literally ran—from task to task,
singing in the midst of her chores or chattering gaily about the people
in her life. Her voice sounded like the bells of a village church, bright
and cheerful and deeply reassuring. As a child, I felt that if Dunty
was there, all must surely be well. She got me through some of the
darkest days of my young life, and, to this day, her memory remains an
unforgettable sign of the real possibility of greatness of soul. Abraham
Joshua Heschel once wrote: "It is gratitude that makes the soul great."
Vera Duncan was one of the great souls.

Despite Vera Duncan's devotion, however, and despite my father's
earnest prayers and my mother's inexhaustible care, death came to our
home anyway. One late autumn afternoon in 1955, in a cot upstairs
in her parents' bedroom, Ollie opened her exhausted eyes to a golden
light and drifted into her final sleep. She was ten years old.

The funeral was held in our living room at 27 Rahiri Road, Epsom. At age 14, I never felt more at home and never less. The people I most loved in the world were gathered there along with kindly neighbors and friends. I was conscious of other times I had sat in this space, reluctantly practicing Beethoven's "Für Elise" on the baby grand or gathered with my siblings around the fire while Dad entertained us with his stories or a tune on his violin.

Yet, at the same time, I felt completely alone, lost in a fog of bewilderment and grief. Seeking solitude, I sat on the floor under the dining room table, out of sight of my sister's tiny coffin, squeezing my eyes to stop the tears from coming. They came anyway. With my head between my knees, I wept for Ollie. I wept for my parents. I wept for myself. I wept for the whole sad world. At some point, my parents realized I was missing from the somber family circle and, inviting me to sit with them, pulled me in close. But it was cold comfort. In my deep, deep sadness, I was beyond consolation.

In a gray rain, we huddled together at Ollie's graveside—my mother, my father, and all of us. Dunty was there, too. Lonely in our own private griefs, yet each upheld by the others, we intoned the melody of a familiar hymn: "Safe in the arms of Jesus, safe on his gentle breast, there by His love o'ershaded, sweetly my soul shall rest." The wind seemed to catch our halting words and blow them back in our faces as heavy clods of damp clay thudded onto the small wooden box. My mother stood there, silent for a time, then turned her face toward the gathering mist.

After my sister Olive died, a tender melancholy, one that has never fully gone away, settled into my heart. Desolation seeped into the crevices of my life and left me bewildered and alone, shivering in the darkness. There were of course loving people around me, but there was only so much they could do to help me bear the weight of my sorrow. They had their own souls to comfort.

"The beauty of the world has two edges," wrote Virginia Woolf, "one of laughter, one of anguish, cutting the heart asunder." By the time I was fifteen, I was already beginning to feel in my blood the power of this universal paradox. In Ollie's brief time on the earth I had been a witness to the joy of life in its sweet, clear-eyed innocence and also its raw, blurred agony. Already torn asunder, my heart was about to feel the terrible beauty of the world cutting yet deeper into my soul. Not once, but twice.

On June 8, 1953, my youngest sister, Alison June, came into the world, followed on March 13, 1956, by my youngest brother, Geoffrey. They were both born—like their older sister—with Hurler Syndrome. Their stories are so intertwined in my memory that I cannot adequately disentangle them, and so I choose to tell them as one, offering snapshots of our life with them in the years after they were born.

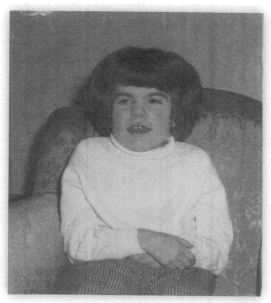

Alison,
"Ali," age 4

On good days, when I'm in my best frame of mind, I recall much about those days that was good. I have dim memories of Alison

Geoffrey, "Jeffie,"
age 5

and Geoffrey as babies, glowing with good health, wriggling with possibility, eyes wide open—as most children's are—to the wonders around them. I remember the soft creek of basinets, the clatter of small toys, the gentle chirp of tiny voices, the urgent, needy cries, and the soothing symphony of laughter, play, and song.

I see them as growing children, when the differences between them were beginning to appear. By now we knew them affectionately as "Ali" and "Jeffie." I have fleeting images of Ali cross-legged on the floor, singing in the softest of tones, repeating the refrains of her favorite songs over and over again. "I'm happy today," she would sing. "I'm happy today, in Jesus' love, I'm happy today. He's taken all my sins away, wop why, I'm happy today." (Her use of "wop why" instead of "that's why" always gave us a small rush of delight, and we loved to quote her).

Wriggling her way into a pile of cushions, she would turn the pages of her favorite children's book, her face pulled in close, her feet bobbing like marshmallows on the end of a stick. Captivated by the stories of Cinderella and Hansel and Gretel, she would take wide-eyed delight in the discovery of each new image and each new word. "Luh-ha-lee," she would say, intending to say "lovely" and pronouncing it like "cuppa tea." "Luh-ha-lee." It was one of the first words she ever spoke, and also one of the last.

Jeffie was, by contrast, a spitfire of compulsive motion. He bounded through the house like a fantastical Puck, laughing, giggling, telling stories, and playing tricks. Nothing pleased him more than performing for an audience. Ransacking his parents' wardrobes for costumes and props, he would create his own original cast of characters: a sophisticated lady teetering on high heels with a string of pearls around her neck, a gardener in oversized work-boots snipping the edges of the lawn with a long-handled trimmer; a fireman in a floppy rain-hat pouring water on an imaginary blaze with a few yards of rubber hose; or a policeman up to his elbows in long, white gloves directing the traffic on a busy street corner. "Get moving, you!" he'd say. "I haven't got all day!"

While there is joy in the memories of Ali and Jeffie in their early childhood days, there is little such joy over what happened in subsequent years as they surrendered to the terrible destiny of their genetic code. We looked on helplessly as laughter turned to tears, as dances of innocent joy and delight turned to ominous falls, and innocent songs turned to cries of pain. The lurid snakes of suffering and death appeared once more and continued to roil beneath the surface, threatening at times to pull us into the depths. The ghostly shadows were back.

In the late hours, another little girl cries out in pain. This time, it's Ali. Long descending agonized wails. Everyone's awake. We hear the hurried words "Ali!" "Ambulance." "Emergency Room." A car engine cranks into life, headlights flash on the bedroom wall, driveway gravel crunches, the sound of the engine fades in the distance. An uneasy silence, worried thoughts, fitful sleep. Deep in the night, car lights once more. Doors bang shut. More whispered words, the muffled strains of a song. "London Bridge is falling down...My fair lady." Ali is asleep now. We fall back into our own slumbers, another despairing prayer in our hearts. My mother's own prayer, in the silent center of her heart, was that of a caressing touch and whispered song.

At times it seemed there was disintegration everywhere, like the collapse of a tunnel in dry sand. A homework assignment laid out for school is trashed and left on the floor. A holiday trip is canceled. A visit to a relative's house is cut short. A doctor comes. Our hopes are briefly raised. He shakes his head in perplexity and leaves. Our small hopes fade. Another doctor, another ambulance ride, another sleepless night. A poopy pile is left on the bathroom floor. We clean it up. Another poopy mess runs down a bare leg onto the seat of the car. We drive to the grocery store and back, then clean it up. A paperback book is bitten and torn away at the corners, terrible tokens of a little girl's physical distress and mental anguish. We put the book back on the shelf.

The sands kept falling. An agitated little boy grabs a carving knife from the cutlery drawer and chops at the keys of the baby grand piano. He finds a screwdriver somewhere and carves deep gouges on the surface of an antique dresser. He opens a can of white paint in the basement and paints his way around the house, over the face of the dark oak grandfather clock, along the side of the garage, and across the polished doors of a neighbor's prized black Vauxhall sedan. He unwraps a pound or two of hamburger purloined from the refrigerator and squeezes fistfuls of it over the dining room window. He pours a bottle of ink into the aquarium and leaves a tiny world of desolation, the white bellies of the fish drifting upside down on the surface of the grey green water. "It's not the end of the world," says his infinitely patient mother. "They're only things."

It's Sunday dinner in 1958: roast lamb with mint sauce, roast potatoes, cauliflower smothered in rich cheese sauce, green peas, a sprinkling of laughter and lively conversation. Then it's time for "pudding" (our word for "dessert"). Eager to lend a helping hand, Jeffie leaps from the table and disappears into the kitchen. With his undersized knuckly hands, he lifts a wide crystal bowl from the refrigerator and promptly loses control. The bowl explodes on the tiled floor. Standing in a mess of broken glass and fruit salad, he wails: "Aaaaaahhhhhhhh." He's heartbroken. His mother races to take him in her arms. "You only wanted to help, I know you did," she says. "Don't cry little boy. It's all right. It's all right." And as the wails subside, we all get busy cleaning up the mess.

My mother lays no blame. Fully aware that her son's serial mayhem is without malice, she sees it as the expression of a body being tortured from within and a brain falling apart at its core. In quiet surrender, she holds him in her arms and sings to him. "Incy Wincy spider climbs up the water spout. Down came the rain, and washed the spider out. Out came the sun and dried up all the rain. And Incy Wincy spider climbed up the spout again." Feeling a warm rush of safety, the little boy settles for a time against his mother's breast and, with trembling lips, joins in the song.

Toward the end, there is no comfort left for him. Compelled by energies he could not understand or control, Jeffie goes on destructive rampages from room to room, bringing dangers and disorders even the serenest of mothers could not bear. She must at last surrender her youngest child to the care of others—a care center for severely disabled children, where Jeffie wears a kind of bicycle helmet to protect him from mortal injury—and it breaks her heart.

At the family table, our father prays for Ali and Jeffie as he had for Ollie. The heavens are silent. The complications of severe disability multiply. The besieged bodies of our siblings get weaker. Each in turn, now passive and emaciated, curl up upon themselves and, taking their last difficult breath, drift away. Jeffie is the first to go. Then, within a year or so, it is Ali.

In each case, we stand by a small grave cut into the green sod and watch as a tiny wasted body is lowered into the silence of the earth. We have no choice but to let them go. Bravely singing of resurrection, we offer our baffled cries to a darkening sky—a cold, and lonely, broken alleluia.

What can I say? For more than quarter of a century, we had been in an intense conversation with suffering and death. There had been days when, riding my bike from school, I would approach the doors of home in breathless silence, hoping for any cue—the strain of a song, the cheery intonations of an ordinary conversation, maybe the radio playing—to reassure me the eyes of one or the other of my siblings were still open to the light of day. But now those eyes were shut forever, and I was confronted once more by the blunt reality of death. For me, the days of easy awareness of the eternal were over. The world was now a much darker place than I had thought in the sweet innocence of early childhood. The idea of a loving God, so easy to accept in the abstract, was now, at best, open to question. Paradise was a fading memory—if not altogether lost.

All this time, my mother had kept alive her trust in life. For twenty-five years she had surrounded her stricken children with tenderest care. She had bathed them, dressed them, brushed their teeth, administered their medicines, changed the linens on their beds, and cleaned up their messes. With loving arms, she had embraced their fragility. With the softest of words, she had calmed their anxieties and fears. With raw, chapped hands, she had washed their soiled cloth "nappies" (diapers) and sung them to sleep at night. All the while she had taken care of five other children, including me, each of whom had felt no diminishment of her affection, each one feeling uniquely blessed by the radiance of her smile and the reassuring warmth of her presence.

Before the ravages of MPS: Ali, Ollie, and Jeffie (pencil sketch by Vicki Marshall)

One dark winter's morning, I woke to a familiar combination of sounds. It was dark outside. A hard rain lashed at the leaded windows and a raw wind thumped in quick bursts under the eaves. I could hear the labored rattle and clank of the washing machine in the washhouse below my bedroom, and amidst the hubbub, I could hear my mother's voice, singing one of her favorite folk songs. "I will take you home, Kathleen, across the ocean wild and wide." There was a haunting loveliness to it, a reassuring quality like the peal of bells in a picturesque English village, and I counted it a blessing.

For my mother, there was a bittersweet poignancy to that particular song. Whenever she sang it, her heart was filled with memories of her late mother, Annie Kennedy, who in 1905 had left her home in distant Cumbria in England's far north for Wellington, New Zealand, where her fiancé, Arthur Elliott, was waiting for her. She remembered how her father had promised to take her mother "back home" someday to the lovely dales of the Eden Valley. I have a photograph of the two of them, Annie and Arthur, suntanned and finely dressed, walking in the gardens of Scarborough Fair—the "Scarborough Fair" celebrated in Simon and Garfunkle's song—on the only trip they ever took back to the country of their birth.

Annie and Arthur Elliott at Scarborough

To this day, nothing so deeply connects me to the courageous spirit of my mother's immigrant parents, their sheer audacity in pursuit of a dream, the sadness of their separation from what they had once called beloved, than the words and melody of that song, "I will take you home, Kathleen…"

There were other songs, too. When the world blossomed with flowers in spring and the fruit hung heavy on the trees, she sang of a place where her own heart seemed in tune with a divinity beyond time. Even now, I can hear her high, pure notes filling the house like light: "I come to the garden alone, while the dew is still on the roses, and the voice I hear falling on my ear, the Son of God discloses." When the world was dark and difficult, she sang of hope whispered in the silent center of her being: "Soft as the voice of an angel, breathing a lesson unheard / Hope with a gentle persuasion, whispers a comforting word." When disappointment came in waves, she sang of other hearts shattered like hers, and took courage from remembering the beauties of other times: "I wandered today to the hills, Maggie / To watch the scene below / The creek and the creaking old mill, Maggie / As we used to long, long ago."

Because of childhood years in such a home with such a mother, I found myself wrestling perhaps earlier than most with intense feelings of life's fragility, while at the same time sensing that I was held in a place of ultimate safety. I knew at some deep, intuitive level that, though life was a contingent thing, I was not lost. Somehow, I knew I was held in time by silken threads of loving-kindness, and there was at the core of my being a place where I belonged. I owed—and still owe—much of that inner sense of confidence to her. My debt to her is such that I can do no less than turn back to other pages in her story.

CHAPTER 2.

Glimpses of a Higher Love

"The sunlit meadow beyond the confining dark."
—*Frederick Buechner*

I like to imagine that my mother's name was given to her out of an intuition that she would grow up to be a woman of remarkable feminine grace. Her given name at birth was Annie Mae Elliott, but from her earliest days everyone called her "Rene." The name Rene is of French origin and carries the idea of rebirth and renewal—"renée" translates as "newly born."

In retrospect, it seems entirely appropriate to characterize that little girl, born to a farming family in the Waikato district of New Zealand, as one who would bring to her family line a new flowering of loving energy. There was about her an infectious vitality, a great forbearance, and deep, unworldly serenity. The very word "serenity," especially when spoken aloud, carries the echoes of her name.

She was a rosy-cheeked beauty, an eighteen-year-old nurse in training, when she met my father. There must have been a day when, riding home on Trixie, her pony, the air fragrant with arborvitae and eucalyptus, she became aware of a shift in tone around the house, an unaccustomed brightness and levity that seemed to have lifted the spirits of everyone on the farm. This new energy emanated from a charismatic young Aucklander, a wise-cracking, story-telling character who had driven 80 miles in his Willys sedan to measure her dad's waist and chest for an expensive new suit.

His name was Torrey Martin. It was in the nature of his job to make business calls on that farmhouse in Manawaru, and so, under a great spreading macrocarpa tree, with dairy cows calling from the paddocks and lambs skipping in the emerald green pastures, their love story began. He saw in her a manifestation of alluring shyness and fresh-faced loveliness. She saw in him an embodiment of handsome, wavy-haired vitality and extroverted, fun-loving good humor.

Before they were married: Rene (pronounced Reenee) Elliott, Torrey Martin.

They were married in 1940 at the St. James Presbyterian Church in Te Aroha and took their honeymoon amidst the dazzling splendors of the west coast of New Zealand's South Island.

It is a great blessing for all of us that, as we set out on the journey of our lives, none of us knows what lies ahead. If we did, would any of us dare the first step? The young woman who tiptoed so prettily from that country church in 1940 was surely blessed in her innocence. She did not know that, among the joys and sorrows to be expected in any human life, she was heading for a sea of troubles.

She knew nothing of how three of her eight children would suffer catastrophic disabilities. Nor did she know of the debilitating asthma attacks that would one day wrack the body of the confident young man at her side, or of his humiliating failure in business, the weight of which would fall equally upon her. She knew nothing of the sorrows to come nor of the unusual grace with which she would be able to bear them.

Newlyweds

I have often looked back on my mother's family heritage, as I did on our 2016 journey to Penrith and the surrounding Cumbrian countryside, trying to find the origins of this remarkable flowering of grace. I've looked at family photographs, unpacking where I could the store of family memories. I've spent hours poring over the records on Ancestry.com and read histories of the English Borderlands that included any references to her lines of descent. After many hours of searching, I have come upon very little that could explain the resilience and loveliness of Rene's life. Some of the clues I found, in fact, seemed to offer contrary indications. But not all. There were here and there signs of fierce, unyielding physical endurance in her ancestral line, and one story that must be told of a great soul and a great kindness.

On her father's side, my mother was one of the Elliotts, a family that had for centuries made their living as farmer-laborers on the harsh, rocky terrain of the Borderlands between England and Scotland. In the fifteenth and sixteenth centuries, the Elliotts were notorious as cattle thieves—reivers—who, under cover of fog and night, mounted daring raids on surrounding hamlets and farms. During those years, when the name "Elliott!" went out through the Liddesdale Valley—now on the Scottish side of the border—hundreds of men, armed with crossbows, axes, and broadswords, would answer the family's call. Faithfulness to the family name (in those days spelled many different ways, including "Elliot" or "Ellot" or even "Allyett") was paramount. Any man who refused the call was subject to a very rough justice: drowning, lynching, or exile.

Riding their quick little ponies into the moonless dark, the Elliott boys would ride for miles—sometimes thirty miles or more—over the untracked dales, descend upon an estate or castle in the English Marches, hold the terrified inhabitants hostage, and guide the stolen herds back to their home base. By means of bloody mayhem and

plunder, and in the absence of border control by hapless English and
Scottish kings, the Elliotts accumulated considerable wealth in cattle
and land. On several occasions they laid siege to the Hermitage Castle,
a forbidding royal fortress in Liddesdale, tossing out the royal keepers
living there and claiming the castle, at least for a time, as their own
family seat. There were many tough fighters among them, but perhaps
the greatest of them all, especially in family lore, was a fierce young
outlaw named "Little Jock."

The Hermitage

There is a story from the mid 16th century about how Little Jock
Elliott came face to face with James Hepburn, Earl of Bothwell, third
husband of Mary Queen of Scots. For some time, the Earl of Bothwell
had been the Keeper of the Hermitage on behalf of the Queen. He
had recently made a successful raid on nearby Elliott lands, killing
numerous fighters and locking up forty Elliott boys in the Hermitage's
dank dungeon.

In a rage of revenge and wounded pride, Little Jock calls for a
counterattack. A hundred sinewy Elliott fighters mount their "hobby"
horses and ride at breakneck speed across the moorlands into the

armored line of the Earl's defenses striking and retreating, and striking again. In the midst of the mayhem, the ground streaming with blood, Bothwell catches sight of Little Jock and yells out a challenge: "Thee and me, Little Jock, you bastard, one on one, for the others." It is one of the more fateful challenges in English-Scottish history. They agree to a duel. White flags go up. Fighting stops. And now it's Little Jock Elliott alone on his grey-flecked borderland pony facing Bothwell high on his armored courser. David and Goliath. For a negotiated truce.

Bothwell is first to strike. He fires a single shot from his gar (pistol) and hits Little Jock in the neck. The outlaw falls backward from his hobby horse, and lies face-down on the rocky ground, clutching a dagger against his ribs. In eager triumph, Bothwell flings off his helmet, and, on foot now, approaches Little Jock's inert body. He raises his sword to strike a final blow across the fallen fighter's exposed neck. In the split second between the ascent and descent of Bothwell's sword, however, Little Jock kicks sideways, springs to his feet, and slashes Bothwell across the face with his dagger, then strikes again and again in quick succession, leaving deep gashes around Bothwell's eyes, neck, and wrists. Bothwell crashes to his knees. Little Jock points his dagger at Bothwell's bleeding eyes and backs away. Jock is helped back onto his horse and, with his cousins and brothers alongside, rides off into the foggy dark. Within minutes, no more than a mile from the scene, Little Jock collapses across the neck of his horse and dies.

Bothwell is grievously wounded. His attendants rush to his rescue, lift him onto a cart, and carry him back to the what they suppose to be the sanctuary of the Hermitage. A terrible surprise awaits them. In Bothwell's absence, the imprisoned Elliott boys have freed themselves and taken control of the fortress. They refuse Bothwell admittance to his own place of refuge. After tense negotiations, the Elliott boys agree to open the doors in exchange for their own free passage from the castle and a return of all stolen lands. The Elliotts ride off to plunder and pillage another day.

The humiliated Bothwell never fully recovers. While recuperating at the Hermitage, he receives a brief visit by the beleaguered Mary Queen of Scots, who rides thirty dangerous miles from Jedburgh through Elliott-held lands to see him. But Mary's visit is not enough to save their relationship or the Catholic cause in Scotland. Soon after her daring expedition, Bothwell is dispossessed of his title and lands by an act of the Protestant Scottish parliament and is hounded into exile to Norway. He dies chained to a pillar in a Danish prison.

Thus it was that the Elliotts, who took no consistent side in the conflict between Catholic and Protestant in Scotland, were not only heavily involved in the long history of lawlessness in the Borderlands, but also played some significant part in the final ignominious fall of Mary Queen of Scots and her consort. The voice of Little Jock boasting cheekily of his victory over the Bothwell is recalled in a 17th-century Borderland ballad:

> *Grim Bothwell frae me got a claw*
> *He'll never forget till he dee.*
> *I'll keep my ain head wi' my hand,*
> *And my neck free from the hanging tree,*
> *As lang as I waiggle a brand—*
>
> *Oh! wha daur meddle wi' me?*
> *Wha daur meddle wi' me?*
> *O, my name is Little Jock Elliott,*
> *And wha daur meddle wi' me?*

The Elliotts paid a heavy price for their distain of the rule of law. In 1603, King James VI of Scotland also became King James I of England, thus uniting the two kingdoms. Among his first actions was to deal with the chaos in the Borderlands. Combining the military forces of both England and Scotland, he took brutal revenge on the Elliotts, hanging numerous heads of families, confiscating lands, and forcing some remnants of the clan into exile in Ireland. He imposed harsh new laws on anyone bearing the name of Elliott, forbidding any single family to own a horse valued at more than thirty pounds, and making it a requirement that any lands left in the hands of an Elliott could only be passed on from father to eldest son. Three centuries later, this rule of primogeniture would be the cause of great mischief in the Elliott family of New Zealand twelve thousand miles away.

After dispossessing the reiver clans, King James I secured the borders, drawing the line between the two countries much as it remains to this day. Thus it was that, in the early 1900s, some of the Elliotts were living in Scotland, others in England, many of them struggling to make a living as laborers on lands they no longer owned. One of these was a young farm worker named Arthur Elliott, my mother's father, who was born in 1885 in Penrith on the English side of the border. As a teenager, Arthur was employed as a stable boy on a Clydesdale stud farm at Gelt Hall in Castle Carrock until 1908, when, motivated by the promise of opportunity in the new world, he boarded the *SS Iconic* bound for Wellington, New Zealand. Thus a new generation of landowning Elliotts began. Their reiving days were long past.

Could this be the family from which my mother was descended? In the 16th century the Elliotts were widely known and feared as the perpetrators of bloody mayhem. According to author George MacDonald Fraser, Borderland visitors described them, along with other reiver families such as the Kerrs and the Armstrongs, as "barbarous, crafty, vengeful, crooked, quarrelsome, tough, perverse, active, and deceitful." They were responsible in part for the appearance in English of the word "bereaved"—the people who suffered such terrible losses at the ruthless hands of the reivers were said to have been "bereived."

In those lawless days, they were also notoriously irreligious. Fraser relates the story of how a posse of Elliott reivers was intercepted in the marches and asked: "D'ye believe in God?" Defiantly raising a battle-axe, one of the them, quite possibly one of my mother's very distant cousins, answered in a thunderous bass: "Nay. We dunna believe in God. We's a' Elliotts."

It's possible perhaps to trace my mother's physical endurance and emotional strength to the reivers in her past, but how is it possible to trace from such roots the surprising appearance of her fresh, verdant faith or her kindly grace?

If I look with some imagination, I sometimes see a suggestion of Rene's tender nature in the eyes of her own mother—Annie Kennedy—whose image appears in a few old family photographs. Along with hints of a sharp intelligence and fierce determination, there is kindness in those eyes. There are traces of kindness, too, in the stories of Annie's wider family.

I remember meeting one of Annie Kennedy's cousins—Joseph Kennedy—on his visit to New Zealand in 1965. Recently retired from a distinguished career as head of the Murder Squad at London's Scotland Yard, he had, over the years, been involved in a series of high-profile criminal cases. According to family lore, he was the officer who arrested one of the principals in the infamous John Profumo-Christine Keeler scandal that rocked the Tory government in the early 1960s. The story goes that Joseph Kennedy approached his man, tapped him on the shoulder, and said, "Come with me, you silly fellow."

Annie Kennedy Elliott with granddaughter (my cousin Marian)

Joseph Kennedy had been known to us, his antipodean family, as "Uncle Joe." A photograph in Scotland Yard files reveals him as a big, burly man with a handsome reddish face and a distinctively hooked nose. Despite his impressive stature and gentlemanly bearing, I remember feeling completely at ease in his company. He approached me, as he seemed to approach everyone, with a ready smile and a hearty, welcoming laugh.

I also remember seeing a great tenderness in him. At some point during his visit to our home on Rahiri Road, our family sang a song in his honor—our own version of Woody Guthrie's classic "This Land Is Your Land." As our harmonies veered uncertainly from two parts to four and back to one, I noticed in Uncle Joe's eyes a certain wistfulness. He was thinking perhaps of the day so long ago when his young cousin Annie had said farewell to her family in Cumbria to start a new life on the distant shores of New Zealand—a journey that promised no return. As we sang the refrain "This land was made for you and me," Uncle Joe allowed the tears to roll down his wide, craggy face. Courage and vulnerability. Strength and tenderness. Inseparably woven together, it seemed, in the Kennedy DNA.

During our visit to Cumbria in 2016, Jen and I drove north from Penrith through the village of Hayton, where my grandmother Annie Kennedy was born, and stopped on the outskirts of the tiny nearby hamlet of How. I knew that located somewhere nearby was How Mill Farm—now divided into three separate properties—where Annie worked as a dairymaid before leaving for New Zealand in 1911. Across the lane, we noticed a family sitting in a circle in the backyard. We asked if by chance they knew of anyone in the area by the name of Kennedy. There was an immediate response. Yes, they knew the Kennedys. Indeed, they remembered Joe Kennedy of Scotland Yard. What's more, an old friend from down the lane—Joan Watson—had had a very personal connection to him. They insisted we hear from her. One phone call was all it took for Joan to join us for a cup of tea. She told us a remarkable story.

During World War I, Joan's father had been sent to France to fight with an English infantry division on the Western Front. During close combat in the muddy trenches of Ypres, a German bullet had torn a crease in his brain, just above the eyes, leaving him paralyzed and severely mentally impaired. After treatment to an army field hospital in France, he had been transferred to a rehabilitation facility on the southern coast of England. He was still there fifty years later—in Brighton, East Sussex—when an unexpected visitor knocked on the door of his flat.

It was Joe Kennedy. Somewhere in the reaches of the old soldier's shattered mind, there was a flash of recognition. Their families had known each other when they were kids in Cumbria running the lanes of Hayton and How. Joe's father, George Kennedy, had been the master of the local railway station, a few hundred yards from where the old soldier had been born. He remembered George, the stationmaster. He remembered Joe, the policeman from Scotland Yard.

Joe Kennedy had taken a very different path to that meeting in the old soldier's Brighton flat. After leaving Scotland Yard, Joe and his wife, Hilda, had moved to the resort community of Brighton, where the winters were less severe. It was there, through mutual family connections, that Joe met up once again with Joan's father. Joe went back to the old soldier's flat many times—almost every day for the best part of a decade—bringing to a broken and lonely old man a comforting presence and a cheery word. Joan spoke of Joe with wistful gratitude, almost reverence, as if he had been a living saint. "Joe Kennedy was a loving, caring man," she said. "One of the finest gentlemen upon the earth." Perhaps here, in this sweet human being, who died in Brighton in 1989, I had caught a glimpse of the spirit of my mother and perhaps found a clue to its origins in the family line.

Many who came to Rene Martin's door, often expecting no more than an hour with her over a fresh cup of tea, felt embraced by an almost unearthly radiance and calm. Many wanted to know how she'd been able to bear such heavy burdens in her days as a young mother.

The answer, she would always say, was gratitude. "There are so many others in the world whose suffering is far greater than mine," she would say. "I'm grateful for the blessings I've been given."

Rene with her young family: (from left) Bryan, Olive, Howard, Cecile, and Ian

Others wanted to know how she kept the candle of faith alive when so often it seemed that a merciful God either did not exist or had abandoned her. "I felt these little ones were given to me for a reason," she would say. "They were my angels, and it was my calling to care for them. My peace comes from acceptance."

After many conversations with her, it was clear to me that by "acceptance" she did not mean resignation—giving up in the face of overwhelming odds—but rather a graceful surrender to what could not be changed, coupled with a trust that some higher purpose was at work. She measured the troubles of her life against the possibilities of what is beyond time. My mother's trust in life was such that even as she watched the light dying in the eyes of the little ones in her care, she placed her trust in the One who made the sun and the stars and who brought light out of darkness in realms beyond our knowing.

She surrendered her life to the grace of greater things. It was the sweet surrender of one who knows that even in the darkness, she could see the bright pinpricks of the stars.

What made Rene's trust in life possible, at least in part, was her spirit of forgiveness. There was much for her to forgive. She forgave her parents for bringing her to birth in a land a world away from their roots in the ancient soils of the English Borderlands, so far from her place under the wide branches of the Kennedy and Elliot families. (Many first-generation New Zealanders felt this sense of loneliness and alienation—they spoke of England and Scotland as "home"—and they too lived by repeated acts of forgiveness).

She forgave her eight children for the pains she suffered in giving them birth and forgave her three stricken little ones for their complicated woundedness and their never-ending neediness. She forgave the people of her religious community who, with one or two notable exceptions, like the saintly Joyce Guptill, failed to see the burdens she bore.

She forgave her husband, the shining star of their social circle, for being just another ordinary guy after all. She forgave him his many faults and laughed supportively at his oft-repeated stories, jokes, quips, and wacky sayings. (There were times, of course, when his clowning gave her no reason for forgiveness at all; she just surrendered to the moment and laughed.)

And she forgave God. She forgave God in the sense that she accepted the circumstances of her life without complaint and came to see the care of her wounded angels as her divine calling, the task for which she was born.

A mother's forgiving love carries within it the possibility of trust in a yet Greater Love that is marked by forgiveness and forbearance. It was true, at least for me. No words come as close to expressing my own sense of the connection between an earthly love and divine love as these from Wendell Berry. I wish I could have written them to my own mother:

> *I was your rebellious son,*
> *do you remember? Sometimes*
> *I wonder if you do remember,*
> *so complete has your forgiveness been.*
>
> *So complete has your forgiveness been*
> *I wonder sometimes if it did not*
> *precede my wrong, and I erred,*
> *safe found, within your love,*
>
> *prepared ahead of me, the way home,*
> *or my bed at night, so that almost*
> *I should forgive you, who perhaps*
> *foresaw the worst that I might do,*
>
> *and forgave before I could act,*
> *causing me to smile now, looking back,*
> *to see how paltry was my worst,*
> *compared to your forgiveness of it*
>
> *already given. And this, then,*
> *is the vision of that Heaven of which*
> *we have heard, where those who love*
> *each other have forgiven each other,*

where, for that, the leaves are green,
the light a music in the air,
and all is unentangled,
and all is undismayed.

I was not the rebellious son that Berry talks of, but I was, in my childish self-centeredness, largely unconscious of the thousand ways I was blessed in my mother's loving-kindness. How often did she, without expectation of thanks or praise, wipe away my tears, attend my sick bed, keep meals warm for me when I was late coming home? I shall never forget how once she ran down the steepest of hills to bring me the school lunch I had left behind on the dining room table. I loved coming home to her. And she was always there, offering me a place of warmest refuge and graceful welcome. I saw in her what it meant to possess a loving heart. To borrow the words of novelist Philip Roth, I felt my whole being "permeated by the quality of my mother's kindness." And so did we all.

Rene Martin in Iowa City with Jen and Howard, Barclay (standing) and Doozie

Despite the gift of such a mother I was rarely as grateful as I should have been. I was offered grace abounding but rarely expressed what my heart truly felt. I did try, feebly, a few times to tell my mother how much she meant to me, but it was a huge debt repaid in pennies. On my return from my year driving my powder blue VW bug on the wide red dirt roads of the Australian outback, for example, I brought a gift for her purchased at a jewelry store in Sydney. It was a silver bead-encrusted brooch in the form of a kookaburra, one of the iconic birds of the desert continent down under. It was, I suppose, the best I could do at the time, but, in retrospect, a mere token when set alongside the incalculable weight of her loving-kindness.

If I could roll back the calendar of my life and do one thing again, I would tell my mother in plain words that I loved her. It is a great regret that I rarely did so. Even in my thoughtless ingratitude, however, I knew I was, as Berry was, already forgiven. I erred safe-found in the generosity of her heart. Like Berry, too, I find buried somewhere within the memory of my mother's forgiving heart a place where forgiveness is already given, and clarity—disentanglement—a music in the air.

There is much more I could say about my mother's life, including that in her later years she became a dear companion to a wide network of friends and acquaintances. She was, in the truest sense, an "anam cara"—a soul-friend—to so many whose lives touched hers: her children, her children's children, her friends, her friends' children, her neighbors, and her neighbors' children. I have no doubt her spirit lives on. It lives on, for example, in the person of her daughter, Cecile, who, despite hardships that are hers alone to tell, has, with her brilliantly enterprising and kindly husband, John, offered gracious welcome and hospitality to unnumbered friends and strangers. In her enduring cheerfulness, in her sweet, reassuring voice, and in the deep wells of tenderness at the core of her being, my sister Cecile bears to this day an unmistakable resemblance to her extraordinary mother. My mother's spirit lives on, too, in the quiet strength and kindly instincts of my three living brothers—Bryan ("Bryn"), Ian ("Tigg"), and Warwick ("Wock").

Reflecting back on the woman who gave me birth, I think of all those who, throughout human history, have lived lives of quiet grace, the humble heroes of the world who kept the flame of hope burning in the darkness and faithfully tended the hearth in places shattered by suffering and death. I include her among those who, in their faithful service to life, possessed souls of true greatness. In the words of poet Stephen Spender, "she wore at her heart the fire's center."

With her gentle whispers and kind caresses, Rene Martin nurtured a loving family into being and traveled a short while with it toward the sun. I was the first born of that creation. Because of her, I found it possible, ultimately, to believe in the existence of an eternal Beloved, whose presence is manifest in all of creation, always and everywhere, the loving center of gravity of all that exists. In her kindly spirit I caught a glimpse of what life could be at its best and what it could ultimately become. It was my first intuition of paradise. Other such intuitions were to come, some of them through my father, to whose story I now turn.

CHAPTER 3.

A Kind of Rejoicing

"There are days we live
as if death were nowhere
in the background; from joy
to joy to joy, from wing to wing,
from blossom to blossom to
impossible blossom, to sweet
impossible blossom."
—Li-Young Lee

have a photograph of my father taken when he was around 25 years old. In his white gymnastics suit, he stands relaxed, strong and confident on the rooftop plaza of Auckland's Farmers Trading Company (the Sears Roebuck of New Zealand). His arms are outstretched on a double-rimmed circular device, the Rhönrad—or aero wheel—invented in Germany in the early 1930s and commonly used in those days for acrobatic entertainment. (Acrobats performed on aero wheels at the 1936 Berlin Olympic games, not as competitors in athletic events, but as ambassadors of German physical prowess.)

He has just completed a daring routine of runs and spins, including single-rimmed pirouettes and 360-degree rolling turns, to entertain the lunchtime crowds gathered six floors up in the warm summer air. Alongside him, his face wreathed in smiles, stands a hearty companion, Jim Duncan, the kind lady's husband, proudly displaying the shiny buttons of his official caretaker's uniform.

Dad on the aero wheel (with Jim Duncan)

A photograph like this can reveal things we didn't know about the past and confirm others that we did know, however imprecisely. This one confirms something I always knew about my father: He was a born entertainer.

Frederick Torrey Martin was a first-generation New Zealander, born into a family that had arrived from England in the last decades of the 19th century. Having traveled 12,000 miles to create new lives for themselves in one of the world's most distant places, they were, to say the least, ambitious, resourceful, and enterprising folk. His father, Samuel, who reached New Zealand in 1882, was the co-founder of a thriving furniture business on the Octagon in the heart of Dunedin (the historic building is still there). His mother Elizabeth was the daughter of an immigrant coalminer, Thomas Hetherington, who'd become the managing operator of a coal mine—one of New Zealand's first—on Saddle Hill near the frontier town of Mosgiel a few miles west of Dunedin.

Elizabeth and Samuel Martin

When Samuel first set eyes on Elizabeth, he was riding the bus on his way to meet a business client. If it wasn't love at first sight, it was something close. Samuel had never seen a face so radiant or eyes so gentle and kind. By the time he got off the bus that day, he knew he was going to marry her. Their union would produce eleven children. My father was number five.

Given the intense religious devotion of both his parents, it is no surprise that my father was named after a well-known American evangelist—Reuben Archer Torrey (1856-1928). Samuel and Elizabeth may well have cherished a hope that one day their son would follow the calling of his famous namesake. Their hope was partly realized. With his outsized personality and storytelling wizardry, my father was to become, in his twenties and thirties, a star on the local evangelical-revivalist stages. He was the go-to guy in his religious community for musical celebration and entertainment.

There was music in my father's soul. As a teenager, he studied violin under the guidance of a private tutor. He took to the fiddle with a natural flair, often filling the home of his youth (and also that of his later years) with the melodies of great classical composers, including those of his favorite, Fritz Kreisler: The Viennese Caprice, Beautiful Rosemary, Love's Joy (Liebesfreud), and Love's Sorrow (Liebesleid). Wandering the house like a strolling musician in a romantic setting, he played the Massanet's "Meditation" from Thaïs, double-stopping with an artist's sensitivity and a showman's flare. He seemed headed for a career in classical music.

Then came the Great Depression and the subsequent collapse of his father's business. Like so many young men of his generation, Dad delayed plans for professional training to help support his family. Turning down a scholarship for study at the Rodeheaver School of Music in Winona Lake, Indiana, he continued to play music with his siblings in the family chamber ensemble—he on violin, his siblings on piano, second violin, cello, and flute.

Martin family ensemble: (from left) Cyril, Torrey, Margaret, Betty, Sam

Increasingly caught up in the family's religious culture, he led the congregational singing at large religious rallies and conventions. Decades before the arrival in New Zealand of big-time American evangelism, well before the age of sound amplification technology, he took center stage with the unlikeliest of stringed instruments—the ukulele— strumming its simple chords with the sunny energy of the South Pacific and the passion of a true believer. Having made himself familiar with hundreds of sacred melodies, he served for years as the cantor, in this case without the ukulele, for the improvised communion services held weekly at Howe Street Hall, the unadorned meeting place of a large Plymouth Brethren congregation. In his long retirement years, he sang a strong baritone in a barbershop-style gospel quartet which included his brother Sam and a friend named Warnock Watson. Harmonizing with his brother and his friends filled his heart with the purest joy.

Over the years, from the days of nursery rhymes and gospel choruses to the celebrations of present day, the music in my father's soul has had a profound effect on the culture of our family. I found it especially touching, for example, when, on one of my regular returns to my native land, my four living siblings and I spent a memorable evening at my brother Warwick's exquisitely crafted home in Taupo with the wide blue arms of the lake spread out before us. Amidst the laughter and storytelling, there was music. Bound together by the ties of blood and memory, we sang song after song, each one in some way reconnecting our hearts to our family story. As we sang deep into the night, I felt that the boundaries between the past and the present had somehow magically dissolved as if touched by a magician's wand.

The lead magician in this case was my younger brother, Ian, who remembered all the old tunes, words and melodies alike, strumming the chords with confident gusto on a borrowed guitar: "Yellow Bird," "White Cliffs of Dover," "When the Quiet Evening Comes," "The

Well is Deep," and so many more. When we got to "When He Cometh, When He Cometh," an Appalachian folk gospel standard we had learned in Sunday School, the emotions, at least for me, surged in a rush of joy tinged with sadness. I could almost hear the sweet voices of my long-ago deceased siblings joining us in the chorus: "They shall shine in their beauty, His loved and His own." The fact that one of them—Olive, I think—pronounced it "brutey," added a touch of lump-in-the-throat nostalgia. Despite half a century of being separated by thousands of miles, pursuing our own callings in life, we were collected once more into a circle of unshakeable belonging. And there, in our memories, was our dad, singing his heart out.

At about the same time as this reunion was taking place, a grandson Torrey never knew was becoming increasingly captivated by the entrancing mysteries of lyric and melody. Inspired by a fellow student, Ben Stancil, while on a semester abroad program at the University of Liverpool, Barclay began writing and performing his own music. I well remember a start of tears as I listened to him perform one of his first songs with the band Potato Moon at a sold-out concert at Unity Temple on the Plaza in Kansas City. With Ken Lovern on the Hammond organ, he let fly with a song about the journey away from home that sends chills through me to this day: "Won't you take me on that golden road /Take me where I want to go?"

Over the years, Barclay wrote many songs, from the joyous "Wishing Well" to the haunting "Ghost Boat" and the deep spirituality of "Eyes of a Child," or the exhilarating breakouts of "Dance in the Rain." With or without his band (The Barclay Martin Ensemble combining the talented musicianship of Mark Lowrey, Erin McGrane, Shay Estes, Guiliano Mingucci, and Rick Willoughby), he performed in venues large and small—the Bluebird in Nashville, The Living Room in New York City, as well as Jardine's, Broadway Jazz

Club, Helen F. Spencer Theatre, the Folly Theater, and the Record Bar, all in Kansas City. With his holiday-season group, The Snow Globes, in joyous harmony with Rick Willoughby and Lindsey Jones, he sang for 20,000 Kansas Citians at the 2014 lighting of the Plaza lights. With guitar in hand, his voice resonant in the brilliant acoustics of the Kauffman Center for the Performing Arts, he sang solo as part of the Virgil Thompson retrospective, with the cameras of PBS rolling.

As Barclay's songs continued to flow from within, he was privileged also to travel worldwide, listening to the music that emerged from the hearts of others in cultures utterly different from his own. Working on the staff of the nonprofit organization Unbound, he recorded the virtuosity of local musicians from Zamboanga, Philippines; Antsirabe, Madagascar; and Bogota, Columbia, and brought their music back to audiences in the United States.

In 2011, after volunteering with the Medical Missions Foundation team in Mali, West Africa, he co-founded with his Malian friend, Tieblecoro Samake, a community health initiative called The Wash Project (washproject.org) in the town of Ouelessebougou, fifty miles from the capital city of Bamako. In 2019, at Christmas, Barclay was in Kansas City with The Snow Globes, offering—as he had for the previous six years—a series of seasonal concerts to raise funds to support Tieblecoro and his vibrant network of community volunteers. These concerts have included Barclay's exquisite adaptations of traditional carols and original songs of the season, along with compositions by his talented bandmates. In his own life, and in all these places across the globe, Barclay has been a contributor to the persistence of song in the world, his music an echo of his grandfather's legacy in the ongoing story of our family.

Similarly influential in our story has been Dad's irrepressible sense of humor. There were days, especially early on, when he was the emperor of fun, telling fantastical stories loosely based on reality, playing practical jokes, boasting the athletic achievements of his youth, challenging his kids to gymnastic tricks or boxing matches, twisting and bending like a clown while playing his violin, doing handstands on the kitchen floor as the coins spilled from his pockets, singing in a rich vibrant baritone, switching his songs from opera ("O sole mio") to spiritual ("Ring dem bells") to gospel ("He's Got the Whole World in His Hands"). He was in constant demand as a cheerleader, master of ceremonies, and stand-up comedian. In our tiny part of the world, his storytelling was legendary.

Dad keeps us all in stitches: with Mum on my 21st birthday

In another time and place, my father might have been a vaudevillian actor or a rubber-faced clown, like Emmett Kelly, with the Ringling Brothers and Barnum and Bailey Circus. There is no doubt he had the talent for it. Overflowing with antic exuberance, he improvised his way through all kinds of public celebrations: wedding receptions, camp meetings, family reunions, and—his specialty— "kitchen evenings."

The kitchen evening was a New Zealand 1950s-style pre-wedding celebration—a wedding shower—to which friends and family brought gifts of household items to help a young couple set up their new home.

Dad was often invited to these events to provide entertainment by "helping" the prospective bride and groom unwrap their gifts and offering words of advice about marriage. "Oooh what have we here," he would begin, as the bride opened a package to reveal a handheld egg-beater. "Looks like something you're really going to need in Mt. Albert! A fly-catcher!" Spinning the handle with exaggerated vigor, he'd send the blades into a frenzied whirr. "This'll get em. You can add the flies to a plum pudding with this." Then he'd go cross-eyed for a moment and dart about the room in search of a fly upon whose unfortunate frame he could prove his point.

With the crowd in a chaos of mirth, he'd extract a gleeful confession from the future bride and groom that now, after his convincing demonstration of culinary genius, they truly—yes, truly—understood what the egg-beater was for. Then he'd tell the bride-to-be she could also use it to cut her husband's hair and would make a fake pass over the lucky groom's neatly coiffed thatch. His imagination on fire, he'd add, "Might also work as a bicycle," and would pretend to "ride" the egg-beater in crazy circles around the room.

Each new gift—a carving set, a baking dish, a set of pots and pans—became the starting point of a new, completely unrehearsed sketch, replete with puns, red herrings, old jokes, new jokes, and flights of fantastical imagination. After improvising in this fashion for an hour or so, he'd leave his jigged-up audience still ready for more.

He had a vast repertoire of sayings, gags, and practical jokes that he sprinkled generously into the mix of his daily conversations. One of his verbal bits was the horribly butchered Latin phrase "Mens tuus ego." He translated "mens" as "mind," "tuus" as "your," and "ego" as "I." Hence, "mind your eye." When he had a strenuous task to perform, say cutting a gnarly ti tree log for a fire, he'd roll up his sleeves, take a self-consciously deep breath, as if about to dive off a cliff, and raising his shiny-tipped axe, would call out: "Mens tuus ego, boys!" It was part warning to his two young sons, whose attendance was required, and part show business. Duly impressed by this display of fatherly erudition and physical aptitude, two little boys would step back in mildly stricken awe. Down would come the axe and chips would fly. "Did you see that, boys?" he'd say, not really asking a question. "Kawka!"

One night, after a particularly profitable day of sales at Torrey Martin Limited—the menswear store he established around 1950 on the northeast corner of Customs and Quay Streets in Auckland— Dad was finding special delight in counting out the contents of the shop's cash register. With an expert pinching motion of thumb and forefingers, and an occasional touch of thumb to lips, he counted out several hundred pounds' worth of paper bills. Wrapping the fat pile in heavy brown paper, he bound the package tight with sticky tape. Then, overcome with exultation at his cash bonanza, he let out a whoop—WOO-HOO!—and kicked the packet toward the ceiling. The precious bundle rocketed toward a mess of hat boxes and surplus stock on a high mezzanine at the back of the store, and disappeared from sight. "Aw, crikey," said Dad. "We'd better go and find *that*."

Someone grabbed a ladder.

After a vigorous laugh-filled search that required us to rearrange the mezzanine storage space piece by piece, we finally recovered what we were looking for behind a pile of cellophane-wrapped white cotton shirts. "OK," said Dad, grinning with anticipation. "Now let's get some chicken chow mein at the Golden Dragon and have a party!"

Around the kitchen table, with a fire roaring in the iron cooking range, we celebrated the good fortunes of the day over steaming plates of overcooked cabbage and watery chicken. Relishing the rare exoticism of restaurant food, we listened with happy skepticism and considerable rolling of eyes as Dad regaled us with fantastical stories suggested by history but mostly fresh from his imagination.

At all such moments of celebration, Dad's stories were apparently inexhaustible. He spun out colorful tales of hard times during the Depression: the devastating collapse of his father's French polishing business in isolated Gisborne, the decision to move to Auckland to start a new business laundering and pressing clothes, and the 100-mile family migration, on bicycles, over dusty, unsealed roads from Gisborne to Rotorua, where they caught the train to the big city in the north.

That particular journey was epic in Dad's imagination. With every retelling, its details became richer and its status as family legend grew—the nights under the stars, the search for welcoming hotels, the patching of ruptured tires, the spills into deep mud, and the singing, in four-part harmony, of hymns and choruses along the way. In the only photograph I have of them on that bold adventure, the touring party appears dressed as if for a formal reception at the mansion of the Governor General, suits and ties for the men, knee length floral dresses for the women. They look at the camera with confident smiling eyes as if to say: "Moving on, first class!"

Bike ride from Gisborne: Dad second from left

One of the other stories Dad loved to tell, always with impromptu variations, was the tale of the car trip to Ngaruawahia, a small town sixty miles south of Auckland, and the incident of the flat tire on the Bombay Hills. To the best of my memory, he told it like this:

In those days, the road up the hills was absolutely crummy. It was full of ruts and potholes…and dusty? You have no idea! So we're on our way to Naggery-waggery (Dad's made-up name for the town) *and, Christmas, was it hot! I have sweat running down my back and my hands are slipping off the steering wheel. The Willys is really rocking around. One of the cheeky jokers in the backseat calls out: "Hey Todd, does this thing have square wheels?" "Oh, for crying out loud!" I say. "What are you talking about? The Willys has perfect wheels; it's the roads! Crikey, they're full of potholes as big as Bolivia. Then I hear something. "Shish! Listen!"* (He puts his hand upon to his ear.) *I pull over to the side of the road and switch off the engine. I hear it: Ssssssss. We're all dead silent now. Yep, we can hear it all right: Ssssssss. I get out and check the tires. Of all the bloomin' luck! We've got a nail in the tire back here. "Get your shirts off, boys," I say, "and we'll fix 'er up."*

(Pretending to roll up his sleeves, Dad continues the story.)

We all pile out of the car. We unload the jack, crank the car up on an angle, take off the tire and remove the nail, tug out the inner tube, find the hole, rough up the spot with sandpaper, stick on a rubber patch, and squash the tube back in. Then we start pumping air in the tire. With a hand pump! Boy, was that HARD WORK! Even for a guy with muscles like mine! (He flexes his biceps and evokes groans of fake admiration.) *Finally, we get the tire back on. "OK, boys," I say. "D-U-N: done! Let's get back on the road."*

"We're dripping with sweat and covered in dust. We crank up the engine, hop back in the car, and take a couple of big deep breaths. "Praise the Lord! We're on our way." Then I hear something. Hey, hang on a minute…What's that?" (He cups his hand over his ears and leans forward). *Ssssssssss.*

"You gotta be kiddin'!" I say. "It's the bloomin' tire we just fixed!" We boil up the thermette (a cylindrical kettle on stilts) *and have a cup of tea. Then we do it all again."*

Another of Dad's favorite stories concerned his epic encounter with Frank Hare's bull. Frank Hare was a prosperous sheep farmer living near Gisborne on the East Coast of the North Island. Frank had ordered a new custom-fit suit from the Farmers Trading Company catalog, and, as a Farmers employee, it was Dad's job to drive to the farm to measure him for it. According to family rumor, Frank also had vague hopes of Torrey catching the charms of his eligible unmarried sister.

Dad drives 100 miles over dusty rural roads and turns onto the gravel driveway of the Hare's fine old green-roofed colonial villa set in a grove of tall poplars. Dressed in her best smock, the eligible unmarried sister meets Dad at the door and serves him a cup of tea and a scone laid out with a doily on a tray. In solicitous tones, she tells him that Frank is waiting for him in the shearing shed, across the paddocks. With a knowing laugh, she also warns him to watch out for Popeye, the bull. Finishing his tea, Dad sets off to meet up with Mr. Hare. Here's how I remember him telling the rest of the story:

I'm in the middle of the paddock, miles from the gate, and there's Popeye. No kiddin'—he's the biggest bull you ever saw—big as a tractor—and he's snorting. Oooooo! He's pawing the ground and lowering his head. Crikey! He's coming straight at me! "OK, Torrey," I say to myself, "Whadda ya gonna do?" There's a rotten fencepost lying there. I grab it. I'm looking straight at Popeye and he's looking straight at me. Whoo-boy! I wait until he gets really close. Then, get this! I step sideways like a chap from Spain and let Popeye have it. (He mimes his expert swing). *Right on his snout. The fencepost busts to smithereens. Tell you what! Popeye changes direction quick-smart and off he goes. Frank saw it, too. "Fair effort for a city bloke," says Frank.* (Dad laughs heartily) *"Jiminy Christmas!"*

To the end of his days, Dad took great pride in his magnificent victory over Frank Hare's bull. "Torrey, the toreador," he would say, then in full-throated baritone launch into the appropriate passage from Bizet's opera: "*Toreador. Tor-or-ree-a-dor.*" Never another word, though, about the eligible unmarried sister.

Dad also loved telling the story of the rotten toheroa. Toheroa are a species of shellfish, akin to scallops, that in the 1950s we could harvest naturally on the wild, windswept beaches of New Zealand's northwest coast. One day, Dad drives us to Bethell's Beach—in his words "a kawka pozzie" (perfect spot)—and sends us out along the seashore after a retreating tide to look for telltale bubbles in the shiny surface of the flat black sand. Beneath each bubble, just inches below the shiny surface, we expect to find a single toheroa. We can see bubbles everywhere.

There was nothing like free stuff to quicken the sense of anticipation in Torrey's tribe. We often descended like the Egyptian plague on the bountiful provisions of nature wherever we could find them in the wilds of our fresh young country—blackberries, raspberries, gooseberries, mushrooms, rabbits, koura, cockles, mussels, oysters, wild apples, or plums. So it was, on this occasion, with toheroa. Itching for plunder, we run from bubble to bubble, digging out the dun-colored shells with short-handled spades. We load our treasures into wet sacks, counting them as we go, and heave the sacks into the trunk of the car. The final numbers are in. By Dad's calculation, we've dug up more than the local laws allow. "What if those cheeky inspectors catch us?" asks Dad. He goes silent for a moment. "Oh, pooh to them, that's what I say! Run quick and hide the extras under the spare tire."

We forget all about what's under the spare tire. A week goes by. It's Friday night after the shop has closed. We open the trunk of the Super Snipe and are instantly assailed by a whoompf of putrid air. Dad's revulsion knows no bounds. He holds his nose and collapses in a full-body gesture of disgust. "Jiminy cricket!" he says. "What a stink!"

Then, remembering the booty we'd stowed away at Bethell's Beach, he bursts into paroxysms of laughter: "Aw, crikey," he cries. "We forgot those bloomin' toheroa! Crumbs!" He thinks for a second or two. "Hey!" he says. "Let's put these little beauties in a box and wrap 'em up. Make 'em look like a nice expensive package someone's left behind. Some lucky joker will pick 'em up and he'll get a nice surprise. It'll be kawka!"

We do it.

We wrap the rancid mollusks in mounds of newspaper and stuff them in a shoebox. We cover the box with crisp, clean wrapping paper and tie it up with a pretty arrangement of shiny silver ribbon. Like seasoned wartime saboteurs, we place the surprise on the Quay Street sidewalk across from Torrey Martin Limited and hide in the darkness to see what happens. Dad barely stifles his giggles of anticipation. "Shhhhh!" he whispers, as if to warn himself against premature disclosure.

Within minutes, a grey-suited man, apparently on his way to catch the ferry, stops for a look. Dad silently coaches him to pick it up. "Go on, go on!" he whispers. "You'll really like it." As if on cue, the man picks up the box, puts it under his arm and casually walks on. Dad 's delight is inexhaustible. Imagining the lucky man and his eager little wife at home opening the box and inspecting its stinking contents, he falls to his knees in a gale of laughter. "Poooooh!" he mocks, holding his nose in an exaggerated gesture of disgust. "What a find!"

On the way home, Dad rehearses our spectacular triumph, while the rest of us, in the backseat of the car, crack up in conspiratorial glee. "So funny, eh?" he says. We have, of course, successfully disposed of the foul-smelling contraband—that's our most notable

accomplishment—but we have done much more. We have struck
a blow on behalf of civic virtue. After all, people shouldn't pick up
packages on the street that do not belong to them. We do however pay
a price for our original sin of taking more shellfish than was our legal
due: the Martin automobile with its cavernous trunk reeks of overripe
toheroa for months.

Friday nights were Dad's favorite nights for highjinks. He loved
thinking up pranks after the 9:00 p.m. closing of the store. One of the
most memorable was the the "monkey mask parade."

In one of his regular scavenger hunts in surplus stores and estate
sales, Dad had once discovered a set of four grinning monkey masks—
bright yellow paper-mache monkey faces that could be fastened to the
face with a rubber band. He'd bought them for a shilling each. Just
for fun.

One Friday night, after we serve the last customer in the store, he
decides we're all going to slip the masks on and drive the car down
the main street of town—Queen Street—with our heads stuck out
the open windows. He choreographs the scene with an artist's eye
for comedic detail—two kids side by side in the front seat, two in the
back, masks just so. Playing the role of circus master and chauffeur,
he takes us on a slow roll through the city's bright neon lights, the
sidewalks bubbling with shoppers, revelers, and people-watchers.

With every wink-wink, nudge-nudge and double-take we evoke
on our way, Dad raises a meaty hand to his face and giggles in pure,
uncomplicated delight. At the teeming intersection of Queen and
Wellesley Streets, shoppers with their bulging string shopping bags
wave at us in happy affirmation. "Bodgies" and "widgies" (the local
equivalent of black-garbed Teddy Boys and Teddy Girls) stare in
disbelief. "Got a banana?" we call out, our muffled voices resounding
fuzzily inside our masks. At another corner a gaggle of kids fling

themselves into a crazy dance, scratching under their armpits: "Yip, yip, yip, yip, yip." "Yip, yip, yip," we answer. "Yip, yip yip," says Dad. "Crikey! Absolutely kawka!"

With Torrey Martin, there were times like that. In such carefree moments, it felt good to be alive, as if the powers of the universe had briefly converged to make the world a safer and more delightful place. They created within me a reservoir of good cheer that, despite my own natural wistfulness, has no doubt fed the springs of my life with healing waters.

When Dad was in his Charlie Chaplin mode, he offered me something precious—a glimpse into the laughter, the sheer fun, at the heart of life. His sense of joy was, for me, a clue to a greater Joy out of which our existence springs. His exuberant good cheer helped me understand why, even in the darkest of circumstances, we human beings find reason for hope even beyond the horizon of time, and why we find inexplicable consolation in the surprising miracle of laughter. To quote a line from Martin Buber: "Laughter is the exultation of possibility."

There was more to Dad, as you might guess, than song and laughter. He was, by any definition, among the kindest of men. During the years he was in business, street people would stop by the door of his shop looking for a handout or a cheery word. He would listen to their stories and, moved with compassion, would more often than not send them off with a pound note in their pockets and a little joke or a pat on the back to brighten their days. He was not always an easy mark, however. Sometimes he knew when inappropriate plays were being made on his good nature, and he reluctantly offered at least temporary resistance.

One night, while Dad was counting up the day's intake of cash, one of his street friends, Harry, leaning unsteadily on the partly-closed frame of the shop's front door, greeted him with a solicitous wink:

"Gidday, Tory!!" he said, deliberately mispronouncing his name to lend it an air of familiarity, "Got a minute?"

"As long as we're not talking about money, like yesterday," replied Dad, pretending not to be a pushover.

"In that case, I couldn't be bothered talking to ya," huffed Harry.

"OK then, Harry," said Dad. "I'll be seeing ya."

"I'll think about it," continued Harry, gathering his coat up around his neck and turning to go. "Maybe ya will, maybe ya won't."

Harry would be back. You could count on it. And next time, no doubt, Dad would slip another pound note into his outstretched hand.

Despite the story, I must also tell about what happened to my father in his later years. I can never forget that the best portion of his life—this good man's life—was what Wordsworth called his "little, nameless, unremembered acts / Of kindness and of love."

If Torrey Martin erred, it was always on the side of compassion. I can never forget the tokens of mercy dropped in needy hands, the sunny friendship offered to lonely neighbors, the jobs created for relatives in need, the midnight rescues of desperate weeping souls, the companionable meals provided to all kinds of wayfarers and newcomers, and the glowing spirit of hospitality with which he opened his home and his heart to the world. He could not have done the half of it, of course, without the support of his long-suffering Rene. Her heart was as big as his.

In the formation of my own view of life and the emergence of my own sense of connection to a greater Kindness, Dad's

Father and Son, 1947

simple daily acts of generosity counted for a lot, as did the music in his soul. They revealed more to me about the grace of newborn humanity than a lifetime of preaching from the finest of pulpits or shelves full of books on theology. And now, with a glance back at the origins of his exuberant spirit, I must tell the rest of his story.

CHAPTER 4.

The Persistence of Song

"Here a kind of singing
And there a kind of rejoicing
And though it is not yet evening,
There is the persistence of song."
—Howard Moss, "The Persistence of Song"

I have often wondered about the origins of my father's bright presence in the world. Was there, somewhere in his line of descent, evidence of unusual ebullience of character, or musical talent, or extroverted religious sensibility? Could he perhaps have been the offspring of circus performers or vaudeville actors or traveling minstrels? Could there be traces in his DNA of aggressive salesmanship, vigorous entrepreneurship, or daring religious activism? I have sometimes wondered if I might find a clue going back to one of the earliest holders of the Martin name—St. Martin of Tours (316-375AD).

Certainly, in St. Martin, there were signs of a passionate religious sensibility and a startling gift for the dramatic. It is said that as a cavalry soldier riding into Amiens with the imperial army of Rome, he came across a half-naked beggar on the side of the road, and,

St. Martin of Tours offers his cloak to a beggar

moved with compassion, cut his cloak in half and laid one half over
the desperate man's shoulders. That night in a dream, he saw a vision
of Jesus speaking with the angels and heard Jesus say: "As I stood in
distress by the wayside this day, Martin clothed me with his robe." In
one version of the story, he awoke from his dream and found his robe
lying across his body uncut and wholly restored.

The link between St. Martin of Tours and Torrey Martin of New
Zealand is, of course, pure fantasy, but there is perhaps a common
thread of significance. There is, at least for me, a wishful convergence
in their stories. Though I have not yet been able to go back more
than three generations in my father's family line, I nevertheless have
found evidence, in some of my forebears, of an unusual combination of
religious fervor and bold dramatics.

A good place to start is with my father's own father—Frederick
Samuel Martin. Born in 1870 in Barnstaple, Devonshire, Samuel
(as he was always known) spent most of his childhood years in
Nottingham St. Mary, now a suburb of Newcastle upon Tyne in

England's industrial northeast. He and his brother Francis worked in their father's furniture shop, where they became skilled in the crafts of French polishing and furniture making and also proved highly adept in the arts of salesmanship and business management.

After emigrating to New Zealand with their father in 1883, the two brothers established a successful furniture store and piano showroom— F. and F. Martin Limited—on "the Octagon" in Dunedin's central business district. (One of the unexplained mysteries of the family is that their mother, Ann, who also worked in the furniture trade, weaving the cane backs and seats for chairs, did not travel with them to the antipodes. She remained in England with her married daughter, Bessie.)

The business in Dunedin was so successful that the two brothers subsequently established their own separate fine furnishing companies. At the height of his success, the younger brother, Samuel, employed 70 workers in manufacturing, sales, and management.

During his years of good fortune, the 1920s, Samuel Martin provided for his family in a manner he could only have dreamed about back home in Nottinghamshire. He and his New Zealand-born bride, Elizabeth, lived in a handsome wooden home in Dunedin's Saddle Hill district, finely appointed with handcrafted furniture and tastefully decorated throughout, with one room—the "blue room"—set aside for visitors. According to family historian Elizabeth Rackley, Samuel and Elizabeth employed a small army of household assistants, including a housemaid, a gardener, a seamstress who made clothing for the children, and private tutors to teach them singing, piano, violin, and cello. One of the girls, Margaret, kept her own horse on the pastures nearby, riding it freely over the surrounding hills.

It was a lively and prosperous family, with religious devotion at its beating heart. Many a meal began or ended with Bible reading and prayers, led with supreme earnestness by Samuel, who insisted

In prosperous times: the Martin family of Saddle Hill

on appropriate displays of piety. If devotional theology was not to the taste of the children gathered in orderly array round the finely polished dining table, he would focus their minds by rapping the tops of their heads with the stubby ends of his fingers. "Give the Lord your whole attention," he would say. "He is worthy! He is worthy!"

Then, in 1929, everything changed. The New York Stock Market collapsed and the Great Depression spread from the United States to New Zealand. The Martin furniture business in Dunedin was hit especially hard. Though Samuel kept the doors open as long as he could, drawing on his own savings to keep his staff employed, in the end it was not enough. He had no choice but to lay off his employees and sell the family estate for pennies on the pound. They were migrants once more.

They packed what was left of their old life into boxes and, wishing upon the stars, made their way to the isolated coastal town of Gisborne on the North Island and, a year or so later, to Auckland, the largest city in the country. Elizabeth and the younger children made the journey by ship; Samuel and the older ones, including my father, rode 100 miles by bicycle over dusty, unsealed roads to Rotorua where they took the steam train—the Rotorua Limited—through the Mamaku Hills into Auckland.

Just as Samuel Martin had naturally found his way into the family's furniture business, he had also willingly adopted his family's religious culture—that of the Plymouth Brethren. "Plymouth Brethren" was the name given to an evangelical movement that began in Dublin, Ireland, in the 1830s and spread first to Plymouth (hence the name) then to other parts of England and the wider British Empire, arriving in New Zealand in 1863.

One of the early leaders of the Plymouth Brethren was a saintly man named Robert C. Chapman. Though born to wealth and privilege, he chose to live among the poorest of England's poor, especially those in the cities who'd been crushed under the iron hammer of the Industrial Revolution. Beginning in and around Barnstaple on the north coast of Devonshire, he devoted his life to the relief of suffering and the search for justice for the economically disadvantaged. "God is love," he is quoted as saying, "and His children please Him only so far as they are like Him, and walk in love."

By practicing what he preached with a kind and forgiving humility, Robert Chapman became widely known throughout England as "the apostle of love." He was also a man of deep spiritual devotion, given to Bible study and prayer, and, like the well-known divine, George Mueller, an inspiring preacher and teacher. Among the many who came under his spell was my grandfather, the young Samuel Martin.

It seems that Samuel Martin was born to follow in the footsteps of the great 19th-century nonconformist divines. Less focused on the economic plight of the poor, he believed that the greatest gift he could give to others—both rich and poor—was "the good news of the gospel" as he understood it. Like his mentors, he saw the world in black and white and divided humanity into those who were "saved" and those who were "lost." He felt his true calling was to persuade everyone he met to join the company of those who were "saved."

Though he had no degrees in arts or science—or theology, for that matter—he was extraordinarily well-versed in the Biblical texts, and preached with uncompromising conviction wherever he could find an audience—at conferences, meetings, in the home, and on the streets.

In Martin family lore, there are many stories of Samuel's religious enthusiasm. According to one story, he was riding his clattering bicycle at a fast clip down a long, steep hill—perhaps Saddle Hill in Dunedin—when he came across a family walking uphill toward him. Determined to engage them in friendly conversation, he tried to bring his bike to a stop. He tugged hard on the brakes, but nothing happened. Careening past the walkers, more than a little out of control, he raised his dusty fedora and called out: "God loves ya. Christ died to save ya. Good day to ya." His voice trailed off in the distance. In Samuel's mind, it was message delivered.

According to another story, he preached an impromptu sermon onboard the passenger ferry between Bayswater and central Auckland. Just minutes into the crossing, the thunderous engines abruptly quit, and the big boat coasted to a stop. The passengers were now adrift in the slow swell of the Waitemata Harbour. In the silence, they heard the captain's voice over the handheld loudspeaker, assuring them that they were in no immediate danger and that help was on the way. Samuel Martin seized his opportunity. He stepped up on a wooden bench, removed his hat, and introduced himself to his fellow passengers. With the light dancing off his round, wire-rimmed glasses, he launched into his improvised remarks.

He told his astonished listeners that, just as they were adrift on the green waters of the Waitemata, they were likewise adrift on the uncertain seas of life. "Put your lives in the hands of the Great Pilot who alone has the power to bring you safely home," he said. "Trust in Jesus as your Savior, and you will be forever found, otherwise you will

be counted among the lost." Then, flashing a big smile, he stepped
down from the bench, and vanished into the milling throng waiting
for the arrival of the tugboat from the city. It may well be that, later
that night in his dreams, Samuel saw a vision of an angel saying to
him, "Well done, good and faithful servant."

Frederick Samuel Martin's life was by no means all about
preaching. In distinct contrast to his fearsome views on the fate of
unredeemed mankind, he looked out on the world with cheerful,
laughing eyes, and in the public square he was a bubbling, effervescent
presence with an extreme extrovert's startling self-confidence. People
called him "Happy Day Martin." My one personal memory of him is
of a kindly old man digging into his heavy coat pocket as we walked
into church one Sunday morning and slipping a barley sugar candy
into my hand. To my mind, it was the best sermon he ever preached.

My father was shaped in body and soul like his own father. In his
cheerful extroversion and unabashed evangelistic fervor, Frederick
Torrey was the very image of Frederick Samuel. Gregarious. Energetic.
Funny. Kind. Intensely devout. Wearing his revivalist faith on his sleeve,
he wisecracked his way into numerous conversations about the life of
the soul, and found ingenious ways to ask everyone he met—Bruce
the milkman; Brookings the bookshop owner; Daya the greengrocer;
Deering the butcher; Smith and Rope and Sargeson the neighbors—
if they had found the true way to salvation. It was a habit as deeply
ingrained as polishing his shoes and gardening in his suit and tie.

In his last years—even when his life was apparently coming
unmoored—Dad made it his habit to offer little homilies to any who
would listen. The words he used were virtually unchanged from those
he had heard from the lips of his own dad. One day in the late 1970s,
on the sidewalks of charming historical Roscoe Village, Ohio, he
approached a gang of heavily tattooed motorcycle riders, dark angels

from the wild side, and offered them a sunny "G'day, boys." After a cursory word or two about the big shiny machines lined up at the curb, and without a thought for decorum or self-preservation, he asked: "You boys go to Sunday School?"

Natural as they were to my father, such interrogations were an intense embarrassment to me. They were as unnatural to me as they appeared natural to him; I shrank from them and sought refuge, when I could, in the counsels of my own solitude. There was undoubtedly a religious calling deep within me, but as I shall later show, it was more of a call to inner quietude and reflective conversation than to the assertion of religious certitudes I did not then—and do not now—possess. In this I was not the son of my father.

Despite my reservations about my father's religious extroversion, however, there were other parts of his character that remain within me as a source of deepest gratitude. I think back, for example, on his lifetime of fidelity to our household and his unsung acts of devotion that kept a fire burning in the hearth. Good memories of him come back to mind whenever I read lines like these from Robert Hayden's "Those Winter Sundays":

> *Sundays too my father got up early*
> *and put his clothes on in the blueblack cold,*
> *then with cracked hands that ached*
> *from labor in the weekday weather made*
> *banked fires blaze. No one ever thanked him.*
>
> *I'd wake to hear the cold splintering, breaking.*
> *When the rooms were warm, he'd call,*
> *and slowly I would rise and dress,*
> *fearing the chronic angers of that house,*

Speaking indifferently to him,
who had driven out the cold
and polished my good shoes as well.
What did I know, what did I know
Of love's austere and lonely offices?

In our rooms, there were no such chronic angers, but there were lowering clouds of sadness and disappointment. And yet, with courageous good cheer, my father continued to do what he could to keep us safe and warm.

I think of cold winter mornings in our cabin beside Lake Taupo. In late August—the frostiest time of the year in New Zealand, especially on the North Island's high volcanic plateau—the temperatures inside the cabin were almost as cold as the chill outside. The air seemed to bite our faces and press down on our blankets. We felt it an act of great daring to step out of our cozy beds onto the bare wooden floor.

Many a day, it was Dad who was first up. From under warm covers, we could hear him splitting wood with his short-handled axe, stacking the grate, scratching away to spark a match, and, with strong hearty breaths, coaxing the ti tree logs into a roaring wall of flame. Soon we could feel the touches of warmth around our ears. Only then would we leap from our bunk-beds and head for the hearth, jostling for a spot in front of the crackling orange blaze. In childish oblivion, I never thanked him for this gesture, one among so many, of his faithful love. But what did I know? What did I know?

While recognizing the paternal origins of my father's religious extroversion and native cheerfulness, I also recognize the part played in this by his mother, Elizabeth. Born in 1869, she was the daughter of early New Zealand pioneers, Christopher Thomas Heatherington, a coal miner from Northumbria, and his second wife, Margaret Watson, the family's Scottish nanny.

I have few memories that serve my understanding of my paternal grandmother, but I do have clear memories of one of her daughters who, I have been told, was made in her image. I speak of my unforgettable Aunt Ruby, the second youngest of the Martin girls.

Aunt Ruby's life bubbled with good cheer; her heart was a song, her voice a pealing of bells, her face a gentle riot of joy. To enter her home was to enter a world of cream-cakes and brandy snaps, endearing turns of phrase, and a hundred gestures of uncomplicated kindness. Seemingly always in agreement with her conversational partners, not for lack of conviction but from an overflow of goodwill, she'd answer with a chuckle from deep in her throat: "Woll, this is royt! This is royt!"

One memorable day, on a visit home from the United States, she and her husband, my jolly Uncle George, welcomed me with a festival of homemade goodness. The teapot was at the ready, as usual, on a lace-covered table in their sunny living room, and every available surface overflowed with layered sponge cakes, lamingtons, and flaky pastries drowning in sugary icing.

Aunt Ruby and Uncle George

In the midst of the celebrations, after reminiscencing among aunts and uncles and cousins, Aunt Ruby pulled me aside, as if to say, "This is a little secret between us," and pressed into my hand a crumpled $20 bill. Knowing as I did the hard economic times she had faced over the years and the long hours she had worked at her part-time job to have a little extra cash in her pocket, I felt as if she had just offered me the heavens and the earth, and was introducing me, in that moment, to Kindness itself. In that moment, too, I believe I caught a glimpse of her own mother's heart and thereby found a clue to the kindly instincts of my father.

It's against the background of Dad's persistent cheerfulness and generosity of spirit, so evident in a thousand gestures of faithful love, that I must now speak of the breaking of his heart.

Big changes in life sometimes occur in the blink of an eye, others come slowly over time like the dying of the day's light. The changes in my Dad's life were more like the latter. By gradual degrees, the man who had begun life with such promise and had brought such rollicking good cheer to his young family began to lose his grip on the wheel of his destiny.

Heartsick from the burden of his love for three multiply-disabled children, he became more and more distracted, disappearing from the household for long hours, brooding, defensive, and depleted. He would sit at the bedside of one or the other of his dying children, comforting them—and no doubt seeking to console himself—with familiar lines from hymns and choruses. "Jesus loves me, this I know, for the Bible tells me so," he would sing. "Little ones to Him belong, they are weak but He is strong." Then, exhausted and at the end of his wits, he would lapse into bewildered silence. His hidden tears were his prayers.

Things were no better for him in the world of business. Faced with increasingly sophisticated competition from other menswear retailers in town, his business began to collapse. He had relied for years on selling through slap-on-the-back friendliness and good-natured cajolery, but there came a time when jokes and wisecracks were no longer enough. A shiny new menswear store—Horace Bull Limited—opened across the street. (Dad called the owner "Horri-bull".) New products came on the market, much better in quality than the nylon shirts he had imported from the Miller factory in Christchurch. The customers who had come in such numbers for Dad's exclusively imported shirts— the first no-iron shirts on the New Zealand market—began going elsewhere. His hail-fellow-well-met optimism was not enough to win them back. He laid off staff and spent hours alone in the store, until he realized the game was up. The menswear and custom-tailoring business he'd built with such promise had to be closed down.

It was a terrible blow to a proud man. Up to that point in his life, he had known little but success in his various public enterprises and little but admiration, verging on adoration, in his personal relationships. Now he was staring into a chasm of failure and humiliation. He valiantly tried other commercial enterprises to bring back the old sense of magic, the touch of triumph, but they all failed. One of these was an ill-conceived partnership with a rag-and-bone flea market operator named Doyle.

I have no idea how they met. It may have been at an auction for manufacturers' seconds and cast-offs, random items well past their sell-by date. They may have begun a conversation over the price of a line of Hawaiian shirts, a batch of work socks, a miscellany of women's shoes, a few reels of heavy-duty electrical cable, or a box of screwdrivers still in their original plastic wrapping. They must have agreed that, since they were in the same business—buying and selling odds-and-ends for a profit—they should go into partnership together. With a small initial investment—a thousand pounds or so each—they opened a store in a rundown factory building on Fanshawe Street near the Auckland waterfront.

When he was not at an auction searching for salable bargains, Dad would be in his shopfront pretending to be busy, rearranging his stock, greeting passers-by with his usual cheerful banter, waiting for customers who rarely came by and even more rarely purchased anything. He would stand at the door and ask anyone who would listen if they needed a pair of sunglasses or a set of kitchen knives—"A kawka bargain," he would say. "You won't do better anywhere in town."

Pressed for more profitable sales by an increasingly imperious and unforgiving Doyle, he began to feel a sense of panic, compounded by guilt. Once more he was staring at failure. Trapped beyond his own powers of rescue, he fell into a despair of futility and indecision. One night, I overheard a conversation in which my father, his strong baritone reduced to a sad lament, confessed to my mother that he had reached the end. He felt helpless in the face of the business's mournful unprofitability and Doyle's harsh blame. He needed to get out of the partnership, but did not know how. My mother's sympathetic suggestions were met with a refrain of ultimate defeat: "I don't know, Rene," he said. "I just…." and his voice trailed off. I imagined him doing something I had rarely seen of him in all the years I had known him—laying his head, in silence, on Rene's kindly breast. I decided to act on his behalf.

Though I was 23 years old, I was scared of Doyle. I feared his temper and his unpredictability. I feared his liquored-up breath. More than once, I'd seen him slumping on our doorstep in an advanced state of inebriation with my mother wiping his face with a cold washcloth. I feared the man's presumption and self-serving neediness. But I loved my Dad more than I feared Doyle and could no longer bear the burden he, Doyle, had been laying on him. Nor could I bear the burden he had been laying—directly and indirectly—on my mother. So it was that, later that same night, I drove the family Morris Minor to Doyle's house and knocked on the door. Doyle answered. He did not invite me in.

Standing there in the dark doorway, with no knowledge of the nature of the arrangement between the man and my father, and even less of the legal issues surrounding their partnership, I simply said, "You need to let my father go."

There was a pause. "What are you talking about?" asked Doyle."

"You know what I'm talking about, Mr. Doyle," I said. "It's about the shop on Fanshawe Street. Dad is feeling trapped and frightened; he's close to emotional collapse, and you know it. He's unable right now to act on his own behalf, so I'm acting for him. You need to find a way to dissolve the partnership with him and set him free. And you need to do it now. Now!" I was virtually screaming. "Now! Now!! Now!!!"

Doyle stared at me in silence for several long seconds, then lit a cigarette. "OK," he said. "Let me think about it," and he closed the door. I turned away and drove home.

The next morning I got a call from Doyle. "It's about the business," he said. "Tell your dad I'll make him a deal. I'll let him go free of all obligations to Fanshawe Street if he agrees to allow me to take ownership of all the stock remaining on the floor." What remained on the floor was a scavenger's untidy dream: rolls of carpet, boxes of past-the-sell-by date popcorn, buckets of stale licorice candies, a line of discontinued house paint, and other odds and ends. His face stricken and somber, Dad agreed to the deal. From that day on, he never went back to the shop on Fanshawe Street and, as far as I know, never saw Doyle again either. Within a few months, the bleak ungraceful storefront had been shuttered, no signs on the battered double doors. Dad and I never spoke of it again.

I felt no sense of triumph. Only a new lightness of heart, ever so slight but palpable. I had for some time felt the humiliation of my fathers's failing business, but the sense of shame had been his far more than my own. I had witnessed his sad efforts to maintain his self-respect in the face of another of life's crushing disappointments. I had come to see my dad as a tragic figure, like Willy Loman in Arthur Miller's play, *Death of a Salesman*.

Like Willy Loman, Dad had been a young man of big dreams and supreme self-confidence. People had adored him. Their adoration, however, had left him curiously unprepared for the inevitable time when the world no longer thought everything he did was wonderful. He was admired when it was cool to be the entertainer—and patronized when the clown mask began to slip. He had been a star in a religious culture that steered its course by its stars. In his later years, when people expected substance, he seemed a lost soul, forever attempting to reignite the spark of vitality, the improvisational brilliance, that once defined him. I felt a great sadness for him.

After all these years my sadness for my dad has never really gone away. It has been intensified, in fact, by my realization that he was, after all, a very lonely man. Outside of his family he had few, if any, real friends. He had many admirers, but none with whom he had a true connection of the heart. While he was happy to be given pride of place at the center of popular attention, he never developed the skill of nurturing the bonds of companionship with his peers. The men he admired most—prominent members of his religious and business communities—tended to exclude him from their most private counsels and treat him with a wink-of-the-eye condescension. Torrey was, it seemed, always good for a laugh, but rarely for much else.

At some point, Dad's appealing showmanship was not enough. It is perhaps emblematic that the only one who was there in the house when he died unexpectedly—of a sudden heart attack on the second floor of their duplex in Titirangi—was his faithful beloved of 40 years. His broken heart had found its ultimate joy in surrender. He was 75 years old.

Despite the shadows of disappointment that hung over the last decades of his life, Dad still found ways to make music even in his grief, and to the end of his days, was still able to join the laughter at the heart of the universe. Even when he was trying to pull on his socks.

I watched one day as he sat on the carpeted floor of his bedroom trying to snag his feet with his socks. Stiffened with arthritis and swollen from the side effects of asthma medications, his aging body insisted on keeping his left foot just out of reach. He tried once and missed. He tried again, and missed. Failing again he began to laugh. "Aw, crikey!" he said. "Crumbs!" After another unsuccessful try, he began to shake with spontaneous mirth, and finally collapsed into a fetal position. Now he could do it. Rocking back and forth, he wrestled the top of his sock over his toes and wriggled it into place. Laughing all the while, he completed the same task with the other sock. The whole adventure had been a bit of fun.

A year or so before his death in 1981, Dad came 10,000 miles with my mother to visit us in Iowa City. As young faculty members, sharing a single assistant professorship in theatre and communications at the University of Iowa, we made an exception to our usual habit of eating at home and treated my visiting parents to an early dinner at the local Taco Bell. To keep things simple, we each ordered the same item from the menu: crispy shell tacos.

It was Dad's first time with tacos of any kind, let alone the crispy shell variety. Following our directions, he unwrapped his taco, seasoned it liberally with extra sauce and took a hearty bite. The taco instantly exploded into fragments, lettuce spilling out onto Dad's

lap, hot sauce and sour cream running across his fingers and onto
the sleeve of his shirt. Fragments of golden shell lay scattered across
the table and randomly over the floor. Dad raised his hands as if
in surrender, searching his sleeves and his lap for what remained of
his shattered meal. "Aw, Christmas!" he muttered. "What kind of a
sandwich is this?" Then, gathering up bits of taco like a bird pecking at
scattered grain, he began to laugh.

There is a passage from Thomas Merton's writings that comes to
mind when I think of my father's ability to laugh in the midst of the
life's messy realities. In the magnificent final paragraphs of *New Seeds
of Contemplation*, Merton imagines the Divine Creator "playing" in the
garden of His creation, diverting Himself in an all-inclusive game of
hide-and-seek, and, like an affectionate parent, inviting his children to
join Him in the forgetfulness of sheer delight. Our Divine Playmate,
he suggests, invites us "to throw our awful solemnity to the winds and
join in the general dance."

*Dad, still
cheerful, dressed
for the beach at
Lake Taupo*

Perhaps Torrey Martin had found the secret. Perhaps at some level
of his being, he had sensed, at the very heart of existence, a certain

playfulness, a never-ending song, a mysterious cosmic dance. Perhaps there was, after all, a comedic divinity that shaped his ends. In later years, I came to see in his life a call to me, his firstborn, to cast aside my own natural reticence and join him in the Great Dance of the Creator. I can hear him now: "Get your monkey masks on, boys. We're going to have a couple of beauty laughs."

In his poem "The Persistence of Song," Howard Moss speaks of a kind of joy that appears as a constant at the heart of human experience. Though his later life bore little resemblance to the promise of his early years, my Dad practiced "a kind of rejoicing." Despite the sad circumstances of his last decades, the years of bitter disappointment and sense of failure, he courageously bore witness to the undying hope in the depths of the human heart and lent his own voice to the persistence of song in the world. He was among those the poet Thomas Lux calls the "joyful ones" whose memory, in my gratitude, I try even now to protect from diminishment and loss.

In the epigraph to his poem "Ode to the Joyful Ones," Lux quotes a phrase from the Anglican Book of Prayer: "Shield your joyful ones." His poem continues as follows:

> *That they walk, even stumble, among us is reason*
> *to praise them, or protect them—even the sound*
> *of a lead slug dropped on a lead plate, even that, for them,*
> *is music. Because they bring laughter's*
> *brief amnesia. Because they stand,*
> *talking, taking pleasure in others,*
> *with their hands on the shoulders of strangers*
> *and the shoulders of each other.*
> *Because you don't have to tell them to walk toward the light.*
> *Because if there are two pork chops*

they will serve you the better one.
Because they will give you the crutch off their backs.
Because when there are two of them together
their shining fills the room.
Because you don't have to tell them to walk toward the light.

In telling my father's story, I have done what I could to shield this particular joyful one from misunderstanding and unfair judgment, and also to honor him. For the best part of his life, it seems, Dad needed no one to tell him—even when his life was dark and difficult—to walk toward the light.

CHAPTER 5.

The Little White Boat

"To hear the faint sounds of oars in the silence as a rowboat
comes slowly out and then goes back is truly worth
all the years of sadness that are to come."
—Jack Gilbert,
"A Brief for the Defense"

Allow me to go back now to my earliest years and pick up a silver thread that weaves in and out of the tapestry of my life. As I have suggested in the first pages of this book, in the course of my days I have occasionally stumbled upon a still, silent place deep within, a place where I have felt reassuringly at home, and where I have taken sweet refuge from the confusing agitations of the world.

Although I have returned to that place many times in my life, sometimes by accident, sometimes by choice, I did not begin to recognize it as a sacred place until after the middle years of my life. In the midst of the events I now relate, that essential life-transforming secret lay hidden within me, trembling with possibility but not yet fully revealed.

I was about five years old, lying on an untidy woodpile in the front yard of our home in Bayswater, gazing upward as marshmallow clouds drifted past the shadowed edge of our bungalow's corrugated iron roof. I had a diffuse sense of a big world coming and going outside of me, past the boundaries of my control, accessible to my eyes but also beyond my reach. Then, momentarily, I felt as if the clouds were solid fixed points in the sky and the woodpile beneath me was moving. The dark triangle of the roof above me became the prow of a ship destined for unknown shores. I felt the thrill of being carried by a gentle wind of some kind into an undetermined but somehow desirable future.

In those moments I became half-conscious of being wrapped in a mystery much greater than myself, surrounded by wider horizons stretching far beyond the tidy quarter acre in coastal New Zealand that had hitherto defined the edges of my life. I sensed a sweet pang of desire to explore those horizons, to go wherever the wind might take me. I felt, as the poet William Wordsworth did, that "the earth was all before me," and even though I should choose as my guide nothing more than a wandering cloud, "I could not miss my way."

At some point in the midst of my reverie, I heard a familiar and beloved voice calling me indoors for tea. Breaking from my dream, I had a vague but unmistakable sense that my intuitions of wonder were somehow connected to other worlds beyond my comprehension, yet also infused with the sense of being not far from home.

My drift of wonder on the woodpile in Bayswater was the first of many experiences when the ordinary has given way to something extraordinary. One of those was a sanctuary in time called summer, memories of which include a modest one-room cabin by a lake—and a little white boat.

I was no different from kids the world over in experiencing the school holidays as a kind of sanctuary. Carried away from the noisy convergences of family, church, and school life, I found my January days—high summer in the south Pacific—to be some of the most peaceful I have ever known. Never before or since have I felt so unencumbered or so free. It can surely be no coincidence that in the midst of these happiest of days, I would sometimes feel my deepest self fall gently into a place of rest that carried a hint of something beyond time. I felt a pervading sense of joy and deep down—even though I could not name it at the time—sensed that my life was held in safety. I felt unusually safe, for example, inside the wooden frame of a little white boat on the rippling surface of a lake which remains in my memory as one of the most beloved places on earth.

Oddly enough for a family living close to the sea, as most New Zealanders do, we chose to travel at vacation time to inland waters. Our destination was Lake Taupo, a clear blue jewel set in the pumice hills of North Island's volcanic plateau. In our English colonial accent, we pronounced it "tao" (rhyming with "cow") "poh." The native Māori pronunciation, which we never used in those days but which most New Zealanders now do, was "Toe-paw."

Lake Taupo, looking south. Watercolor by Marion Ratcliffe

Sprawling at the feet of the snowy peaks of Ruapehu, Tongariro, and Ngauruhoe, Lake Taupo and its surroundings were—and are—a spectacular playground for trout fishing, boating, skiing, swimming, picnicking, wild raspberry picking, and relaxing in hot pools gathered from steaming thermal springs. On many a day, looking south across 26 miles of sun-kissed water, we could see Ngauruhoe ("Mount Doom" in the movie *Lord of the Rings*) exploding from its conical peak, great plumes of ash streaming westward across a pinky-orange sky.

Our residence in this magical place, at least for the most vividly remembered years of my childhood, was a bare one-room cabin (or "bach") situated a stone's throw from the sandy crescent of Two Mile Bay. Clad in fibrolite and roofed in tarpaper, with unpainted floorboards and plain wooden bunkbeds, it was a tiny monument to thrift and simplicity.

We thought it was a palace. We loved it like no other in the world. The fact that the toilet (or "dunny," as we called it) was a shed over a hole in the backyard, the perfect gathering place for midges and flies, only added to our sense of its quirky holiday charm. If, in the course of our deliberations in the dunny, we left the door open, we could look out over the bracken-clad hills, tracing the mandalas of the punga ferns, watching entranced as once in a while a single red deer, ears alert, would gaze at us over a flimsy wire fence. The dunny is now long gone, a victim of the trend toward anything new, but the cabin still stands to this day as part of a much larger development bearing the name "Accent on Taupo."

Along with the cabin there was a small rowboat. I never knew how it came to be ours. It just seemed always to have been there. Dad may have purchased it from a friend, perhaps from our elderly neighbor Percy Mercer, who had a knack for accumulating potentially useful odds and ends, including rolls of faded tarpaper which he was pleased to sell to us to protect our cabin from the rain. Dad loved buying stuff from Percy; he always felt he was getting a bargain. As it turned out, the tarpaper hc purchased from Mr. Mercer was well past its use-by date. It leaked. During a heavy rain, we all rushed to our stations to catch the drips with well-placed pots and pans and tin cups. Percy, however, could see no fault in his tarpaper. The problem, he thought, was with the roof's wooden underlay, the sarking. "It's that darn sarkin'," he said.

No matter. Dad's acquisition of the rowboat—probably designed as a tender for a bigger boat—was a stroke of genius. It gave us all, his boisterous progeny, a good reason to get out of the house and explore the various delights of the lake. As Rat says to Mole in *The Wind in the Willows*, "There is nothing—absolutely nothing—half so much worth doing as simply messing about in boats."

The particular boat in question was a six-foot pram dinghy, painted white, with a flat front that butted the waves. We kept it upside down on the lakeshore pumice, not two hundred yards from our cabin door, and had no doubt in those days that we would find it each day, untouched, exactly where we had left it. I especially enjoyed the early mornings when I had it to myself. It was the easiest thing in the world for me, a twelve-year-old kid, to turn the hull right-side up, drag it to the water's edge, and let it float free. I loved the sensation of the boat taking to the still water, breaking away from the grinding constraints of sand and rock, and just letting go.

As the boat went, so did my heart. There was within me a sweet sense of release. I'd jump aboard while the forgiving little craft rocked precariously from side to side. I'd slot the oars into the oarlocks and, with my back to the direction I was headed, dip the blades into the water and pull away from the beach with a strong, easy rhythm. It gave me exquisite delight to hug the shoreline, listening to gentle waters buff-buffing against the blunt bow. *Kersssh. Kersssh. Kersssh.*

Some days my goal was distance; others it was depths and shallows. I would elbow the dinghy as close as I could to a rocky point and, with a final pull on the oars, let the little craft drift on the glossy surface of the bay. Peering intently over the side, I would watch entranced as the wonders of the lake's bed slowly floated by—moss-bearded rocks, sparkling grey gravels, soft waving waterweeds, darting brown cockabullies (tiny brown fish, native to New Zealand), motionless freshwater lobsters ("kōura" in Māori), wavy striations in perfect symmetry on the sandy bottom. Everything was bright and clear in the crystal deep.

I had no idea how long I would drift. Half an hour? An hour? I did not know. I felt I was suspended between two skies, floating on glassy stillness. Then at some point, my tiny craft would bump lightly against a rock or beach itself on the sand with a gentle tilt. I would feel the kick of an oar, and my reverie would end. I had been for a time in my heart's deep home. I had felt a reassuring presence, something beyond myself but companionable, infused with beauty and peace.

Many years later I would read of another young boy who found his peace in moments like these. Remembering his meanderings on the lakes around his boyhood home, William Wordsworth wrote in *The Prelude*: "*Oh! then the calm / And dead still water lay on my mind / Even with the weight of pleasure, and the sky / Never before so beautiful sank down / Into my heart and held me like a dream.*" I, too, had been held like a dream, and now, almost seventy years on, the pleasure of it still bears echoes of the Eternal.

Another such moment occurred in what was for me one of the unlikeliest places on earth in the unlikeliest season of the year. It happened one winter's day at grammar school.

Winters in Auckland were, as I remember, a curious mix of warm sunshine and clinging cold. One day we'd be running the leafy streets (most native trees are evergreens) or sledding the volcanic hills in shirtsleeves and shorts; the next we'd be wrapped against the wind in our lambswool jackets or gathered in the kitchen near the coal-burning stove. The cold was not like that in the American Midwest where the air hammers your skin, icy and hard, but the kind that presses down on you like a heavy, wet blanket—not quite freezing, not quite warm. Many a July day, I would arrive at school feeling damp and miserable and arrive home seven hours later feeling, well, damp and miserable.

It was on such a July day that I experienced an unlikely breakthrough of joy. It occurred in a music class where, in theory at least, we were to be coaxed from our spiritual lethargy into something higher and better. Our teacher was the venerable Gerald Lee, a crumpled Burl Ivesian figure with tired, wary eyes, wire-rimmed glasses, and a thatch of grey crew-cut hair. In our youthful irreverence, we called him "Gerry." On this particular day, Gerry announced that he was busy with other things and wanted us to listen to a piece of recorded music. No need to write anything down, he said. No reason to take notes for an examination. All we had to do was listen.

Gerry placed a scratchy vinyl disc on the record player, turned up the volume, and allowed the music to drift over the classroom. It was, as I recall, Edvard Grieg's "Piano Concerto in A Minor." Despite my dad's minstrelsy around the house with his violin, I was not in the habit of listening to classical music, nor was I, with my shirt clinging damply to my skin and my socks squelching in my shoes, in any mood on that particular day for exultation. But nevertheless something magical happened.

Almost at once, I was captivated by the beauty of the sounds, and I began to listen—really listen. Grieg's melodies and harmonies, especially in the adagio passages, aroused deep feelings in me, like those I had felt as I drifted in my rowboat on the surface of the lake. Once again, I entered a quiet inner place, where I felt wistfully at home and surprisingly free. In a sense, it was another Wordsworth moment, a moment when "the earth and every common sight / to me did seem / Appareled in celestial light / The glory and the freshness of a dream."

My brief encounter with the music of Edvard Grieg in that faraway classroom is long past, but its echoes somehow live on. To this day, I cannot forget that for a brief time, I had been carried away in a kind of waking dream, where, at the silent center of my being, I heard the whispers of something that seemed beyond time and circumstance. As philosopher Abraham Heschel once wrote, "Inspiration passes; having been inspired never passes." I had been moved, however unknowingly, into an alternative economy—a realm I have come to call the economy of grace. I only wish I had found the words to let the honorable Mr. Lee know. It might have done his tired old heart some good.

There were other times when, momentarily at least, I stumbled upon similar sanctuaries for my soul, where I tasted the very fruits of the everlasting. There were the moments at the top of Mt. Eden where, after a steep climb, I could stand with the vastness of the city falling away at my feet. There were the clear nights on One Tree Hill when I thought the stars of heaven joined the stars of the city in an almost touchable panorama of twinkling light. There were the mornings when from the chalky cliffs of Orere Point I could see the pink sun rising from the edge of the Pacific Ocean, a clear disk cutting its way out of the blue waters. I felt my heart at ease when I dug my toes into black sand and watched the ocean swells crash at the feet of Lion Rock in Piha or, sitting on the pumiced shore of Lake Taupo, felt the gentle tug and wash of the waves.

I was aware of something similar when I first heard the hefty thunder of Huka Falls and felt the cool spray on my face. I felt it, too, when I first smelled the sweet pungency of eucalyptus wafting among the orange roofs of Sydney or when I caught glimpses of bright red and green as native parrots flashed across the outback deserts of Australia. In more recent years, as I shall later tell, I have found myself in touch with something beyond the ordinary in the unforgettable beauties of the Blue Ridge Mountains of Western North Carolina.

There were, of course, other times when I was aware, as Wordsworth was, that there was trouble nibbling at the edges. There were occasions when the boundaries of my inner sanctuary were threatened by fear, a fear that also carried—at some intuitive level— hints of other powers greater than myself. The little white boat, as it turned out, was not always a sanctuary. There were times when it became a source of great peril.

One summer's day, after one of my drifts of wonder around the point at Two Mile Bay, I set out with my younger brother Bryan ("Bryn") on what was for us a big adventure. We were no doubt encouraged in this by the arrival of a 2.5 horsepower Seagull outboard motor, a convenience we hoped would propel us across the lake further than ever we had dared before. We set out confidently toward Rangatira Point about four miles to the southwest over deep, clear water.

Getting there was nothing but fun. Our confidence in our navigational skills grew as we guided the dinghy through a mild chop, enjoying the thrill of finding the best angle to attack each successive wave so that the rock of the boat was bow to stern rather than port to starboard. In self-assured exhilaration, we reached Rangitira and, beaching the boat in a secluded bay out of the wind, sat on the warm sand for a picnic of thick white bread sandwiches layered with butter, slices of bologna and tomato sauce, along with salty potato chips and warm lemonade straight from the bottle. We spent companionable hours exploring the shoreline and skipping pumice stones over the surface of the bay. We felt, for a time, like masters of the universe.

Getting home from Rangitira was a different story. We knew the winds on the lake were unpredictable, especially in the afternoons, but we were not prepared for what happened that particular day. As we broke free from the shelter of the cove and rounded the rocky point into open water, a cold wind slapped us with sudden fury and the waters churned in frenzy around us.

We had no thought of turning back; we needed to get home. White-capped waves loomed above us like mouthing beasts. At full throttle, the little Seagull engine roared hot and loud, while the boat's flat bow butted its way into the lurching swell. Icy spray lashed our faces. Shifting our weight fore and aft, side to side, we fell into anxious silence and cast our eyes nervously toward the friendly cluster of homes sheltering in the sunlight on the far shore. We dared not look back; the waves at our stern seemed to be rising in anger against us, as if energized by some malevolence determined to bring us under. Without fully realizing it, we were juggling with our fate. We weren't quite sure we were going to make it home.

Then, as if called into existence by a touch of Prospero's magic staff, a majestic apparition loomed up alongside us, gleaming white, its powerful engines roaring over the tumult. The men on board, perhaps remembering their own youthful encounters with Taupo's wilder moods, waved knowingly to us, slowed the engines, and pulled the heavy bulk of their craft in front of us, a boat's length from our clumsy bow. They seemed to know, by sailors' instinct, where we were headed. Confidence returning, now mixed with a suitable humility, we settled gratefully into the path of their wake, a smooth roiling triangle of turquoise and white, and followed them to the shelter of our home bay. Gratefully, we waved them goodbye.

There were of course other homey pleasures waiting for us in the summer world surrounding that lovely little bay—a mere nick in the variegated edges of the great lake—and it is with the luxury of time's distance that I turn back to them in my heart's memory. I turn next to those magical days of summer and add to them visitations of delight I have known at other stages of my life: intimations of joy that have built a confidence in me that life is stronger than death, goodness stronger than evil, and light stronger than the dark.

CHAPTER 6.

Visitations of Delight

"What does a visitation of delight do, but confirm the
reality of the soul, the redemption of experience,
the affections of hope, of gratitude to the light,
and to the unheard music that light contains...?"
—Derek Walcott, *"The Elegist"*

I still think with great longing of those summers at Lake Taupo. The little white boat was just one of the pleasures of our simple living there. The very air seemed to echo in shades of blue and the dawning of each new day brought the promise of thrilling new adventure.

Carefree, we wandered along Taupo's lapping shores, digging holes in places where hot water boiled up from thermal springs and luxuriating in the tiny saunas so easily created.

On early mornings we fished for trout as the sunlit mist drifted lazily over the lake's still surface.

On sizzling afternoons, we dived into the cold, crystalline waters from the unpainted wooden jetty of our wealthy neighbor Robert Laidlaw and rode with him toward the Western Bays in his roaring twin-engined speedboat, the *Piri Pono* (now housed in the New

Zealand Maritime Museum in Auckland).

In the bracken-covered hills, we hunted rabbits and took potshots at tin cans in hidden pumice valleys.

We hiked past boiling mud pools and roaring geysers of hot steam and lit fires for "sausage sizzles" on untrodden beaches.

In the twilight of windless evenings, we netted freshwater crayfish at the lake's edge and feasted on the tasty tails, boiled in water, dipped in vinegar and sprinkled with pepper.

Among the liveliest diversions in this childhood paradise were our games of croquet on the bach's wide front yard, dubbed more appropriately the "croakey" course. The croakey course offered us the most unpredictable of delights. With scythe and shovel, we rendered the ground as flat as we could, creating a patch of earth that seemed less like a croquet player's green than an obstacle course designed by tipsy leprechauns. There were hazards everywhere: obstinate clumps of dry tussock grass, thick stalky roots of thistle and broom, pumice mounds, and gravel traps.

Despite the fact that we used professional-grade hoops, mallets, and balls—garnered by Dad during one of his frequent scavenger hunts—no croquet shot on this course was a sure bet. The best of players would line up their mallet with earnest concentration, scrutinizing it, as one of our friends would say, with an "intense scroot," and would strike the ball with crisp precision only to see it pitch off at a disconcerting angle or come to rest with a thud against a stiff lump of crabgrass. By the same logic, a badly aligned shot would take a 90 degree mid-course correction and end up perfectly on target, eliciting an epic dance of self-congratulation.

These matches often lasted for hours, long into the deepening shadows, and were invariably accompanied by cascades of laughter and mini-marathons of good-natured ribbing. Relatives and friends and friends of friends stopped by in crowds to join in the festival of fun.

Among the dearest of my companions in those days was a freckle-faced, redheaded kid named Harvey. He broke into my life like a burst of jazz from a suddenly opened door. The first time I met him was late evening in the summer of 1956, the sun setting orange over wide expanses of the lake and the snowy heights of Ruapehu, Tongariro, and Ngauruhoe.

As I slipped the gate-latch of a bungalow set pleasantly off one of Taupo's wide, pumice streets, I saw the silhouettes of two kids about my age dancing like agitated trout flies in a garish yellow light. For some reason, they were whacking the clapboard walls of the house with fat stuffed socks. I heard squeals of delight and fusillades of self-congratulation: "Zero in for the kill" and "Ya got 'im, Harvey" and "Grouse, man!" Without a word of introduction, the redheaded kid handed me a sock. "So many moths, man, so little time." I, too, began whacking away at moths on the side of the house. I had just met Neil McNaught (cleverly nicknamed "Zero") and his buddy—soon to be mine as well—Harvey Rees-Thomas. I can still hear his eager voice: "Grouse, man!"

The word "grouse," as it turned out, was in 1956 the superlative of the summer. According to my new friend, everything unusually cool was "grouse." A fine-tuned Jaguar Mark 2 screaming down the Waitahanui Straight at 100 mph was "grouse." A spin-out on a dusty pumice road was "grouse." A cruise on the majestic Piri Pono on the mirror surface of the lake was "grouse." A swim in the turbulent warm waters of a thermal beach was "grouse." A miraculous croquet shot over stubby tufted grass was "grouse." A rainbow trout leaping clear in the morning light was "grouse."

Beyond his penchant for superlatives, my new friend was a kid of supreme self-confidence, unquenchably extroverted, verbally adept, and endlessly inventive of ways to prank the world.

*With Harvey
Rees-Thomas, 1962*

It was probably Harvey who came up with the idea of blitzing the "Honeymoon Pool" in the nearby thermal zone of Wairakei. Blitzing the Honeymoon Pool was a spontaneous lark involving an endless succession of testosterone-driven teenagers, including me, bombing the natural hot water pool, butt-first, until the bedraggled honeymooners cuddling at the edges had no choice but to find alternative versions of Shangri-la. It was, of course, a kids' prank, but nevertheless it did my heart some good to be part of it. With his swagger and bravado, my new friend from Wellington had begun to tug my cautious being into life. At first, I was an awestruck observer on the edge of the kid's seemingly limitless social circle. To my mind, he seemed larger than life and also somehow master of it, like an urban Tom Sawyer with pockets full of swagger and a head full of insider information about how the world worked.

Harvey was the leader of the band. Like others in his charmed coterie, I cautiously joined him in his highjinks—jumping off crumbling cliffs, aquaplaning or skiing behind friends' boats, kicking up white dust in fast cars on curvy back roads, skimming pumice rocks until tiny Two Mile Bay was bobbing with white disks, soaking in thermal pools, and raiding the family refrigerator. We thought it "grouse" one afternoon to mash oatmeal, stewed plums, leftover casserole, ketchup, marmite, vinegar, and creamy sponge cake into a garish puddle. Knowing the concoction thus created would be vile, we tasted it anyway—in fat spoonfuls—and exploded in dramatic protestations of feigned disgust.

Then came a great mercy for me. After one of those warm Taupo summers, the redheaded kid invited me to stay with him and his family at their home in the hilly Wellington suburb of Roseneath. I took the train from Auckland's grand old station through National Park into the buzzing heart of New Zealand's capital. My friend was there to meet me. Driving his father's car at a fast clip through the city's squirrelly streets, he offered nonstop commentary on the virtues of his hometown—the best BMW car dealer here, the tastiest fish and chips there, a building designed by a family friend to the left, that kind of thing.

Then, after the usual initial pleasantries among teenage boys and parents, we set off on a wild tandem ride through the hills on his cherry red motor scooter. The motor scooter in question was, I noted, the same model and color as my own—a red 1960 model 150 cc Puch—shiny with potential for adventure. Harvey wanted to demonstrate for me what he called the "double scrape." I swung myself onto the pillion seat and, sensing possible mayhem, gripped the passenger handle in front of me and held on tight. Like a mad jockey, Harvey thrashed the squat machine at breakneck speed down one of Wellington's world-class hills, winding his way through a series of S-bends down The Crescent and along Grafton Road toward the harbor.

Whooping like a kookaburra, Harvey leaned in hard and deep on the first left-hand turn, touching the metal of the running board against the concrete of the carriageway. I felt the scooter lurch—just a touch, as more than a touch could spell disaster—and heard the rasp of metal against road. I caught a glimpse of sparks below me, heard another whoop, and silently noted that we had completed a single scrape.

Still at full speed, the six-horsepower engine screaming, Harvey now swung the scooter hard right in preparation for the next turn. Again I felt the lurch—just a touch—and heard the telltale rasp, saw the sparks. We had now completed the double scrape. No time for self-congratulation, though. Harvey had already rolled the scooter as far as he dared for the fast-approaching next turn to the left. And so on down to the sea.

The double scrape escapade was one thing, the slipstream affair was quite another. It happened on a 200-mile trip between Taupo and Auckland, in the days before the motorway that now eases the journey between Auckland and Hamilton. The top speed of the Puch—in retrospect so well-named for its pokey performance and its emetic looks—was 45 mph, though Harvey and I swore we could, with the wind at our backs, get our machines going much faster. Two hours out of Auckland, on a wide stretch of road leading into the picturesque village of Cambridge, scooters at full throttle, I took the lead.

Harvey was now some distance behind, weaving his machine left and right, every now and then dropping out of sight. As the wind snapped at my jacket and the engine roared in my ears, I was in full sensory overload, as if being shaken in a can of assorted nuts and bolts. Then, suddenly and unexpectedly, the racket became a high-decibel roar, and a towering truck slammed by me on my left. What came next was unbelievable.

Tucked close in behind the multi-wheeled monster—six feet from its hefty rump—was Harvey, head lowered to the level of the handlebars, a fiendish grin on his face, red hair whipping like flax in a coastal gale. He hurtled by me at preposterous speed, the scooter shaking as if it would blow apart as he screamed: "I'm slipstreaming the guy!!" Locked inside the pocket of air behind the blast of the big-rig—a common tactic among racecar drivers—he vanished in a tangled fury of madness. Eventually the calm of mere speed returned and we separately wondered if he had not broken a record of some kind, perhaps (if the Guinness folks are interested) the world land-speed record for motorized ducks, cherry red and Austrian-made. We also wondered if he might have saved a bit on gas as well.

Over the next three years, mostly at Harvey's initiative, we kept in touch by telephone and letter and, on subsequent visits to each other's homes, ventured deep into the waters of youthful philosophical speculation. We asked ourselves all those diverting questions teenagers ask from the safe distance of innocence and easy abstraction: Why is so much of the world—at least the world we could see—so bewildered and broken? Why do innocent children suffer? Does the terminal distress of my siblings at home render pointless the living of their lives. Will praying make a difference? We talked into the wee hours about God and religion, law and politics, science and art, family and friends, the disappointments and the hopes of life. As we talked, I sometimes felt again that deep silent place within me where there was a kind of sanctuary for my soul. At the time though, I could not name it as a sanctuary and, in youthful forgetfulness, thought little more about it. I was not yet connecting the dots.

There was another connection I missed. I realize now, with the perspective that time alone can give, that it was here, in this happy playground of friendship with this redheaded kid, that I first began to discover a voice of my own. With his infectious energy and generosity of spirit, he coaxed me into a bigger life. In his affirming company, buoyed by his generous hyperboles—"Howard, that's brilliant, man; that idea could change the world!"—I felt myself truly recognized, even honored, that my thoughts were enough to shift the direction of a conversation.

To my shame, I was much less capable of offering the same kind of affirmation to him. It's a poor excuse, but in all honesty, he didn't seem to need it. Everybody else in his life seemed to be lining up to offer him company. A couple of years after we first met, the staff and students of his high school named him "head prefect"—an honor that carried the same kind of prestige as that of class president in an American high school. He was later recognized as one of his country's finest science educators and appointed, at an absurdly young age, headmaster of Wellington College, one of New Zealand's most distinguished public high schools.

It has been one of the regrets of my life that over subsequent years we drifted apart, in no small measure because I myself had not yet learned the indispensable skill of reciprocity in friendship. But there was more to it than that. By moving to America, I had put a great physical distance between us, and the two of us had followed different callings and taken different paths. Over the years, we stayed lightly in touch, occasionally recounting for each other the stories of our lives, but, willing as we may have been, we were rarely able to reach back into the sense of connectedness and spontaneous fun we had shared as teenagers.

On a recent return to my native land, as I was putting final touches to this memoir, Harvey and I met up again for coffee at The Cove cafe in Taupo. The familiar waters of the lake lapped gently a few feet away from our table. It was as if we were kids again, riding our cherry red motor scooters on the pumice streets of the town and messing around in boats on the very stretch of the lake that now lay before us. We shared our joys. We shared our sorrows. For four hours, we talked heart to heart, and in doing so, with coffee cups in hand and pastries at our elbows, we set a seal on the six decades of our friendship.

These memories of a dear friend of my early years bring to mind another beloved companion of more recent days, Phil Dibble. It is no exaggeration to say that Phil, now in his early eighties, combines Zorba's rollicking capacity for life with more than a touch of James Thurber's zesty wit. With his shock of white hair, his ruddy weathered face, and grizzled beard, I swear he looks like Ernest Hemingway. I'm not the only one to say so. As the resident Hemingway lookalike at the annual meeting of the American Ernest Hemingway Society, he takes pride in being a stand-in for the great—and long gone—man himself, and almost as an afterthought, in offering papers and essays on various obscure bits of Hemingway lore.

Phil Dibble thinks of life as a one great unceasing conversation, a lighthearted exchange that embraces everyone—and every dog—within the sound of his voice. If he walks into one of his favorite hangouts—like the very European Aixois Bistro in Kansas City's Crestwood neighborhood—or arrives for an "occ-<u>ay</u>-si-on" of some kind, for example, a book reading or a concert, he simply starts the conversation, commenting on this or that ("nice hat"), quoting lines of poetry, offering quick summaries of books and movies, breaking into bits of French or German, confessing his sins both real and imagined, reminiscing about his adventures and misadventures in love or religion or surgical practice, and always, it seems, enjoying to the highest degree the pleasure of not taking himself too seriously.

Many an early morning, he'd pick me up on our way to communion at Grace and Holy Trinity Cathedral, greeting me with a hearty "Yo, Howard. What's new?" or "Guten morgen, mein Freund" or maybe "A blessed sabbath, good sir!" and we'd spar with words, sometimes, but not always, attached to thoughts, all the way to the door of the church. In 2017, his daughter Kristin Webster wrote a tribute to him that included the following: "Morning Ritual:

sing tribal songs, do unusual dance moves, blast 'Spanish Flea' by
Herb Alpert & the Tijuana Brass; all before 5:30 a.m. and preferably
with teenagers still sleeping." Speaking for myself, I can't imagine
a better soundtrack to the movie of Phil's life than Herb Alpert's
"Spanish Flea." In his company, it was difficult, if not impossible, to
feel overburdened by life's cares. To adapt one of his favorite quotes
from Albert Camus, it was as if, even in the depth of winter, he had
"discovered that there lay within him an invincible summer." It was—
and is—good to be around a man like that.

There are beloved people who come into our lives as companions
for a season, and then there are those who have been there from the
beginning. One of those who has been with me throughout my days is
my younger brother, Bryn. In this moment of writing, I have reason to
recall with renewed gratitude his dearly-loved presence in my life.

*Bryn and
Howard, 1946*

Born just two years after me, Torrey and Rene's second son, he
was given the name Bryan Kennedy Martin. Like his namesake,
Bryan Bell, a family friend, he seemed to leapfrog his way through
life, his face flickering with welcome, his body poised like a boxer's

for kindly interaction, his speech peppered with gentle laughter, acute observation, and gut-grabbing comical wit. Even as a child he was as physically courageous as anyone I have ever known.

From earliest years, Bryn climbed higher trees, jumped off steeper cliffs, took the toughest hits, faced down the greatest challenges. He stood up to bigger boys on the playground, took "marks" in rugby (like fair catches in American football) knowing he would be crushed by the furious onrush of opposition players. He threw himself like a mad gymnast to reach impossible balls on the tennis court and played himself to exhaustion in heat that was good only for frying eggs on the asphalt.

The tougher the going, it seemed, the more his delight. He eagerly showed up for contests where the odds were vastly stacked against him. He bobbed and weaved his way into a boxing championship at Auckland Grammar School, for example, without ever having taken a boxing lesson in his life. Many years later, in his late fifties, he rowed his heart out in a rowboat tug-of-war in Nova Scotia, laughing for the sheer fun of competing against the much younger Canadians, taking equal joy in both victory and defeat. My task as older brother was to join in where I dared and watch over him where I did not.

One day, when he was maybe five years old, Bryn climbed the fig tree at the back of our house on Landscape Road. In the moist temperate climate of New Zealand's North Island, fig trees can grow to great heights. To my child's eye, the smooth, springy branches of the fig tree seemed to reach to the sky. Their height intimidated me, but they were like catnip to my adventurous little brother. Standing on an apple box to reach the first curving limb, he grasped it with his tiny hands, swung up to a standing position, then picked his way through the figgy tangle, branch after thinning branch, till he could pick the fruit from the topmost twig. Swaying confidently in the light breeze, he seemed to be up as high as the house.

My brother and me outside Dad's store on Customs Street

As I watched in nervous apprehension, I began to feel queasy. How will he get down? What if the flimsy branch breaks? What if he falls? I called out to the kind lady: "Dunty, come and see Brynnie. He's up the tree, really high." I heard a snap and held my breath as Bryn's tiny feet dangled in space and he wriggled to find a purchase among the thrashing leaves and falling fruit. Dunty looked up and blanched. "What a good boy, Bryan. You climbed the tree by yourself. Now, be really clever and come back down for Dunty. Slowly…there's a good boy." Her heart thumping, she watched his every move and talked him down. "What a careful boy," she said again. "Hold on tight. Slowly now. What a good boy!" Then as his feet touched the ground, she begged, "Please tell Dunty you'll never do that again." Bryn answered, "I climb to the top."

Bryn wasn't much older when he discovered his love of horses. In those days, there were farms in the family on our mother's side and horses were still being used for haymaking and delivering milk to the dairy factories. We were welcome as guests at them all, especially in the early 1950s during the summer holidays before Taupo. I was enchanted by the beauty of the countryside, with the sweet scent of arborvitae wafting in the air, but I was nervous and insecure around the animals—especially the towering solid workhorses, the skittish dairy cows, and the sniffing dogs. While I was terrified around these creatures, Bryn was never more at home. On many an early morning, he would steal over to where the horses were resting in the shade and gaze in wonder at them. Climbing onto a wooden platform, he would stroke their faces, wrap his arms around their necks, and put his nose to their flanks. "Get clother to her, mummy," he once said in his childish lisp. "Horthies thmell nithe, don't they?"

By the age of seven, this town-raised kid was riding confidently around the paddocks, whispering to his mounts, deftly guiding them where he wanted them to go, breaking them into a canter, and bringing them to an easy standstill. It all seemed so natural to him, as if he had somehow acquired, through his very genes, a special sense for the equine spirit. It may well have been, quite literally, true.

In the lore of his mother's family, there are stories to suggest that his maternal grandfather, Arthur Elliott, was a genius with horses, a kind of "horse whisperer," employed at an early age at one of the registered Clydesdale stud farms, Gelt Hall, just south of Carlisle in Cumbria. After his arrival in New Zealand, sometime around 1920, Arthur mustered a herd of 150 dairy cows a hundred miles on horseback from Hāwera in Taranaki, along the west coast beaches north of New Plymouth, navigating thunderous surf on one side and high rocky headlands on the other. With his brother, Robert, and his young son, Bill, he led the cattle safely up the shallows of the Awakino River to a railhead where he loaded them onto a train bound for Frankton. From there, he escorted them along country lanes to a lush new farm in Manawaru in the Waikato. By any measure, Arthur Elliott was a first-rate horseman, deserving of greater public recognition than he ever received. His grandson, Bryn, was of the same class.

I have often wondered why Bryn never became a horse breeder and trainer. The answer, most likely, is this: the breeding, training, showing, and racing of horses was not part of the religious culture surrounding him, and so the young horse-whisperer turned his considerable gifts to other callings. Instead of becoming a horseman, he became an award-winning builder and for a few years the owner of a beautiful sheep farm, an 800-acre, stream-threaded property near Korokonui at the heart of New Zealand's North Island.

Bryn's whole life, it seems, was about love and laughter. As a preteen kid, he loved rag-tag games of ping-pong, rugby, and cricket. He would in crack up in gleeful delight during long rallies at the table, or giggle infectiously at a clever shot with the cricket bat, and whoop in modest triumph when he "sold a dummy" (a fake pass) in pickup rugby games. He wisecracked his way through endless rounds of "croakey" on the world's roughest lawn at Two Mile Bay, swung happily on the low-hanging branches of the pohutukawas in Cornwall Park, and with shouts of sheer joy rode wooden sleds down the bumpy, green terraced mounds of One Tree Hill.

Five decades later, in exultation over a newfound romance, he cartwheeled his way down the pristine slopes of Sand Dunes National Monument, the light in his eyes matching the shimmering glow of the early morning sun. He enjoyed few things more than a "beauty laugh"—a moment of unrestrained hilarity—and there was in his laughter a natural sweetness. You can tell the difference between laughter that comes from wonder and laughter that does not. Bryn's laughter came from wonder, all exuberance and pure delight.

My brother took naturally to the outdoor life of a builder, but he didn't always love his work. Arriving at a wet building site on a dark winter's morning was a hard world away from a cozy bed at home near the olive groves of Cornwall Park. Nevertheless, he seemed always to find things to enjoy on the job. With an instinct for the foibles of human nature as well as the cussedness of inanimate objects, he brought home a world of comedy from his adventures in the construction zone.

Bryan Kennedy Martin was the William Shakespeare of planks and ladders, peppering his speeches with brilliantly original turns of phrase and mangled quotations from the Bible of King James. Casting his eye along a length of two by four pine, he would say: "That's as crooked as Potiphar's undies!" Peering at some anomaly of measurement and, remembering the famous quote from Joseph of Arimathea, he would call out to no one in particular, "How can these things be?" If there seemed no immediate solution to a problem, he would ask, using a deliberately botched quotation from the Psalms, "Wherewithal shall a young man cleanse his faaayce?" Running his hands over a misfitting 45-degree joint, he would announce: "Ooooooh…a mouse'll break his leg on that!" Then, heartily mispronouncing the name of Thomas Didymus, the eighth disciple of Jesus, he would add, "Thomas Diddy-mouse…you poor little jock!" That would set up his reflection, in fake Scottish dialect, on the relative advantages of being a mouse: "And I'd rather be a moose than a raaat! Raats is a no gooood!"

Even in the toughest of situations, Bryn used humor to conquer his fears and put the world to rights. As a young apprentice carpenter, just out of Auckland Grammar School, he was bossed around by the foreman, a tough little bantam rooster named Lanigan, who mixed his old-school instruction with gruff insults and unsparing demands. Bryn was not to be intimidated. He liked to think of Lanigan as a cartoon character like Mickey Mouse with his knobbly knees and skinny legs planted in oversized boots that turned up at the toes. Hilariously mimicking the boss's gruff manner and slushy diction he would call him "Mishter Schlanigan." "Mishter Schlanigan!" he would say. "Legs like twigs and boots as big as China! Mishter Schlanigan…you little beauty!" And he would hobble around in a circle pretending that one of Mishter Schlanigan's boots was stuck in concrete.

The little daredevil who swung precariously from the topmost branch of the fig tree grew up to be the young man who danced without a safety harness across narrow planks on building sites several stories high. He scaled steep cliffs high above raging West Coast surf, took turbulent runs on the big breakers at Raglan, and kayaked Class 4 rapids in swollen National Park rivers. At the pool of the old Terraces Hotel on the Napier Road just outside Taupo, he once double-sprang the diving boards, leaping from the five meter board onto the three meter board and catapulting high into the air before cannonballing into the green thermal depths. Years later, on a camping trip in Colorado, with his older brother and two young nephews begging him not to do it, he pushed past a group of wary young daredevils debating the wisdom of a 20-foot leap, and took a blind headfirst dive into shallow untested water. He emerged unscathed, laughing in triumph.

The only time I ever saw Bryn refuse to take a challenge was on a lazy summer's day at the sliding rock a few miles out of Cashiers, North Carolina. With his wife Sheryl, Bryn had come to visit us in our cabin high up in the Blue Ridge Mountains about an hour southwest of Asheville. We had introduced them to our folksy neighbors—Fred and Sammi Lee Franks—whose cottage lay alongside the creek in the picturesque Glassyrock Valley. The topic of moonshine came up and Fred admitted that he had a fair supply of what he called "white lightning" in the back room. Advising us that he wouldn't want the local preacher to know about his stash, he asked if we'd care for a taste. "Sure, Fred," we said, more out of politeness than conviction. "We'll give it a try."

Fred disappeared for a moment and came back with a mason jar filled with moonshine, clear as water. I took a tentative sip from a plastic cup, a mere touch of the tongue, and felt a bitter burn. I sipped no more. Bryn, on the other hand, confident in his ability to face any challenge, took a good strong swig, blinked his eyes a couple of times, then gamely finished what was left in his cup—a short knuckle's depth of pure North Carolina mountain hooch. That was all it took.

Over the next few minutes, Bryn went into a blurry-eyed meditation. By the time we stood at the top of the sliding rock, suited up and ready for the 30-foot glissade over smooth granite, Bryn was in another world. He stood there transfixed, his face a lighter shade than pale, unwilling to step into the gentle wash of falling water, totally uninclined to take the ride. The white lightning—190 proof, "the fastest wrecking drink on the planet"—had struck. "Come on, Brynnie," we called. "It's an easy ride." It was a no-go. We drove him back to the cabin where he took a long, restorative nap. Surely in his dreams he found a way to make sense of the fact that in taking one challenge—a hearty gulp of bootlegged moonshine—he had rendered himself incapable of taking the other—an easy trip down the watery slope of the Cashiers sliding rock.

In a sense, my brother Bryn was—and remains—the other side of my very self—my sweet, mischievous, kindly, laughing alter ego. As children and teenagers, we were companionable opposites. Where I was timorous, he was fearless; where I was serious-minded and introspective, he was happy-go-lucky; where I was clumsy with bat and ball, he was all grace; where I was solitary and tongue-tied—more often than not deciding what to say seconds after it was too late to say it—he was a gregarious chatterbox equipped with a steady flow of surprisingly original wit. Where I stood beneath tall trees and looked up, he climbed his way to the top and looked down. Where

I froze in terror on insecure high places, he scampered blithely from ledge to ledge or beam to beam, holding out a firm, welcoming hand to me when I was stuck, wrangling me back to safety. Where I stood outside doors and wondered, he opened doors and ran inside with his glistening eyes wide open. As separate selves, we managed to come through life with our share of successes and failures, but combined into one self, we'd have been better than a box of birds. In his brotherly companionship, I sometimes touched a deep inner place of reassurance about my prospects for life.

Bryn, on the coast of Maine, summer 2001

Throughout his life, Bryn has been one of those who bring into our lives "the brief amnesia of laughter." Like his gregarious father, he's been one of the joyful ones. The joy he brought into my own life has been in its effect much more than a brief forgetting of the world's troubles; it's been a kind of unveiling. My younger brother has been, quite naturally and unintentionally, one of my first teachers in the healing presence of laughter and the restorative powers of honest good cheer. His welcome presence, whether in the ease of summer or in the more challenging days of winter, has built up within me a reservoir of good cheer that remains to this day a source of confidence that my very existence is sustained by a Great Joy.

As I write this, my brother is ill and I ponder the real possibility that he will leave this life before me. Yet I choose to believe that there will be a time beyond Time when we will laugh together, my brother and I—and indeed all of us—in an unimaginable symphony of Joy.

I would, in the course of my days, meet other such joyous companions, some in living face-to-face encounters and others in the insubstantial, but not inconsequential, realms of my imagination. There was a time, for example, when I met a party of those joyful ones quite by accident in the pages of a book.

On a dark, rainy lunch hour in 1956, I stepped into the Auckland Grammar School library, a modest greystone building set apart from the main buildings of the campus like an English country cottage. The place had a welcoming air, a feeling of coziness and warmth; it offered a sense of refuge and a promise of new worlds to be discovered. Randomly browsing the shelves, I found myself in the fiction section and happened upon Jerome K. Jerome's *Three Men in a Boat*. I sat down at a wide oak table and began to read.

I was soon at the passage where the storyteller imagines the absurd misadventure of three nerdish camping amateurs—J., George, and Harris, along with Montmorency the dog—setting up a tent in the rain on the banks of the Thames River. The canvas is, of course, soaked and heavy, and it flops about, tumbling down on them and clinging to their heads. Just as one of them gets his side of the tent beautifully fixed, the other gives his side a hoist and the whole wet mess falls soggily to the ground. In utter confusion, they toss their mallets to one side, and begin chasing each other around the tent site yelling things like, "You've got it all wrong, you stupid ass!" and "No I haven't; it's YOU that's got it wrong, you bally idiot!"

As I read all this, I was, in a matter of seconds, seized by convulsions of barely suppressed laughter. I read a sentence or two and simply cracked up, read on, and cracked up again. My insides lurched in quick spasms. Tears welling up in my eyes, I looked for mercy from the prim librarian at the desk. Receiving none, I read on, shuddering inwardly until the muscles under my lungs ached. It was almost too much; I had never read anything so downright hilarious.

What is the function of laughter in human experience? How do I explain the sense of liberation that attends it, the vitality it engenders, the sense of hope it inspires? Surely it is true that laughter—whole-hearted, honest laughter, as opposed to the demonic cackle of cruelty or derision—is one of the most natural means of grace in our lives. It is an impulse which enables us to transcend the limits of our ordinary thinking brains. By it, we reach into a place where there are hints of something eternal, something ultimately welcoming and benign.

Our surrender to honest laughter may well be a means whereby we let ourselves go into the embrace of a greater Joy. If, as Jungian psychologist Helen Luke said, there is laughter at the heart of the universe, then surely our own laughter—guileless and deep—is a means of getting to that heart. "Laughter," writes the inimitable memoirist Anne Lamott, "is carbonated holiness."

Such thoughts have led me in later years to believe that studying and teaching the arts of comedy—especially those designed specifically to evoke honest laughter—was a kind of calling, even a sacred one. I do not remember being aware of any such hints of transcendence when, as a small boy in pajamas, I laughed at the antics of Charlie Chaplin during family film night, 8 mm Kodak projector and all, but I do remember feelings of restful liberation that were beyond the ordinary. In short films like *The Tramp*, the loose-limbed little chap on the flickering screen took me somewhere else—and that "somewhere" felt both good and right. Safe.

It became my hope, in my later years as a professor and arts educator, to offer in the classroom moments where my students could feel the goodness and rightness—and safety—of that "somewhere" else. In that sense, I would come to think of my teaching as a means of nurturing spiritual life, an introduction to the care of the soul.

During my undergraduate days and those that followed, I kept stumbling upon other places where I felt the liberating effervescence of laughter. I felt it in the jaw-snapping double-takes of Lou Costello on film and in the fantastic verbal gymnastics of Peter Sellers, Spike Milligan, and *The Goon Show* on radio. I felt it, too, in the brilliant verbal doodlings of James Thurber, who became my frequent companion in the emotional turbulence of my college years and the source of some of the best lines I offered in my speech as best man at the wedding of my redheaded friend and his delicately beautiful bride, Jeny.

I'm still caught off guard by nonsensical Thurberian assertions such as, "I would be the last person to say that madness is not a solution," or "Hens embarrass me; owls disturb me; if I am with an eagle, I always pretend that I am not with an eagle." I found exchanges like the following from Thurber's *The 13 Clocks* both senseless and, at precisely the same time, reflexively hilarious:

> *Something very much like nothing anyone had ever seen*
> *before came trotting down the stairs and crossed the room.*
> *"What is that?" the Duke asked, palely. "I don't know what*
> *it is," said Hark, "but it's the only one there ever was."*

There was no gap between my apprehension of the absurdity of this little scene and my outburst of helpless laughter. I couldn't— and can't—explain it. It just cracked me up. It took me many years to see the connection between the laughter so instantly evoked by James Thurber's humor and that evoked by the subtler, more deeply embedded inventions of the great comedic novelists and playwrights.

I would come across many such inventions over the years, and each one still lives in my memory as a witness to the dearest aspirations of my being. Is there a sense of lightness and goodwill and laughter—a sense of overcoming—in the greater horizon beyond time and space? The comedic inventions of great writers have often reminded me it is so. Among them I include the warmhearted character of Joe Gargery in Charles Dickens's *Great Expectations*.

Here's how I met Joe Gargery. In the darkening hours of a foggy Auckland afternoon, I watched, as an overwhelmed and frightened 14-year-old, one of the first movies I'd ever seen: *Great Expectations*. I had become a member of the school's film club as a way of getting around the unwritten rule that good members of our religious community did not go to the movies for fear of moral contamination from the dubious values of Hollywood. I was thrilled with expectation as the first images flickered onto the screen.

I was instantly transported into a world of new imagination. At its heart was a character named Joe Gargery, the long-suffering husband of Pip's sister. Out of the grim Dickensian world of prison ships, convicts, poverty, arrogance, violence, and despair emerged Joe's kindly and reassuring presence.

Joe was like an angel of mercy to me. Speaking to the heart of Pip's loneliness, he says, "There's room for Pip with us at the forge." Joe's words of gracious accommodation seemed to be addressed to me. They pierced the gloom of my own troubled mind and the dankness of those imprisoning classrooms like sunlight breaking through the clouds. There was, it seemed, room for me at Joe's forge, too.

Later in the story, Joe offers to an increasingly undeserving Pip a cheery reminder of the existence of faithful friendship and hope for better things in the future: "Dear Pip, old chap, you and me was ever friends. And when you're well enough to go out for a ride— what larks!"

With the kindness of Joe embedded in my heart, I continued on through the story of Pip, Estella, Miss Haversham, and the others, feeling much more able to cope with the darkness that pervaded of the rest of the story and the heaviness that had so often gathered around my own young life. Joe's promise, though buried in a make-believe world, was for me a promise that was somehow real. It was an inkling of faithful friendship and better times ahead.

I was in grammar school when I met Joe Gargery; I was at university when I met another unforgettable character, again from Dickens—Sairey Gamp. I was introduced to her in an undergraduate English literature class, taught by Professor John Reid. At a memorable point in his discussion of *Martin Chuzzlewit*, the professor stepped out of lecture mode, that staple of university education, and became an actor. After introducing Sairey Gamp as one of Dickens's greatest comedic creations, he set the scene. Then, with a combination of surrender to the plum-ripe quirkiness of the character and knowing intimations of his own delight and wonder—sidelong winks, wry smiles, and a "get this" turn of the head—he brought her to life in the place where imagination and feeling converged.

I put down my pen, abandoned my critical mindset—the one I would need to pass the end-of-year examinations—and let myself be carried off into Sairey's fantastic comedic world. Astonished by her inexplicable ability to transcend the dark realities of her existence—the ravages of poverty, loneliness, ignorance, and addiction—I sensed a lifting of my spirit, a lightening of my heart, a welling up within of something that felt like joy. I was carried away, almost beyond recall, by the image of her bewigged pate, "a row of bald old curls that could scarcely be called false they were so very innocent of anything approaching deception." I was entranced by the torrent of nonsense spilling from her teeming crosswired brain and liquored-up lips.

Her defense of her supposed "friend," Mrs. Harris—the bottle of gin she kept on the mantel for frequent "conversations"—was a brief but brilliant triumph of silliness over rationality. The silliness of a genius, though, has a way of verging on the sublime:

> Leave the bottle on the chimley piece, and don't ask me
> to take none, but let me put my lips to it when I am so
> dispoged, and then I will do what I'm engaged to do,
> according to the best of my ability…. Rich folks may ride on
> camels, but it ain't so easy for 'em to see out of the needle's eye.
> That's my comfort and I hope I knows it.

To this day, Sairey Gamp lightens my spirit and makes me laugh. I'm carried away by her hopeless mash of knowing self-deception and butchered metaphor, and the place I go seems to be a place of joyous anticipation and freedom. The comedy lies not in the person of Sairey, however—in real life she'd be merely pitiable and sad—but in her creator's magnificent evocation of her. She lives in an imagined world of comedic possibility. What does it matter that there is no such person as Sairey Gamp in the real world? She arises from somewhere in the human spirit. The genius of Charles Dickens found her somewhere. So much the better for me and, I think, for all of us.

The place where I met the kindness of Joe and the sublime silliness of Sairey were places in my heart. All I had to do was let a film or a book take me there.

I am no different from any other in wondering what my life is ultimately for and how to live it well. Along with philosophers, theologians, poets, artists, and contemplatives throughout history, I have wrestled with these questions for as long as I can remember, and yet the answer has always seemed just over the horizon, just beyond my grasp.

Seven decades later, I'm still asking questions, and the answers still seem beyond mortal reach. The difference now, I suppose, is that I see the questions in a different context—a lifetime of exploration and experience, a patchwork of disappointment and hope—and see them less as a cry for definitive answers than as part of a deep inner resonance that comes from another realm. As Thornton Wilder put it in the words of one of his characters, "We all know that something is eternal."

There was always, or so it seems, a sense of something eternal deep in my bones. From the visions of delight I had known in my childhood home sprang an awareness of the pervasive presence of the Eternal and a sense, however subtle and undefined, of calling to a sacred journey. From my early encounters with sickness and death, including my sense that, in one way or another, we are all broken by life, came a sense of respect for the mysteries beyond my comprehension.

It's one thing to have inescapable youthful experiences of wonder and mystery and another thing to know what to do with them. In the light of the great paradox of beauty and suffering, how should I shape my identity in the world and find my own sense of calling within it?

To answer such questions, I soon found I was obliged to step away from the safest place I had ever known and take my own faltering steps—as every human being must—away from the "paradise" of childhood. As years went by, another world began to crowd in around me and, bit by bit, I lost touch with what was deepest and most lasting within. The blizzard of the world, as Leonard Cohen puts it, was upon me. It was time to turn away from the sanctuary of the little white boat—away from the comforting presence of the joyful ones in my life—and face the incoming storm.

CHAPTER 7.

Lost in the Noise

Behind our lullabies,
the hooves of terrible horses
thunder and drum.
—Carol Ann Duffy, "Queen Herod"

Philosopher Alain de Botton once observed that "we are all made to live before we can even begin to know how." After the wrenching passage from our mother's womb, we are cast as struggling innocents into a vast and alien country, with no idea how to cope with its complications and contradictions. Utterly dependent on our families of origin for physical survival, we are almost equally dependent on our surrounding culture for a sense of our place among the teeming multitudes of the earth.

Over time, of course, we begin ever so slowly to discover what it takes to get through the vulnerabilities of childhood, the tumultuous uncertainties of adolescence, and the shocks of adulthood. But we travel blindly much of the time and there's no doubt it's an easier journey for some than for others.

I remember hearing stories of parents throwing their children into the lake to teach them how to swim. Despite the kindness that anchored my existence, I felt like one of those terrified little ones, tossed into a sea of contradictions and ambiguities, bewildered, overwhelmed, thrashing my way toward… what?

There's nothing like bad news to impress upon a tender soul the fragility of our dreams of paradise. While the sense of wonder was somehow at the core of my being, I recognized that there were also contradictory powers, other mysteries with which I had to reckon.

Pervasively in the background of my young life, like the set of an absurdist play, was a feeling of loneliness and alienation. I simply felt out of place in the world. By the time I had become more or less reconciled with the ghosts I heard at home in the nighttime, I was confronted by other specters that appeared in the daytime. Going to school was one of them.

Not only did I walk unwillingly through the doors of my academies of learning, but it was there, in those acrid, oily classrooms, I first felt the cold blast of exclusion. It was, in reality, an exclusion by default. No one deliberately set out to make me feel unwelcome. I was not bullied, as some children are, by unthinking peers. Yet as a shy kid, trembling with nerves, I felt alone and apart. The world seemed overwhelmingly complex to me and seemed to bear secrets that were not mine to share.

I remember one day standing alone on the edge of a grassy field at Belmont Primary School—it would have been 1948—watching classmates play a pickup game of cricket. I heard energetic voices and laughter. I saw kids confidently taking turns with bat and ball, boisterously agreeing or disagreeing on the rules, seemingly carefree in their sense of belonging and apparently assured of their right to be in the game. I was conscious of being alone.

Standing there on the edge of the field, my mind raced with questions: How did it come about that these kids were in the middle of the action and I, entirely unseen, on the outside? How did they get chosen to be in the game? How did they know the rules? Where did they get the bat and ball and the wickets, and how did they learn to use them? I stood there watching for a long time until the bell sounded for our return to the classroom and I went back to another loneliness.

My bewilderment at feeling like an outsider to the secrets of the world—a sense that haunts me still—was amplified in those early years by other dark clouds gathering on the horizon of youthful consciousness, creeping like the harbor mist through the doors and windows of my life.

I was born, for a start, during the darkest days of World War II. There were reports of ruthless conquering powers and incomprehensible casualties. In the Libyan desert alone, three thousand young New Zealanders were killed or wounded in action or taken as prisoners of war. Though I knew little of Hitler's march across Europe, the fall of France, the Dunkirk evacuation, the battle for North Africa, or the D-Day landings, I sensed fear in the air, a dark foreboding as the adults around me tried to make sense of the serial catastrophes unfolding in bloody places like Egypt, Greece, Italy, and the beaches of Normandy.

I remember blackouts imposed for fear of Japanese invasion— curtains drawn, no lights on in the house. I remember taking a bath in a tin tub on the kitchen table, with water heated in pots on the gas stove, and a single guttering candle to light the darkness. I remember ration books for lamb and butter, men leaving for places unknown with no guarantee of return, and, lying randomly around the house, published photographs of London burning and jackboots marching.

I also heard stories of terrible inhumanity—and remarkable resilience—in the zones of war on the other side of the globe. One of them concerned my uncle, Vine Carey Martin, who'd been captured

by the Nazis in North Africa and forced into service as a doctor in
Stalag IV-F concentration camp in Hartmannsdorf bei Chemnitz,
Germany. In those terrible years—1942 to 1945—he had been witness
to inconceivable cruelty, starvation, humiliation, disease, and death.

*Dr. Vine C. Martin
(center) in Stalag IV-F
concentration camp*

I learned much about his harrowing war experiences in later years,
when as a beloved mentor to thousands of young New Zealanders,
he turned the nightmares of his life into cleverly improvised tales,
brilliantly droll retellings of life and death behind the barbed-wire
fences and in the shadows of the ghastly searchlights. For his services
to the physical and spiritual welfare of the youth of New Zealand, he
was honored by the Queen as a Companion of the Queen's Service
(QSM), receiving his award in 1994 from the hand of New Zealand's
Governor-General, Dame Catherine Tizard.

After the war, I would sometimes lie awake at night with troubling
thoughts of another kind of catastrophe—the polio epidemic—which
had been spreading around the world and had arrived like a poisonous
tide on our own distant shores. Its appearance seemed random and
mysterious, but its outcomes were severe, leaving many, including the
child of one of our neighbors, strapped in steel leg braces, struggling
for breath in iron lungs, unable to join us at play on the streets.

I recall a fretful drive to the farming country north of the city,
where we stood in hushed silence by the bedside of a young woman

named Clarice, weak and pale, lying motionless in a darkened room, crippled with poliomyelitis. I remember standing under the dark spreading wings of a macrocarpa tree, waiting for the adults to say their bewildered goodbyes, brooding on the thought that Clarice, the sister of a dear family friend, might never leave that dark place. It was true. When she died, I imagined the blinds of her bedroom still drawn and the macrocarpa branches swaying lightly as she passed.

The specters that troubled my mind at elementary school continued to haunt my days in high school. Dickens would have had a field day with the banalities of a grammar school education in New Zealand in the 1950s. In his oddly paradoxical role as moral mentor in a state school, the headmaster—at school assembly—would sometimes read the "love passage" from First Corinthians: "Now abideth faith, hope, and charity, but the greatest of these is charity." Then, immediately after prayers, he would administer uncharitable thrashings to boys who had dared at any point to break the rule of absolute silence. On many a morning, the tense silence of the first hour of class was broken by the swish and thwack of the cane on the humbled buttocks of those who had dared a whisper.

I myself was once beaten in this way by a master of English language and literature for forgetting to do my homework. Ordering me to bend over at the top edge of a steep set of stairs, he caned me with such explosive force that I barely avoided tipping forward and tumbling into the stairwell's abyss. With waves of cold, dark nausea coursing through my brain, I staggered uncertainly back into the nervy stillness of the classroom, wounded as much by feelings of humiliation and injustice as by the electric shock of the wicked bamboo rod.

In those years, it was rare to find a mentor who was genuinely kind. The pedagogical orthodoxy of the day seemed to call for cajolery and intimidation in an atmosphere of fear. One incident stands out in my memory. It was, once again, the hour of morning assembly. The text for the day was excerpted from the wisdom literature of the Bible, no doubt a passage about mercy, justice, and compassion.

Quite suddenly, the silence was shattered by a loud, throaty wail. There was a clatter of benches and a convergence of loud footsteps, followed by more dissonant wails, more confusion, and a broken chorus of urgent, whispered voices. Within a couple of minutes, the hubbub and the cries became less audible. We waited in stunned silence. No comment from the stage. Apparently unfazed by the drama unfolding before his eyes, the headmaster paused briefly, then continued to read, droning on in rote piety from his biblical book of wisdom.

One of our peers, we later learned, had suffered an epileptic seizure and been carried off to an open classroom nearby. What sticks in my mind, though, is the fact that nothing was ever said about the whole episode, nothing about the boy who'd been at its center, nothing to explain what had happened to him. The dignity of the assembly, the maintenance of rank-on-rank order, had been of primary concern—the fate of the boy apparently of little consequence. I was troubled not only by the suffering of my classmate, but also the harshness of a world that seemed so indifferent to his pain. I still wonder what became of him.

Day after day, I emerged from the dark halls of learning with my eyes blinking as if adjusting to an unaccustomed light, with no greater love of praiseful things, or of life itself for that matter. I thought still less of my fellow human beings, who, on the whole, seemed a surly, self-absorbed and uncivilized lot. I'm sure that I appeared the same to them in my defensive grumpiness and my occasional flashes of explosive pugnacity, which showed up in surprising ways on the rugby field, or in one case, in a fist fight with an English kid named Malcolm (for which I was escorted to lunch-hour detention in the "prefects' lounge").

I was still in grammar school when I found the stone-cold face of death staring at me once again—this time from outside my family circle.

The memory of that day strikes like steel to my heart. First the howl of an engine at high speed, then a scream of brakes. The pale stricken face of a fifteen-year-old kid appears out of a swirling cloud of white pumice dust. "Where's Ken Rees Thomas?" Dumbly, blankly, one of us calls out. "Not here! Why?" The kid calls back, "Got to find the doctor." The engine roars again, wheels spitting gravel, and the car is gone. I feel a shiver of foreboding.

It had been one of those near perfect days at Lake Taupo. Crisp, clear air, snowcapped mountains sharply outlined against a blue, blue sky, gentle waves sparkling in the sun, all contained in a cathedral of summer sounds: the glissading chorus of cicadas, broom pods snapping in the midday burn.

The kid and his older brother had taken their family motorboat to Acacia Bay on the western shore for some waterskiing. They had done this together many times and had become, over the years, accomplished skiers, already confident on a single board, fully capable of fast running starts and long graceful curves to the beach. There was no reason on this lazy day to expect anything but a day of fun on the water.

With the kid at the wheel, the older brother had sliced the water confidently for some time, his ski slapping rhythmically on an easy chop, and after numerous wide, sweeping turns, shoulders close to the surface, had indicated it was time to come in. The kid had pulled the boat toward shore then turned out sharply to slingshot his brother into his landing. There were other craft parked nose-in along the bay, and the skier's simple plan was to glide in close to the parked boats, then take an exhilarating curve around them before beaching on a long stretch of open sand beyond.

Perhaps he was a second late letting go the rope. Perhaps he had misjudged his speed or distance, or in a moment of indecision, had changed his line of approach. Nobody will ever know. There was a sudden fury of wild water, a blunt thud, and silence. The older brother had met the outboard motor of a parked boat at full force, waist high, and his body now lay unconscious and inert across the rocking stern.

Word of the accident finally reached the doctor. In him there lay some hope. One of a circle of family friends who summered around the margins of the lake, he knew the two brothers well. He also happened to be one of the most accomplished thoracic surgeons in the country. By now the older brother was on his way by shrieking ambulance to the hospital fifty miles away in Rotorua, and the doctor was soon racing in a fast car to be at his side. He would be forever too late. There was nothing he could do; the force of the impact had ruptured the boy's liver and spleen beyond repair. The older brother was already dying. His name was Gordon Bain. Seventeen years old.

Silent and dumbstruck, I helped carry Gordon's coffin down the steps of an indecorous wooden church and on to its appointed place in the darkness of the earth. It was all so inexplicably final. The screaming face of tragedy had appeared in my life once again. I was fast becoming aware that suffering and loss were not just themes in my own story, but were unavoidable strands in the tapestry of other lives as well, universal realities in the human condition that would require all my efforts to understand. I would need a story of some kind—a really good story—to help me get there.

Gordon Bain, 1960

The death of my childhood friend was, of course, not the first time I had felt in my blood what poet A. E. Housman called "an air that kills." But I was perhaps aware, if not then, at some later time, that the "happy highways" I had once traveled were now forever gone.

In all fairness to my schoolboy self and the school that for 150 years has been recognized as one of New Zealand's finest, I must confess to moments of contentment—and even inspiration—among my otherwise unhappy days there. One of those bright spots was my friendship with a freckle-faced kid named Charlie Bockett. Charlie ran freely with me around the school's Spanish mission-style main building, laughing as we sprinted across its park-like grounds. He joined me in joyfully unskilled games of handball on the fives courts and chattered away as we waited at the "tuck shop" to buy our favorite lunch: a Broadway pie (a delicious combination of meat and spiced gravy), a donut (a big round fist of dough laced with jam and whipped cream), and a Coke.

Also tucked away fondly in my heart is the memory of a visit by the American political economist John Kenneth Galbraith, advisor to Franklin D. Roosevelt and one of the architects of the post-WWII American economic boom. Standing six feet nine, he towered like a great grey eagle above the lectern of the assembly hall, offering folksy anecdotes and considered wisdom from his life in international affairs.

I have never forgotten Galbraith's closing words, as clear and freighted with meaning now as they were then. "Gentlemen," he said. "The wholeness of your life is like a three-legged stool. The kind a milkmaid uses in the cowshed. There are three essential parts— mind, body, and spirit. To live your life at its best, to stay in balance, you must pay attention to all three. Strengthen your body. Expand your mind. Nurture your spirit." What he meant by the "spirit" that required "nurturing," I did not know. Yet, at some level, I think I did.

Despite such bright interludes in my years at school and the sunny sanctuaries of contentment I found in quiet places and in unexpected laughter, there was still within me a pervasive sense of sadness and fear, a lingering sense of contingency, an unshakeable sense that death was poised on my shoulder and hidden there under my pillow at night. Many a day at school, I bit my nails and teased my unruly hair in anxious expectation of a phone call to the school office announcing the final passing of one of my siblings lying stricken in their beds at home.

Looking back now, I recognize in all this not just an abiding sadness but also the specter of childhood depression. There was a black dog snapping at my young heels, and I could not quite shake him. He would be back from time to time throughout my life, and to this day I can feel him pacing on the edge of consciousness, head down, ready to pounce. Over the years, I've had to be watchful to keep him at bay.

I must speak now of a matter that pains me to reveal, about how, in my first decades of life, the very power that might have been my greatest source of consolation became instead a cause of even greater inner disquietude, complicating my search for reassuring sanctuary in the silent core of my being. I speak of my early experience of a certain kind of religion. I speak not of all religion—but rather of religion in one of its many unhappy manifestations, a form of religion that in large part determined the culture surrounding me in my earliest days.

In her 1986 book, *To Dance with God* Gertrud Mueller Nelson offers the image of a child playing sandcastles on a beach beside a vast ocean. With her back to the surging expanse of untamed water, the little girl digs a pint-sized moat around the perimeter of her castle. She designs the channel so that she can let in as much of the ocean's power as she can manage, open enough to let the water in, but small enough to protect her castle from being overwhelmed. The waves crashing on the beach behind her now flow easily around her sandy construct one teaspoon-sized rill at a time. Feeling safe, the little girl looks on with wonder and delight.

The image of the little girl at the seaside suggests a way of looking at the relationship of the soul and the great ocean of religion. The rituals and creeds of our various traditions are intended to function as thoughtfully crafted channels allowing the curious soul to experience as much of the vastness of the Eternal as it can bear.

Imagine a situation, however, where an unthinking adult brings a bulldozer to the child's playground, turning the tiny moat into a vast trench into which the sea's wildness pours with overwhelming and frightening force. Imagine a situation where religion enters a child's experience by the force of a lumbering tractor rather than the delicacy of a teaspoon. It happened to me.

As a child and as a fledging adult in my teens and early twenties, I more often than not felt overwhelmed, rather than gently nurtured, by religion. A great flood of religious dogma and practice overwhelmed the tiny channels of my interior life.

The people of my inherited religious community, many of them gracious and kind, had built an austere but persuasive culture around the reading and multiplication of words. They seemed to believe it literally true that, as the Gospel says, the word was in the beginning. The sayings of Jesus were the word of God; the Bible was the word of God; the letters of St. Paul were the word of God; inspired preaching was the word of God. They took the metaphor as a literalism: the "word of God" was a matter of words.

Like a member of a secret society, I was initiated into this culture by repeating words. I was affirmed in my faith by listening to words. I gained recognition among my peers by being a multiplier of words. I expressed my sense of identity by attending eloquent displays of words—sermons, seminars, conferences, Bible studies, books, magazines, pamphlets and "tracts." I joined others as they prayed with words and marked my sense of belonging by exchanging familiar verbal clusters such as: "born in sin," or "justified by faith," and "saved by the blood."

Along with those around me, I believed such phrases were the keys to unlocking the secrets of the heart, but, at least for me, they became hard shells around the seeds of faith. For me, as for the people in R. S. Thomas's rural Wales, God was trapped in a cage of words, "crammed / Between the boards of a black book."

When you grow up surrounded by a particular cultural tradition, especially an intensely religious one like mine—it's relatively easy, as David Brooks writes, to get the basic concept of it down, but not so easy to discover its humanity and grace. As William Saroyan once put it, "Life is an art, not bookkeeping. It takes a lot of living for a man to get to be himself."

I was no different from many others in assuming that hearing is believing, that information is insight, that what's given is what's received. I made the easy assumption that, by virtue of its being held with conviction by others, the religious culture of my family of origin was also, in its entirety, right for me. It was not so.

The danger lay precisely in this: that being a compliant kid, I learned well how to copy the religious behaviors of others but— except in moments of reverie in solitude—had little notion of hearing the call of the eternal for myself or knowing how to make my own unique response to its whispers. Out of the distractions of this kind of religion, I was, as poet William Stafford puts it, in danger of "following the wrong God home."

I was essentially following the wrong God home, for example, by agreeing to become a spokesperson for religious ideas received from others, offering in public what I did not fully understand in private.

I allowed myself to be drawn into a circle of well-meaning people who, as one theologian put it, "knew their Bibles better than the human condition." Mesmerized by the fierce eloquence of the elders of the tribe, I became a copycat religious enthusiast, feeling oddly entitled, even as a teenager, to instruct others in the unambiguous certainties of inherited belief.

I became engaged in all kinds of wordy religious enterprises: teaching Sunday school, leading evangelical clubs at college and university, coordinating theological forums, traveling across vast swaths of New South Wales to offer guidance to the leadership of high school religious societies. On Sunday nights, at the age of sixteen, I could be found standing under the awning of a van, designed like a mobile foodcart, gripping a piano-accordion while amazingly gifted orators, including my dad, exhorted "sinners" on the streets to "give their hearts to Jesus." In later years I could be heard speaking of faith to large groups of young New Zealanders in venues throughout the country.

One of these groups was an innovative outreach project called "Drift Inn," designed to make an attractive and persuasive case for a thoughtful kind of Christianity. It was led with great flair by a charismatic young Aucklander, John Hawkesby—still a dear friend—who later became one of New Zealand's best-known media personalities. I felt honored to work with John and his wife, Joyce, and to be the speaker at some of Drift Inn's wildly popular convocations. But, from the safe distance of time, I realize that here, too, I had only the faintest inkling of what I was talking about. I am grateful that, while Drift Inn did not last, the friendships born there, including those with Stan and Doreen Thorburn and Raymond and Helen Miller, still have a gentle but lasting presence in my life.

The problem with all these enterprises was this: I was telling stories that had not yet become part of my own inner life and repeating

John Hawkesby at "Drift Inn," 1967

clichés borrowed from sources outside my actual lived experience. My words did not arise hard-won from the silence of my heart. The more I talked, the more I lost touch with the quiet whispers within, the still, small voice of the Kind, the Gentle, and the Eternal.

In the background of my life, like a radio left on as acoustic wallpaper throughout the day, I was hearing the echoes of other voices: superstar writers (like Francis Schaeffer), Biblical scholars (like John Stott, F. F. Bruce, and J. I. Packer), platform performers (like Tony Campolo), religious celebrities (like David Shepherd) and missionary heroes (like Jim Elliot). I had become an eager participant in an endless round of conferences and teach-ins and had eagerly devoured the contents of religious journals and magazines. I had read words by the tens of thousands, my bookshelves bulging to the point of collapse.

But I had misunderstood what my reading was for. I had accumulated ideas for their own sake, rather than for their transformative powers. I had not realized, as Marcel Proust once observed, that reading is on the threshold of the spiritual life but does not constitute it. "It becomes dangerous," he wrote, "that when, instead of awakening us to the personal life of the mind, it tends to take its place, when the truth no longer appears to us as an ideal which we can realize only by the intimate progress of our own thought and the efforts of our heart, but as something material deposited between the leaves of books like a honey fully prepared by others."

In all fairness to my younger self, I must admit that part of my obsession with reading about religion was itself an expression of my hunger for depth. In a sense, I was reading to save my life. A book can be a sanctuary, a quiet place of reflection, and I found that I enjoyed the sense of living inside the eloquent words of writers like C. S. Lewis, Dorothy Sayers, G. K. Chesterton, William Barclay and W. Phillip Keller. There is no doubt I found moments of deep reassurance there.

Even these moments, however, were as likely as not to be overwhelmed by an impulse to read yet more so that I would not fall behind in the race to be in the know. It was more important to me to be able to say I had read an admired author than to listen for the echoes of the Eternal through the words on the page. I simply could not distinguish between those experiences that were part of my ambition for mastery and those that genuinely resonated on the strings of my most secret heart. In my confusion about what was truly good for me at the core of being, I had succumbed to a spiritual disorder. I had unwittingly overturned what Leonard Cohen called "the order of the soul."

At some level of my being, though, I knew that the path I was on was not the right one for me. I was often troubled by the gap between what I heard others saying (and was myself repeating) and my own felt experience. One summer's night, for example, when I was about 13 years old, I sat in a Bible camp meeting at Auckland's Eastern Beach, dreaming of pretty girls and sunlit beaches, barely listening to yet another lengthy discourse on a dense and lofty passage from the Bible. On this occasion, the speaker, coat buttons popping with scholarly erudition, had chosen a text from the book of Revelation: "And unto the church of the Laodiceans write: 'These things saith the Amen, the faithful and true witness, the beginning of the creation of God: I know thy works, that thou art neither cold nor hot. I would thou wert cold or hot. So because thou art lukewarm, neither cold nor hot, I will spew thee out of my mouth.'"

Like an actor in a Greek tragedy, the preacher expounded the text, offering long, confident orations on the cowardice of doubt, repeatedly evoking the image of an avenging God disgorging the faint of heart from his mouth. This was a God, it seemed, who withheld grace where there was doubt, refused forgiveness where there were heartfelt questions, and threatened to lower a crude boom of punishment on those who struggled with paradox and ambiguity. Lord have mercy! What kind of God was this? This vengeful God was *not* the One I had sensed from time to time at the silent core of my being and had long intuited from the gentle touch of my mother's hands or my father's kindly and forgiving presence. The dissonance was so great that I felt I could bear it no more. I had to get away.

I stood up in silent protest from the hard-backed wooden bench, walked to the exit past rows of solemn upturned faces, and stepped out into the warmth and freedom of the night air. Feeling the crunch and bite of pipi shells under my bare feet, I ran in the darkness to the flimsy shelter of our family tent and lay down on my creaky wooden cot. Resting there a while, I peered out through the heavy canvas flap and drank in the peace of the distant stars. I might well have imagined I was in my little white boat again, my head resting against its flat prow, undiminished and undismayed once more. It had been an act of forsaking and, at the same time, an act of return.

That desire for inner freedom and a welcoming quietness reappeared in my life throughout my teenage years and early twenties, including the times when I myself earnestly and unknowingly contributed to the disharmony within me. Paradoxically, it was that search for my inner home that took me away from my physical home among the cabbage trees and punga ferns of my native land, away from the beloved people around me, and nudged me toward another country across the vastness of the blue Pacific.

Something else was at work as well. In luminous moments of my young life I had been captivated by the power of music and poetry and fiction and theatre to open my imagination to bright new worlds. At the end of my third decade of life, I felt it was time to intentionally explore the possibilities of those powers in a new place where I could be free of the constraining elements of the past. Leaving for America was more than a youthful adventure, though it was undoubtedly that. Like my walkout from the camp meeting nearly two decades before, it was an act of forsaking in order to return, an instinctive gesture of self-preservation, and a quest for new birth.

CHAPTER 8.

Journey to America

"Though Eden is lost
its loveliness
remains in the heart
and the imagination."
—Mary Oliver, "Fireflies"

I grew up with beaches everywhere. The city of Auckland is situated on a volcanic isthmus, a thread of land between two oceans. To the west lies the Tasman Sea, 1,500 miles of uneasy water separating New Zealand from Australia. To the east is the great Pacific, a vast blue wilderness unbroken for 5,000 miles to the coast of South America.

The West Coast beaches are wild and windswept, great open gashes of black sand, edged with tussock grass. The salty air is electric with raw power, as huge swells crash in tumult and run to exhaustion up the long flat reaches of the bays. These beaches—Karekare, Whatipu, Muriwai, Piha, and so many more—are havens for people who love the wind in their hair, pioneer types, surfers, hikers, long-line fishermen, and motorbikers who, at Ninety Mile Beach, can ride at low tide on a single strand stretching northward, as the name suggests, for nearly a hundred miles.

The East Coast beaches are different. New Zealand's eastern shores, especially in the north, are broken by welcoming inlets, sprinkled with islands, and edged with crescents of golden sand.

A beach on New Zealand's east coast

If New Zealand ever tips into the sea, it will be the East Coast that goes first. On weekends and holidays, people flock eastward, lying out on the golden sands flecked with white seashells, body-surfing the gentle waves, gathering the cockles and mussels, walking their dogs, and puttering around in boats. Under the great spreading pohutukawas, they open up their picnic baskets for Marmite sandwiches on Vogel's bread and relax under the southern sun, with a glass of DB lager or a bottle of Lemon & Paeroa (a refreshing combination of lemon juice and natural sparkling waters) winking frostily at their elbows.

Like many New Zealanders in the summer months—December, January, and February—our family took many weekend trips to the beaches of the East Coast. In our case, though, there was no DB lager. We kids were offered lemonade while Dad boiled water in his battered thermette for a cup of tea poured into enamel mugs.

It's odd how memory collapses multiple recollections into a select few. I can't recall the details of all the visits we made to the East Coast beaches when we were young, but I have clear memories of one. We had driven for what seemed hours in the family sedan, crammed with two long-suffering parents and half a dozen kids, wriggling and chattering and singing in the back seat. We bumped our way over twisting, unsealed roads until, with a growing sense of destiny, all eyes on the horizon to be first to see the ocean, we pulled up under a line of Norfolk pines, opened the doors, and spilled out into the briny freshness of the air. Beyond a verge of flat crabgrass, the warm sand felt like velvet under our bare feet, and we wriggled our toes into the cooler layers beneath. While my siblings scampered on to put their feet in the water, so cool and fresh, I did something else. I began to run.

I ran and ran. Faster and faster. My feet seemed barely to touch the sand. I felt a lightness as if I were flying, the wind hissing around my ears in a roar that rose and fell with every footstep. Exhilaration flooded my body. An effervescence rose in me as if bursting from an undiscovered spring. For a few fleeting moments I felt like the world's fastest human, fast enough to play on the wing for the All Blacks, the New Zealand rugby team, headed for the goal line to score a try. I thought I heard the crowd roar and ran even faster, my joy so great I felt it could not be contained. I leapt toward the sky. I felt as if I could shout loud enough to crack open the surface of the earth.

That's how it felt for me to break free from the boundaries of my life in the country of my grandparents' dreams and run breathlessly toward the widening horizons of a new continent and a new life. Now I shall tell the story of how I got there.

Sometimes a chance encounter is no more than a fleeting thing making barely a ripple on our consciousness. Briefly it is there, and then it is gone. Sometimes, though, a completely unplanned encounter can change a life. So it was for me when, on an ordinary day in an ordinary year—1960—I found myself watching a rag-tag company of actors perform a series of short scenes from Shakespeare, bite-sized excerpts from some of the Bard's greatest comedic hits. I was a young first-year teacher at the time, keeping a nervous eye on my students in the auditorium of the Normal Intermediate School. I was soon to be lost in wonder.

As I watched the actors on stage, I was somehow carried off to new and deeply desirable worlds, away from the ordinariness of the classroom, with its measured routines, dusty blackboards, standardized curricula, and tests. I plunged instead into fresh realms of beauty and imagination. By some strange alchemy, I found myself now in a colorful princely court, now in a sun-flecked forest, now on a wondrous island, now in a yet-undiscovered country where the unbelievable became believable, where fantastical creatures appeared and disappeared, and impossible transfigurations abounded.

As the performers stepped in and out of character, in and out of scenes, I was taken by the atmosphere of festival and celebration pervading their world and the new worlds they created. There was a lightness in the air, a freedom, a sense of risk and danger, and I felt a hunger for it. What would it be like to be part of such a world, I wondered, to live for a time inside such magical spaces? What would it be like to be part of an enterprise that took people on journeys from one vividly imagined world to another? A tiny seed had been sown in my heart.

A year or so later, I was in the theatre again and once more my imagination flared into life. In the company of a new love—Ondra Galbraith, my sweetheart of university days—I watched a touring production of *My Fair Lady,* more than slightly overwhelmed by the dazzling energies of light and sound and the near magical evocations of human personality emanating from the stage—the insufferable condescensions of Henry Higgins, the charming gaucheries of Eliza, the confident absurdities of the "dustman" Alfred P. Doolittle, and so much more. I felt enclosed in a kaleidoscopic world, a fantastical place bursting with intensity, flickering with light, pulsating with new ways of seeing the comedy of the human experience.

Once again, fresh questions burst into my mind. This time, though, they were questions about the illusory world of the play and the transactions of human life being presented there: What separates the sophisticate from the "guttersnipe"? Is admission to "high society" merely a matter of proper speech and dress? What are the qualities of a person of truly noble character? What insecurities underlie the unattractive human manifestations of snobbery? What unfortunate distortions of reality cause otherwise flawed and mortal beings to assume the pretense of superiority over others?

I had made a life-changing discovery. The theatre was more than entertainment, though it was certainly that. It was also a roiling nexus of energy that challenged me to step outside the habitual boundaries of mind and heart, that picked away at easy assumptions and made the unthinkable thinkable.

It was also a civilized form of people-watching, and I loved watching people. Going to the theatre was a bit like sitting anonymously in an airport terminal or a busy train station—observing people go by, wondering about them, constructing in my mind the story of their lives. It was also, I must add, a great conversation starter, very helpful in getting a lively exchange going with my super-smart girlfriend.

Undeniably potent as a starting place for healthy conversation was a show I watched a few months later at Auckland's Mercury Theatre: *The Happy Haven*, by English playwright John Arden. It was not, as it turns out, a great play—certainly not, I am told, one of Arden's best—and I must confess to feeling a bit lost and out of my depth. That didn't diminish my sense of excitement at being there, however, in the vibrant dark of the theater; I savored the slight whiff of anarchy that surrounded the whole experience. Yes, I struggled to get a sense of the story, but I also felt my heart stirring for the miserable lives being represented on stage. *The Happy Haven* was anything but happy.

The happy haven of the play's title turned out to be a badly run nursing home in a gritty English industrial town where the residents, incapacitated by age and infirmity, conspire in a brief but unsuccessful revolt against new rules being imposed on them by the medical staff. Resigned to the bleakness of their existence, they prefer to remain undisturbed in their familiar routines. Once more, I was bombarded by new questions—questions about the infirmities of old age, the bleakness of lives that have run out of options, the loneliness of places like the happy haven. There was so much more to the world than met the eye, so much more below its bright surfaces.

At some point in my studies at the University of Auckland, I found myself in the Great Hall beneath the university's distinctive filigreed greystone dome, watching scenes from Shakespeare's *As You Like It*. This was no professional production but a company of students my own age skillfully transforming the black-draped proscenium stage into what I could believe to be another place and time. Briefly under the spell of these actors, I was transported to 16th-century France, in the Forest of Arden where Rosalind finds her love messages from Orlando hung prettily on the trees.

Once again, I was drawn to reflect on the oddly different world of the theatre. It seemed a place of unfamiliar marvels, like a cross between a circus and a town hall meeting, where I could meet interesting people from other times and places and watch their relationships being worked out for good or ill. I felt like a privileged

The University of Auckland

voyeur, a participant in a wide-ranging gossip session about the human condition.

By now, I was beginning to consider being a part of this world. I wanted to hear more of the theatre's stories and learn more about how the theatre goes about telling them. In English classes at university, I read a small library of (mostly English) plays and read numerous scholarly essays about plays like Shakespeare's *Hamlet*, Shaw's *Man and Superman*, and Arden's *Serjeant Musgrave's Dance*.

But studying a play in an English classroom is not the same as watching it come to life on stage. It is even less like actually playing the characters represented by its words. After watching a production of *Hamlet* in the theatre one night, I realized I had learned more about the wintry spirit of Hamlet in those absorbing hours than I had in all my previous studies. It was a revelation to be present with Hamlet in the very room where, burdened by questions of destiny, he fumbles away his best chance to do what he knows he is supposed to do.

There was something about the actor's art that brought words to life and turned abstractions into living realities. It seemed that whereas in religion there was a tendency to turn flesh into words, in the theatre there was an instinct to do the opposite—to embody ideas in the multi-dimensional actualities of character and story. I decided I needed to learn more about this form of art, to learn what I could about how actors go about creating the characters that lived on stage before me, and to learn how theatrical artists put together the storytelling spectacles that had so entranced my imagination.

Since university courses in theatre were not available to me in those years—there was no department of drama at the University of Auckland, no courses offered in acting or directing or design—I decided to look for a teacher elsewhere. That is how I met the singular John Thompson, one of the finest of New Zealand's citizens, and a great teacher of speech and drama.

At some long-forgotten public event, I heard John give a moving performance of works by Shakespeare, Keats, Housman, and others, including New Zealand poet James K. Baxter. I remember thinking: If I could someday read a poem like Housman's "To an Athlete Dying Young" as he did—even if I could, just once, find a fraction of the beauty he found in it—I could die a happy man. I looked for his name in the Auckland phone directory, called his studio, introduced myself, and asked if I could become his student. Thus began two years of excursions into new realms of feeling and imagination.

In our first class together, John asked me to read some lines for him. He placed a copy of John Donne's poem "Death Be Not Proud" in my hands and gave me a few minutes to prepare. I offered him my most polished rendition of the words on the page. There was a long pause. John wrote a few notes on a pad. Then, looking up through his tumbling grey mane, he said, "Well, Mr. Howard Martin." Pause.

"It was a good reading, fluent, if a bit hasty—I think the reverend Dr. Donne would agree with me on that—but, my dear sir…where is the emotion?"

It was as if he was breaking a long-hidden secret. The arts of poetry and drama were about feeling. They were not just about ideas set down with rhymes and rhythms, they were also, and primarily, about the heart. *My* heart. Poems—and novels and plays—were about my own inner life, my own life of felt imagination. They were also, by extension, about the inner life of every person I knew and indeed every person on the planet.

I now felt I needed to learn how to find the emotions at the heart of literature and—just as important—in my own heart. John became the guide in my search. He praised and scolded and prodded and cajoled. He begged and pleaded. He paced the studio like a long grey cat, listening, watching, waiting. I would read a few lines and he would pounce. "That landed with a heavy thud, did it not, Signor Martin?" he would say. "The poet speaks with confidence, does he not, but are there no doubts? No mortal fear lingering in his brain? Once more, kind sir, if you do not mind." I'd try again. If the Muse was with me and the burden of my efforts fell less heavily on his ears, he'd spin on one heel with the graceful agility of Fred Astaire and say, "Aha! There! That's more like it. Yes. Yes. Yes."

Week after week, he led me through the shifting voices of great poems, like William Blake's wistful "Holy Thursday," all of them plump with new meaning. He coaxed me into the emotional heart of powerful dramatic monologues, like Romeo's fateful farewell to his sleeping beloved ("Ah dear Juliet, why art thou yet so fair?") or Tom's unhinged denunciation of his mother Amanda in Tennessee Williams's *The Glass Menagerie* ("You will go up, up, up over Blue Mountain with seventeen gentlemen callers! You ugly babbling old witch!").

Wide eyed at the vistas opening to me, I felt, as John Keats did, "like some watcher of the skies / when a new planet swims into his ken." With persistent good humor, John nudged me on. Showing great forbearance toward my religious naivete and social innocence, he guided me through the successful completion of licentiate and teacher's degrees from Trinity College of London. Then, quite unexpectedly, he cracked open yet another door.

As we stepped out of his studio one late December afternoon, with newspaper boys calling in the distance, John lit a cigarette, took a deep draw, let the smoke drift lazily across his oaken face, and, quoting E. B. White from memory, said, "You may grow old, good sir, and trembling in your anatomies, you may lie awake at night listening to the disorder of your veins, you may miss your only love, you may see the world about you devastated by evil lunatics, or know your honor trampled in the sewers of baser minds. There is only one thing for it then—to learn. That is the only thing that never fails." He paused. "You must continue to learn, Howard Martin, learning is the thing that never fails. But it's time for you to go new places and find new teachers. I want you to consider graduate studies at a university...in the United States."

Why he suggested the United States for me, I will never know. He himself had been trained at the Central School of Drama in London and sounded for all the world like a classically trained English actor. Why would he not suggest I move to London? Like all great teachers, however, he knew by intuition what was best for this particular student. Having taught me what he knew, he wanted me to move on to other teachers in the great creative maelstrom of the New World rather than Old.

I remember the very moment I decided I leave for America. I was mowing the family lawn under the shade of a spreading puriri tree on Crescent Road, with the One Tree Hill obelisk shining above me in the westering sun. Borne into a meditative state by the easy repetitive motions of mowing, cut off from all other sounds by the roar of the motor, I heard my own inner voice saying, "John's right. It's time to go."

Our home on Crescent Road in the 1960s

The very next day I was in the small library of the United States Consulate in Auckland, poring over its collection of American university catalogs. Knowing little about American geography and even less about American university rankings, so significant in young Americans' college choices, I decided to apply to three schools, one in Massachusetts, one in Michigan, and one in North Carolina. Led more by intuition than by information—though I had noted the presence on the North Carolina campus of the poet Randall Jarrell and been impressed by the reputation of its programs in dance and theatre—I chose University of North Carolina at Greensboro (UNCG).

In early August 1970, I flew out of the sun-splashed islands of New Zealand to Hawaii and Los Angeles and thence by Greyhound bus up the California Coast to San Fransisco and on through mountains, deserts, and fruited plains to a tobacco and textile town in the American South near enough to the continent's eastern coast. It was worlds away—about as far from the sheltered South Sea islands as an innocent wanderer could get.

I had always loved the idea of America, especially its image as created in me by the movies I had seen at Auckland's Civic Theatre, the magazines I had paged through in barber shops, the folksy confabulations of Norman Rockwell glimpsed in bookstore windows, and the colorful illustrated books I had read as a child. When I thought of America, I thought of safe, leafy neighborhoods where people made snowmen in winter and burned piles of red leaves in the fall. I thought of idyllic steepled villages, sleek cars, lovely sun-tanned women, cozy college campuses built around grassy quads, sexy drive-in movie theaters, and folksy soda shops. By the time I was twenty, I had developed aching romantic crushes on a succession of American women, all hopelessly distant from the reality of my life—a lovely raven-haired actress in a movie, a shapely pinup in a glossy American magazine, a pretty red-lipped singer in a Billy Graham-style gospel team from California.

I had also developed an inexplicable yearning for the American landscape—the palm-lined beaches of Florida and California, the sensuous curves of the Appalachians, the vast golden wheat fields of the Great Plains, the jagged purple mountains of the desert Southwest, the redwood columns of coastal Oregon. A natural dreamer, I would shift my gaze from my elementary classroom lessons to a poster pinned on the wall. It showed an orange and red train marked "Santa Fe" running a straight rail past the startling red mesas of New Mexico sharply set against a cloudless azure sky. I thought it would be heaven to be in that country, on that train, on my own journey, in a place that looked like that.

In a sense—and for this I am eternally grateful—my dreams actually did come true. In time, I would attend graduate school at one of those cozy college towns (Ann Arbor, Michigan) and become a professor at an even cozier town (Iowa City, Iowa). I would take my sons on camping trips through the prairie wheat fields to the palm-lined beaches, through the Rockies to the Sangre de Cristos, around the Great Lakes to Mount Rushmore and the Grand Tetons and beyond. I would find my way to one of those idyllic villages (Westwood Hills, "the most beautiful little city in Kansas") where I would live with good neighbors for the best part of four decades and more. I would spend many summers in the breasted Appalachian hills and build a cabin there in the flowering Blue Ridge Mountains. With my two sons alongside, I would a sit on a train through the tall red mesas of New Mexico on our way to Las Vegas (NM) in the very heart of mythical cowboy country. I would fall in love with one of those pretty American women and in partnership with her make a home in the very heart of the land I had dreamed about.

Sometimes, even in our ignorance, we blunder into grace. How could I have known that the steps that took me toward an unlikely Southern tobacco town would bring me to a place that brimmed with such undreamed-of possibility? "New beauty," wrote naturalist John Muir, "meets us at every step of our wandering."

It's not the whole truth, of course. Our journeys across new frontiers do indeed reveal new beauties, but they also, in the great paradox of existence, reveal new reasons for letdown and disappointment. Arriving in America, I was again to feel, most keenly, the two-edged beauty of the world—its laughter and its anguish. In the next chapter, I tell the story of how that strange beauty soon tore my own heart in two.

CHAPTER 9.

American Dream and Reality

*"A test of what is real is that it is hard and rough.
Joys are found in it, not pleasure. What is pleasant
belongs to dreams."*
—*Simone Weil,* Gravity and Grace

The realization of a dream is never without cost. At some point, every construct built in the mind must meet the test of what is actual and real. Because in our mortal selves we are not "such stuff as dreams are made on," all our dreams must meet the test of dimensional existence, the stubborn requirements of flesh and blood. We are slow to discover—especially in the days of our youth—that life is most healthily lived in acceptance of what actually is, not in the fantasy of what we wish it to be. So it was for me when I came to America.

For all its beauties and sense of adventure, the real America turned out to be something other than the one I had for so long been seeing in my head. It was shocking to arrive on these shores to find myself face to face not only with its bright side—its stunning landscapes and exhilarating creative energy—but also with its shadow, its overwhelming vastness, its crass commercialism, its unreflective racism, its gun-obsessed paranoia, its cruel gap between rich and poor, and its stubborn religious fundamentalism.

There is of course a dark side to every nation on earth. Despite its staggering natural beauties and its friendly, well-educated people, New Zealand has its own uncivilized beer-drinking mentality, its idolatrous obsession with its national rugby stars, its rough and ready social conventions, its high rates of juvenile addiction and suicide, its dangerous roads, and its bullying educational culture. The difference for me was that America's dark side carried a kind of menace I had not experienced before. Tensions were, of course, especially high in 1970 amidst the protests against the war in Vietnam, but there was also a pervasive air of embedded racial antagonism and, never far from the surface, a hint of violence.

My first views of Greensboro, North Carolina, were from the windows of the lumbering Greyhound bus that brought me in stages from San Francisco across the plains to Chicago, then south into the Carolina Piedmont. On my way into the city, I rode past great looming textile mills and tobacco processing plants, furniture factories and huge, white-cupolaed Baptist churches with sprawling parking lots, leafy country club districts where the faces were mostly white, and blocks of red-brick tenements where the faces were mostly black.

Stepping out into the heavy, humid air at the Greyhound terminal—almost always in the most dilapidated section of big American cities—I had little sense of the freedom Americans so famously and loudly acclaimed as the hallmark of their land. There was a tension in the air and a sense of exhaustion in the late summer haze. It was not what I had expected.

The town of Greensboro had recently been in the news. Before leaving for the States, I had seen a photograph of President Lyndon

Johnson stepping out of a limousine onto the streets of Greensboro, the car sleek and black against an impressive urban skyline, the Stars and Stripes snapping crisply on the hood. My adolescent fantasies of America were reinforced by that photograph, easily seducing me, in my innocence, away from the historic truth that lay behind Johnson's visit.

The truth was this. The city of Greensboro had been one of the flash points in the civil rights movement of the 1960s, when four young black men had staged a sit-in at the Woolworth's store on Elm Street. Inspired by the peaceful protest practices of Martin Luther King Jr., the "Greensboro Four," as they were later to be known, sat at the Woolworth's lunch counter and waited for service. When the courtesies extended to others were refused to them, they stayed anyway, remaining at the counter all that day, coming back the next day, and the next. Their story caught the attention of the national media, and soon there were similar sit-ins at lunch counters all over the country.

It was a tense and difficult time when the cruel realities of America's long history of racial discrimination had once more come to the world's attention. Consciences had been quickened. Four years later, the Civil Rights Act was passed by Congress and signed into law by President Johnson. The President had come to Greensboro to recognize the courage of the Greensboro Four and to celebrate the monumental changes they had set in motion. I arrived in the American South amidst the aftershocks of that turbulent time.

It was not long before I myself felt those aftershocks. Soon after arriving in town, I stopped at a gas station to refuel my recently acquired automobile. It was a powder blue 1961 Oldsmobile Dynamic 88 with over 200,000 miles on the odometer. I had paid $200 for it, including tax. It was a big brute of a car, with heart-stopping power and a staggering appetite for fuel. With gasoline at 27 cents a gallon, however, I could fill the tank for less than five dollars.

As I worked the pump on one side of the station, I noticed a young African-American man emptying the trash on the other side. Somewhere behind me, I heard a deep-throated roar, then saw a flash of red as a souped-up convertible Mustang pulled at speed into the lane opposite mine. There was a fierce screeching of brakes and a cry as the Black kid leapt sideways. The driver—white, middle-aged and paunchy—burst out of his car and screamed, "Get out of my way, you lazy son of a bitch." He spat out the N-word and slammed his car door shut. Surely I was dreaming this, but no, there I was, still pouring gas into my battered blue American fantasy car. There was something so reflexive, so irrational and primitive, in the hatred I had seen on display that I felt I had arrived on an alien planet.

It was, of course, a turbulent time in America for other reasons as well. The spirit of rebellion surging through the youth cultures of the 1960s—the spirit of Haight-Ashbury and Woodstock—had found a unifying cause in opposition to the war in Vietnam. In 1970, the massive incursion into Cambodia was already shaking its eastern hills, and student protests were increasing in number and intensity. On May 4 of that year, national guard troops had opened fire on a crowd of 500 demonstrators at Kent State University, leaving four students dead on the campus Commons. In response to the widely published images of this event, an estimated 450 colleges and high schools, including the University of North Carolina at Chapel Hill—just forty miles from the Greensboro campus where I was going to be a graduate student—had been shut down by angry student protests.

While the mood of rebellion was spreading like fire through college campuses, the rest of the country was still deeply divided over both the civil rights movement and the war. Feelings on both sides ran deep. In Greensboro, the people of the conservative, white middle class were barely able to comprehend the changes demanded of them by the Civil Rights Act of 1965 and largely held the line in support of Nixon's Vietnam strategy. Many of them, still Confederates at heart, looked with fear and loathing on the anti-establishment opinions and nonconforming lifestyles of the current generation of students. They considered kids with long hair and tie-dyed shirts as a threat to the American way of life—"hippies"—like the drug-addled crazies on the West Coast, perversely breaking the norms of civilized society and overturning the old order. Not six weeks into my sojourn in Greensboro, I myself felt the sting of this distain.

The sign outside the barber shop read: "Walk-ins Welcome." An encouraging invitation, and a timely one: I needed a haircut. Though I wore no tie-dyed shirt or red bandana, my hair fell closer to my shoulders than to my ears, in my case more a statement of economy than of style. To some, I suppose, I had begun to look like one of those unwashed liberals causing so much trouble everywhere. For my part, I had no inkling that, in the political climate of the day, my grooming was in effect a political statement and some kind of threat to the established order. I opened the barbershop door, somewhat reassured by the tinkling of a bell, and stepped inside.

Instantly, I felt a chill in the air. No one looked my way. The man with the scissors maintained a studied focus on the greying thatch in front of him. I sat in a chair and waited. "Just a matter of time," I thought. Half an hour later, I was still sitting there, flicking distractedly though the dog-eared pages of sports magazines, watching as customers came and went. Finally, I stood up and walked toward the man with the scissors. He did not look up.

"Ken ah hep yew?" he inquired, in his thick Southern drawl.

"Well, yes you can," I answered. "I'm just wondering if walk-ins are actually welcome here. I'm hoping to get my hair cut."

There was a pause while he continued to snip away.

"Maybe a lohwng tahm a'fore we can git to ya in this here shop." he said. "Ya may wanna trah somewhere's else."

I got the message and left.

Walking back to my rented room on Kensington Road, I felt as desolate as ever I had in my life. Was I, in fact, an unwelcome alien in the land I had dreamed about? Had I been deluded in my decision to move here? The answer would be slow in coming, but when it came it did so in showers of unexpected grace.

First impressions are often pretty accurate. Sometimes they are not. We do well to test them out. A handsome face can sometimes hide a disdainful heart. A gruff exterior can sometimes belie a kindly spirit. So it was for me in 1970 when I arrived in Greensboro.

My first impressions of the Piedmont city had been one thing—a shock of reality sufficient to burst the bubble of my dreamy illusions of America—but what I eventually found there was something else altogether. In due time I was to discover, folded into its apparently unwelcoming heart, some of the dearest treasures of my life. Foremost among them a beautiful woman, who, though she did not know it yet, was waiting for me in a house called "Mayflower Lodge" not far from the university campus. Other treasures came in the form of new teachers and new friends.

Within two weeks of my arrival in town, I walked across the flowering campus of the University to begin my studies. One of my first courses was taught by the classy and brilliant Kathryn England, an extraordinary speech professor and theatre director who became to me in my early days in America as John Thomson had been in New Zealand. With image-laden insight and forbearance, Professor England coached me through my first fully staged theatre production—a University Players' production of Bernard Shaw's *The Devil's Disciple* in which I played the role of nefarious Dick Dudgeon who barely escapes being hanged for treachery.

Professor England took a personal interest in my professional development, driving me home each night after rehearsal, discussing our work in the rehearsal room, reviewing my progress, and offering words of encouragement. "It's coming!" she would say, as I stepped out of her car into the humid Carolina air. "We'll keep at it till we get it right." I took it as a hint that I still had a long way to go. For Professor England's sake, and for the sake of the work, I was determined to get there.

One night, in a moment of rare prescience, she asked if I was getting to know people in the university community. Had I met anyone on the dance faculty yet? With a twinkle in her eye she added, "There's a woman there I think you should meet." I later found out that the woman she had in mind was an instructor in dance named Jennifer Lowe.

I cannot forget the evening in 1970 Jen first changed my world. At my invitation, she stopped by my place on Kensington Road after a dance faculty reception at the university. She rang the bell. I opened the door. I stood there transfixed, unable to move. Sheathed in a red floral minidress, belted to match, with her hair swept up in an elegant Grace Kelly roll, she stood there like a vision, perched gracefully on high heels, statuesque in the backlight of a Kensington Road street lamp. My heart was already lost and for her part, she seemed somehow to be unaware of my own shock.

Fumbling, stumbling, lumpy, and miscued, I showed her into the living room, invited her to sit, and went immediately into the standard New Zealander's if-all-else-fails backup plan: I offered to make her a cup of tea. She accepted.

I stepped out of the room to put the kettle on the gas, furiously running a checklist of cookies or other sweet treats I could serve to make this appear a social occasion befitting of the apparition in the next room. Without asking whether she took milk in her tea, as New

Zealanders always do, or if she needed a spoonful of sugar, I quickly scanned the refrigerator to see what was on the shelves and flipped open cupboard doors in quick succession looking for cups and a pitcher. Somewhat reassured, I moved back into the living room.

O ye heavenly powers! There she was again. Her back was arched upwards like a ballerina's, her hands folded on her lap, her long, elegant legs, folded duchess-style, seemed to reach halfway across the room, and her face had a divinity to it that barely concealed a kind and already forgiving bemusement. Even now I can hear what must have been going through her mind: "Never been around a New Zealander before…This fumbling awkwardness is…maybe just a national trait…if nothing else, this encounter could be an interesting study in comparative anthropology."

Jennifer Lowe (1968)

I pretended nonchalance. The kind of casual indifference a man projects when he wants a lovely woman to think he's been in this situation before. "No problem," I reasoned with myself. "I have women who look like a young Vanessa Redgrave sitting on my couch all the time." We exchange small talk. The faculty party. How I got from New Zealand to

North Carolina. How she got to Greensboro from Orrville, Ohio. Did I know Orrville was the home of Smucker's jams and jellies? Had she heard of the black sands of New Zealand's West Coast or the boiling mud pools of Rotorua? The kettle whistles. I get us a cup of tea. Milk? Sugar? A line of poetry comes to my mind—perhaps a bit of William Wordsworth—and, despite the hour, she shows flickers of interest.

I rifle through the stack of books on my desk and come up with a slim volume of poems, a few by Wordsworth. I read her some favorite lines: "Earth has not anything to show more fair / Dull would he be of soul who could pass by / A sight so touching in its majesty." She still seems interested enough. I read a few more lines. We talk some more. I'm reminded of another poem. I read it to her. She seems to be staying with me. Maybe, I think to myself, she's the kind of woman who thinks listening to Wordsworth in the living room of an awkward foreigner is the essence of a fun night out. I now know of course that I had been quite wrong in this. Listening to me read poetry had not been an act of engaged fascination; it had been an act of kindly, if slightly puzzled, forgiveness.

I don't remember how we parted that night—a hug and peck on the cheek maybe—but I do recall that at some point she called me "professor." I took it as a compliment—suffused with a delicious touch of irony that was itself a revelation—and suggested we get together again sometime. She seemed agreeable and the next day, around lunch time, I showed up at her doorstep. She welcomed me in for toast and eggs. Except for the fact that, in scrambling the eggs, she had burned her hand on the skillet, a fact she dismissed as a trifle, I began to think things were going quite well. She surprised me by suggesting we take a picnic some weekend at one of the Guilford County lakes.

We made a date and, on the appointed day, drove out to the lake in "Buttercup," her yellow VW bug. By the end of our lazy time, stretched out on a blanket not far from the water's edge, I realized I had fallen in love with this elegant creature and had allowed myself to think, unlikely as it seemed, that I had become something more than an awkward specimen of male ineptitude. In sweet surrender, she allowed me to kiss her. Let it be said of me, no matter what else I may or may not have done in my life, that there was a day, precious in my memory, when, as the poet Leigh Hunt so tenderly expressed it, Jenny kissed me:

> *Jenny kiss'd me when we met,*
> *Jumping from the chair she sat in,*
> *Time, you thief, who love to get*
> *Sweets in your list, put that in!*
> *Say I'm weary, say I'm sad,*
> *Say that wealth and health have miss'd me,*
> *Say I'm growing old, but add,*
> *Jenny kiss'd me.*

We were married in Greensboro on May 19, 1972, our families from Ohio and New Zealand present to witness our vows. Jennifer Lowe had become Jennifer Martin. I called her Jen. With tin cans rattling from the bumper of my baby blue Oldsmobile, cleverly nicknamed "Bluey," we set off for our honeymoon on the Outer Banks of North Carolina, somewhere near where the Wright Brothers took their famous first flight.

Our wedding day, 1972

Jen has done more than her share to help me find a place to belong in America. She has done it with her uncomplicated grace, her kindness, forgiveness, and self-discipline, always made sweeter by the presence of flowers. Wherever we have lived, there have been flowers: flowers in the garden, flowers in the window-boxes, flowers on the dining room table, flowers on the shelf above the kitchen sink, flowers in the nooks, flowers in the crannies. One especially memorable summer's day, there were also flowers on a picnic table.

As far as I am concerned, there is no more romantic place on earth for a picnic than the mountains of western North Carolina. With their mysterious feminine beauty, lush forests of oak and elm, shady groves, fast running streams and tumbling waterfalls, summer cascades of laurel and rhododendron, they provide a thousand cozy sanctuaries for restful retreat. We got to know these mountains well, working for five consecutive summers on the outdoor drama *Unto These Hills,* in Cherokee, North Carolina, on the southern edge of the Great Smoky Mountains National Park.

*The Great Smoky
Mountains*

On a Saturday night, after performing the last show of the
week, Jen and I would often drive away from the company village
in Cherokee to explore the natural wonders and sweet small towns
hidden in the hills around us. We hiked up Clingmans Dome,
tubed down the Oconaluftee River, stopped at the old soda
fountain in Bryson City, stepped up into the cool spray of Mingo
Falls, clambered over the ruins of Mingus Mill, trod the squeaky
floorboards of the Mast General Store in Waynesville, roamed the
pioneer village at the entrance to the Smoky Mountains National
Park, plunged into the folksy madness of Gatlinburg, drove slow,
gorgeous miles on the Blue Ridge Parkway, and stopped for lunch at
the Pisgah Inn, with the misty ridges of the Southern Appalachians
lying in folds at our feet.

One vividly memorable day, we packed a cooler—Jen always loved
an abundance of ice—and drove off into the hills for a picnic. We
found a rustic table set in a leafy cove somewhere near Fontana Lake
(the lake attractively featured in the movie *Nell*). While I unpacked the
car, Jen laid a checkered cloth over the table's rough-cut timbers, then
disappeared for a time. Minutes later, she returned with a bouquet
of blue and white forget-me-nots, and, after arranging them in a tiny
vase, placed them at the center of our little feast.

It was a simple gesture, but suddenly it meant the world to me. In
this arrangement of flowers on a table in the woods, I saw how much
depended upon the presence of the feminine in the world and how
much I needed this particular presence—this particular woman—in
my life. As I write these words at the Broadway Café in Westport,
Missouri, I do the math. Jen and I have been together 43 years and 152
days. To this day, wherever she is, I am at home.

The love of a mother is one thing; the love of one who chooses to
love you is another. In both cases, though, the experience of faithful

forgiving love lays a foundation for recognizing the source of love, the great Love at the heart of all things. At least, it does for me. In words far more eloquent than my own, Frederick Buechner calls the first stirrings of married love "an anguish of longing" for Beauty and Being beyond time.

I often go back in my mind to the loveliness of the mountains where Jen first picked those flowers for our picnic table. The Blue Ridge Mountains, which embrace at their southern end the Great Smoky Mountains National Park, provided the perfect setting not only for romance but also for feelings of mystery and wonder. In *Look Homeward, Angel*, novelist Thomas Wolfe describes them as a "vast rich body of the hills, lush with billowing greenery, ripe-bosomed, dappled by far-floating cloudshadows."

How many a time have I watched as a thin layer of early morning fog poured like milk over the layered blue breasts of the Blue Ridge Mountains of North Carolina? How often have I stood under the lacy curtain of Dry Falls and listened to its sweet, silvery hush? How often have I walked along woodland trails between high flowering walls of white rhododendron? How often have I watched in silence as the evening shadows fell on the sheer granite cliffs of Whiteside Mountain or Lonesome Valley? How often have I wandered the picturesque streets of Highlands and Cashiers with their shady nooks and flower boxes, their colorful coffee shops, galleries, and fruit markets?

I see them still in my mind like glimpses of paradise and wonder if I would ever have lived to see such beauties if I had not first gone to study at the University in Greensboro, North Carolina. By choosing to pursue my graduate studies in that unlikely Southern town, new wonders had opened to me, including—just four hours' drive away on Interstate 40—that lovely corner of the world that remains as deep in my heart as any place ever has.

Four decades after our first drive together through those mystical hills, Jen and I decided to make a summer home there among the flowering rhododendrons and mountain laurel, among the bubbling streams and tumbling waterfalls. For a dozen years, from 2003 to 2015, that summer home, its windows open to graceful folds of the Blue Ridge, became a beloved place of welcome for many of our family and friends who dared the twisting unsealed roads to get there. The story of the building of the cabin—and of the salt-of-the-earth people who were our neighbors there—is one I must save for another time.

Our memories of any place, whether positive or negative, are more often than not associated with the people we meet there. I met more than my fair share of warm-hearted and welcoming people in my first heady months in the American South. Jennifer was but the first of many. There was, for example, a strikingly handsome couple named Bob and Alice Voorhees. They defined for me the true meaning of Southern hospitality, introducing me to the sweet, gritty pleasures of cornbread, still warm from the oven. In May of 1972, they opened their home—a cozy cottage set among the blossoming magnolias, redbuds and dogwoods—for our wedding, the prettiest celebration of marriage I ever attended.

There was a gracious belle of the old South, Mrs. Paul White, who lived next door to my lodgings on Kensington Road. I never knew Mrs. White's first name; it seemed improper to ask. On hot summer days, with the scent of bougainvillea in the air, she served me iced sweet tea on her cozy screened-in porch, her little dog Brown Sugar nipping at her elbows.

There was the urbane George McSpadden, chair of the Department of Romance Languages, who over long lunches helped me navigate some of the complexities of race and religion in America and, with his kind-hearted wife Jane, introduced me to a widening community of generous, thoughtful, creative Americans.

And then, popping up out of the Carolina blue, was one of those unforgettable characters I could only have met in the South: Mark Clark.

Mark and I got talking one night at a downtown coffee shop and—in a gesture of great trust and generosity on Mark's part—became roommates for a year in a budget rooming house, painted green, on Paisley Street a few blocks from Greensboro's downtown. Our lifestyle can only be described as "grad-school grunge," and our cuisine best characterized as variations on the theme of meat and potatoes with a side of canned green peas. Think of the possibilities!

With Mark Clark, 2018

Often at the end of the day, we would drive to a bar on the edge of town and talk into the wee hours. I introduced Mark to the oddities of New Zealand culture: the old British school tradition of caning recalcitrant boys across the buttocks with a vicious rattan cane, the oddness of celebrating Christmas in the heat of summer with artificial trees covered in artificial snow, the unnerving experience of driving through bobbing flocks of sheep on the country highways—that sort of thing. In turn, he introduced me to the fine taste of Michelob beer, to the difficult pleasures of hunting wild game in the backwoods of Mississippi and Alabama, and above all, to his latest discoveries in classical history and literature. Fiddling casually with his battered tobacco pipe, he would quote gems from Plato, Aristotle, Cicero, Homer, and Virgil, his passionate discourses occasionally erupting in bursts of laughter, as if his joy in learning could barely be contained. There was delight in his eyes.

I felt then, and feel to this day, a great sense of kinship with Mark. His religious search was similar to mine. His sense of humor was uncannily matched to mine. His sense of awe at the new horizons opening before him was also like mine. He brought a welcome touch of joyful comradeship to my days in Greensboro, and I have no doubt he infused that same buoyant spirit into his years as Professor of Classical Languages at Southern Mississippi and Mississippi State Universities.

Mark Clark is without a doubt the only professor of classics in the world who at age 70-plus still hunts wild bear in the forested uplands of New Brunswick. Last time we met, over a July lunch at the Bass Pro Shop in Jackson, Mississippi, he was on his way to deliver the pelt of a bear, fresh from the Canadian woods, to a friend a few miles up the road. I'm not a hunter and never will be, but I consider this hunter—a hunter of wild game and great ideas—among the dearest of my American friends.

And then there was a true American original named Patricia Griffin. I had never met anyone like her before, nor have I since. The ultimate Carolina Piedmont mama-bear, mistress of "Mayflower Lodge"—the house on Mayflower Drive where Jen was living when I came to town—"Griffin" (as her many friends affectionately named her) was a winemaker, storyteller, people-connector, anti-fashionista, and a non-conformist mathematics instructor at the university, where she taught for the best part of five decades. With her quirky imagination and infectious good humor, she infused life at the lodge with a spirit of casual celebration. No doubt she did the same in the calculus classroom. Lodgers came and went at the Mayflower—Claire, Jonesy, Jean, Schmeet, Frankie, Jen—and none left without lifelong admiration for the mistress of the house.

With the happiness and welfare of her lodgers in mind, Griffin appointed herself impresario of what she dubbed the "perfect supper," and it is now my honor to spell out what she meant by perfection in the preparation of the evening meal.

"Perfect supper" was an assemblage of the following ingredients: a hot dog on a white bread bun, baked beans heated up from the can, oven-baked potato fries from the frozen food section of the Kroger store across the street, and a side salad of iceberg lettuce with a scattering of cherry tomatoes smothered in Good Seasons French dressing, all served on paper plates. For Griffin such evident perfection was never complete without the taste of a Pabst Blue Ribbon beer (PBR), sipped straight from its frosty can. The whole enterprise was designed with rough mathematical exactitude to conform to Griffin's first rule of cuisine: "No meal, formal or otherwise, should take longer to prepare than it does to eat." In the case of perfect supper, the preparation time was about nine minutes and a longish swig of PBR.

At home and in the classroom, Griffin loved to talk, and I for one was enchanted by her folksy way of saying things. She had an endearing habit of supplementing her languid Southern drawl with all kinds of phonological inventions and grammatical mischief. She called Jen "Jennry." Her parents were "MG" (Mama Griffin) and "PG" (Papa Griffin) and her younger sister was "BG" (Baby Griffin). The piece of land she owned outside of town was "the fram."

Griffin's purpose in buying "the fram" was to build her own log cabin there. After the papers had been signed, Jen asked her what she would like as a "fram-warming" gift. In her perfect country Carolina accent, she replied: "Oh, Jenry, yieew don't need to do thay-it! Ah wish ya'll wouldn't bother. Ah rilly rilly do." Jen remained adamant, however, and Griffin finally conceded: "OK they-in. What ahd rilly lahk is a drohwin' naaf."

In translation, she wanted a "drawing knife" to strip the bark off logs for her cabin construction project.

With the willing assistance of friends from near and far, Griffin cleared the land of honeysuckle bramble and built a two-story log house out of the ruins of a one-room cabin that had long since collapsed under the weight of time. In loosely organized teams, Griffin and her friends harvested logs for the house from the trees growing in profusion on her 36 wild acres—loblolly pine, maple, oak, and yellow poplar.

They stripped the bark with the "drohwin' naaf," and treated some of the foundation lumber with used engine oil from their own cars. They built enclosures for chickens and rabbits and kept a goat named "Giles" on hand to help clear the honeysuckle and trim the surrounding grass. "Bilbo" the dog got in the way wherever he could. With her boundless curiosity, honest hard work, and witty turns of phrase, Griffin turned "the fram" into a destination of joyous hospitality.

In the first spring, Griffin and her friends planted an acre of butterbeans and another of chickpeas and welcomed her neighbors to harvest whatever they needed. Later they planted strawberries, this time as a cash crop. Discovering in due course that the land produced more crops than cash, they let the whole place return to the wild. This was ultimately how Griffin preferred it. Surrounded by all that natural beauty, and content in the simplicity of her days, she lived there until her death in 2021 with her partner, Francie, hidden away in their sun-bleached log home.

What I have said about Patricia Griffin barely begins to describe her generosity and charm. She was an extraordinary woman, a genuinely folksy character who could only have come from the American South. If heaven is peopled with women like her, sign me up. The same goes for a long-treasured woman who came into my life as one of the added blessings of my marriage to Jen.

There is a fragment of folk wisdom that goes something like this: "People will probably not remember what you say; they may remember what you do; but they will never forget the way you make them feel." It is a commonplace that deserves far more attention than it gets. I will never forget the feeling of welcome I received from one who was soon to become my sister-in-law: Rebecca McHenry Lowe, affectionately known as "Becky." Though her physical presence is gone from us now, (taken too soon in 2015 at the age of 62) Becky remains in my memory forever as a special instance of unusually joyful presence in the world.

It was Thanksgiving 1971 when I first met her. I'd driven all day from North Carolina through the mountains of West Virginia to east central Ohio over snowy November roads. My destination was a pretty little farmhouse just outside of Coshocton, Ohio, where I was to meet, for the first time, some of Jen's family: her brother, Denny, his wife, Becky, and their one-year-old daughter, Jennifer. It was country dark when I arrived—a silent and moonless cold.

As I inched up the long, curved driveway toward the farmhouse, the snow hissing and squeaking under the tires, I felt an odd and unexpected sense of loneliness. Where in the world was I? I'd followed a map (no GPS systems in those days) across hundreds of miles of the vast American interior to reach a place that seemed no more than a stab of light in a great surrounding darkness. Who were these people—Jen's people—I was about to meet? What was I to expect from the strangers beyond columned porch that now shone white in the focused beam of the headlights?

I pulled the car to a stop and crunched through the snow to the entrance. Before I had time to ring the bell, the door swung open in a burst of warm yellow light, and I stepped into another world.

It was a glowing Thanksgiving carnival, a wonderland of orange, yellow, red, and brown—sparkling lights, cardboard turkeys, basketfuls of yellow squash and dried cornstalks, tiny orange mini-pumpkins lined in a row, rag dolls, flags, pennants, handmade plates and coffee mugs, and, grinning proudly on the kitchen table, a plump carved pumpkin, big as a basketball. There was Jennifer, elegant as always, wrapping me in her arms, her kindly brother, Denny, shaking my hand in unaffected welcome, and her infant niece Jennifer reaching for the baubles tinkling above her tiny wooden crib. And at the smiling heart of it all was Becky.

Becky Lowe with Barclay (left) and Doozie

With an unselfconscious mama-bear hug she drew me instantly into her circle of belonging. It was as if I were her long-lost brother. In a flurry of open-hearted questions, eyes sparkling with genuine interest and affection, she implored me to tell her about, well, everything—my trip north in the snow, my decision to travel to America, my first date with Jen, my family in New Zealand, and so on and on.

And while this cheerful inquisition was proceeding, Becky was making frequent trips to the kitchen and returning with arms full of delectables to rejoice the heart, if not to save it from ruin. Out came the chips and dip, the sliced carrots and celery, the bunches of grapes, the popcorn and pretzels, the ten varieties of pop and beer, the second and third rounds of chips and dip, the pastries, the cookies, and the aromatic zucchini bread fresh from the oven.

In the course of that night and many subsequent visits to her home, through her unbounded kindness, her unfailing good cheer, and her words of comfort and affirmation, Becky Lowe made me feel truly welcome. I can never forget it. There are uncounted others who, if you ask, will say the same about her. With wholehearted passion, she lived out the creed she professed on a decorative banner fixed to the wall of the home she had filled with so much joy until the day she died: "There is little in life that cannot benefit from a little love, a little time, and a stick of butter." In Becky Lowe's case, there was more than a little of them all.

I have happily digressed into an exploration of the people and places I encountered in my first two years in America and how the desolations I felt when I first arrived gave way in time to consolations of unexpected joy. But my purpose in America was theatre, and I continued to discover it in what must surely be one of the most dramatic cultures on earth—dramatic, sometimes, to uncomfortable extremes. It was theatre that reset the boundaries of my life and reseeded the fields of my imagination.

CHAPTER 10.

In the Verdant Hills and Dark Valleys

*"Remember that even the road to terrible battles
always passes by gardens and windows and children
playing and a barking dog."*
—*Yehuda Amichai, "The Third Poem about Dickey"*

By the early days of September 1970, I was already well-launched into my studies at the University of North Carolina at Greensboro. Under the guidance of professors with academic and professional credentials from all over the country, north and south, east and west, I willingly entered exciting new worlds of communication theory and practice, dramatic literature, theatre history, acting, directing, and design.

I worked on the construction of sets and props and became increasingly familiar with the dimly-lit backstage life of the theatre the audience does not see. I watched dozens of shows—most memorably a heart-stopping production of Harold Pinter's *The Dumb Waiter*—and feasted on the apparently limitless bounty of music, film, and dance being offered on campus by professional artists and talented students.

Then came an unusual challenge, one that almost brought me to my knees in surrender, yet at the same time shook me to my existential foundations and set my imagination free to ask new questions and think new thoughts. I was cast as Vladimir in a production of Samuel Beckett's *Waiting for Godot*. I had no idea how formidable the mountain I was about to climb.

It presented a sturdy challenge from the start. Despite John Thomson and Kathryn England's work with me to develop a dramatic speaking voice, to find a character, and embody the emotions of a text, I was by no means ready to immerse myself transformatively, as actors do, in the utter otherness of another personality, moving and speaking out of that other person's inner reality. Nor was I experienced enough to sustain this mysterious fusion of self and other for nearly three hours on stage. Learning the lines, one of the first technical tasks of any actor, was, in itself, a titanic struggle.

Look at the text of *Waiting for Godot* and you will see what I mean. Vladimir, otherwise known as "Didi," and his fellow lost soul Estragon ("Gogo"), interact in broken, discontinuous sentences and quick single-word riffs, making frequent apparently illogical transitions. I needed to have my "lines" overlearned to the point where they flowed instinctively from some deep place within, every one of them in the correct order and crisply on cue.

I woke every morning for those six weeks reaching for my increasingly dog-eared paperback script. I went to sleep every night with the script dropping out of my hands. I walked for miles on the streets of Greensboro repeating the sequences to myself. I spent hours on weekends running lines with friends, including my not-quite-yet fiancée, Jen, who fed me the cues with sacrificial patience and had them memorized before I did. Despite a growing anxiety that troubled my dreams, I finally patched and cobbled the role together. With the ready assistance of the much more talented and experienced actors on stage—and the encouragement of a fine young director, Bruce van Blarcom—I was able to offer a passable representation of Beckett's sad, earnest, lost little clown. Enough at least to earn cautious praise from the local press.

The challenge of playing the role of Vladimir, however, was of lesser significance to me than my encounter with the story itself. Beckett's play grabbed me by the scruff of my innocent neck and plunged me into a searing world of honest and courageous new questions, some of which had been hidden in the depths of my heart for a long time. The world of the play was one of desperate souls hoping not to be forever lost.

In the opening scene, Gogo is sitting under a lifeless tree trying to get one of his boots off. He and Didi have been wandering in a barren wilderness, hoping for someone they call Mr. Godot to tell them where they are and where perhaps they are going.

Howard (foreground) as Vladimir in Waiting for Godot

Gogo tugs at his boot with childlike earnestness, totally preoccupied with the task at hand. Didi, however, more fully aware of the peril they are in, makes brooding observations about their own particular predicament and the larger predicament of all humanity. Why do we feel so alone and so lost? Why do we find life such a struggle? What reasons can we find to keep going? Why do we keep hoping someone—or something—will turn up to show us the way? What do we do while we wait to be saved from our uncertainty and despair?

After much ineffectual wrestling, Gogo finally gets one of his boots to come free, then the other. Having rid himself of his bothersome boots, he feels a great sense of relief, his animal-self flooded with satisfaction.

Didi, on the other hand, continues to ask his anguished questions. Why are the questions (about life) so many and the answers to few? Why do our myths and religious stories leave us in such confusion? Why is it, for example, that in telling the story of the crucifixion of Jesus, only one of the four Gospel writers speaks of the dying thief being "saved"? Why do people persist in believing the witness of one of the writers rather than the other three? Wriggling his blistered toes in the dirt, Gogo bursts out: "It's because people are bloody ignorant apes."

Now that the saga of Gogo's boots is over, the two citizens of nowhere find what diversions they can to pass the time while they wait for "Mr. Godot." Some of their games are endearingly childlike ("What did we do yesterday?"), others more ominous ("Let's hang ourselves off the branch of this dead tree.") Their feelings fluctuate from hope to despair and back to exhausted hope. Occasional surges of courage are soon quashed by insurmountable obstacles. False leads mysteriously appear and just as mysteriously disappear. One of them takes the form of a strange pair named Pozzo and Lucky.

For Gogo and Didi, even the most bizarre of companions can bring at least temporary relief from despair. Pozzo and Lucky are indeed bizarre: Pozzo an obese, arrogant "master" and Lucky his pathetic cowering slave, attached to his master by a chain around his neck.

Far from being the rescuers the two lost souls were hoping for, however, Pozzo and Lucky turn out to be lost themselves. They are enigmatic frauds, offering little more than disconnected fragments of discourse and a stream of seemingly erudite nonsense pouring out of Lucky's servile brain. His unhinged monologue quoting nonexistent scholars pokes devastating fun at the false prophets of the world who pretend to have definitive answers to the great questions of life but are no closer to understanding the deep existential cry of humanity than croaking toads in a backwater swamp. I had known a few Pozzos in my day.

This powerful scene, and the others that followed, put me in a deeply reflective state of mind. There was a bit of me in all of Beckett's characters. Despite the grace bestowed on me as a child, I had felt, like Didi, a deep sense of existential loneliness, especially when I heard the ghosts crying at night and felt firsthand that the powers of death were stronger than the powers of life.

Like Gogo, I had been obsessed with inconsequential things, practicing the art of living other people's lives, tugging at the books on my bookshelves, wanting to become another C. S. Lewis or Paul Tournier or Francis Shaeffer or someone else like them.

Like Lucky, I had surrendered without protest to intellectual and emotional bullies, especially of the religious type. Like Pozzo, I had spoken words I did not understand with a certainty I did not possess.

I had begun to realize that the dilemma of Beckett's two sad clowns was a shadow of my own deepest dilemma and most likely the hidden dilemma of every human being who'd ever breathed God's air. In the face of the ravages of time and the inevitability of death, we wander alone on a dry, featureless plain, vulnerable to the false promises of loud voices, yet at the same time clinging to fleeting intuitions of hope. Somewhere beyond the dark we all seem to have a memory of the lights of home and some kind of rescue.

It's hard from this distance to judge if thoughts like these were already present within me as I worked on the show or were rather the result of a growing self-awareness in subsequent years. One thing I do know is that, by immersing myself in this play, I had learned more than I could by simply reading it on the page. By the engagement of mind, body, and heart, I had found some of its truth, and some of its truth had found me.

I was exhilarated by the whole experience and also, by the time it was over, utterly spent. Beckett's masterpiece had demanded of me everything I had—physically and emotionally—and I had given it. The falling of the final curtain was like a benediction. It had already become clear to me that I was not going to be an actor, but I was going to be interested for a long time in the theatre's profoundly challenging interpretations of human existence.

I would go on to play other characters in university and semi-professional productions: Oscar Hubbard in the *The Little Foxes*, for example, or Ravenel in a Broadway mystery from the 1950s called *Monique*. I directed a few plays and designed the lights for others. Because of my budding romance with Jen, I also had the opportunity to play a role in an unusual outdoor drama and live for a time among theatre folk whose exuberant extroversion and wild imaginations brought a riot of newness into my life. It was as if a magical hand had switched my perception of my fellow human beings from black and white to technicolor.

The play was *Unto These Hills*, an outdoor drama performed every year in the Smoky Mountains of Cherokee, North Carolina. Written in

1949 by Kermit Hunter, it tells the tragic story of the forced removal of the Cherokee people from their ancestral home in the southeast corner of the United States to the vast open lands west of the Mississippi.

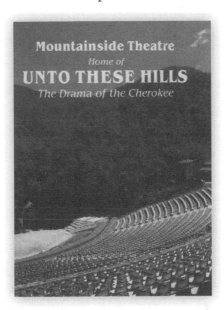

Mountainside Theatre,
Cherokee, North Carolina

It's a story of great injustice and terrible suffering, of people tricked by an illegitimate treaty, let down by a feckless president and Supreme Court, hunted down by armed U. S. government soldiers, herded like animals into stockades, and forced to walk a thousand miles on what became known as the "Trail of Tears." On their tortured journey west, 4,000 Cherokee died from starvation, exhaustion, disease, or hypothermia in the freezing winter temperatures.

The dramatized version of the Trail of Tears—told under the stars in a natural hillside amphitheater—was a brilliant and moving spectacle. A live choir hidden in the forest augmented the amplified sounds of the music; actors appeared from among the trees, lit from below; dancers in bright native dress turned and swirled with white eagle-feather wands; battle scenes erupted in simulated fire; a single drum beat marked the steps of the Cherokee as they trudged slowly across the wide sandy stage and disappeared into the surrounding forest.

The telling of the story was made even more poignant by the presence in the cast of many local Cherokee people. Ranging in age from seven to seventy, they were members of the Eastern Band of the tribe whose ancestors had escaped the removal by hiding in the hills or had at some point made the perilous journey from Oklahoma back to their ancestral lands. Among them was Amoneeta Sequoyah, the medicine man of the tribe and the descendant of one of the most celebrated of Cherokee chiefs. (Amoneeta's story is briefly told in Peter Matthiesson's 1984 book, *Indian Country.*)

Jen with Amoneeta Sequoyah (1968)

In a nightly ritual before the show, Amoneeta exercised his powers of white magic "to keep the rains away" from the Mountainside Theatre, for which valued service he was paid a few extra dollars a month. Many in the wider Cherokee community—and in the theatre company—believed his powers were real and there were many anecdotes, apocryphal or not, to back them up. One summer, for example, Amoneeta was released from the drama for breaking company rules. The very next night the show was rained out. That rainout was followed by another, until inexplicably there had been twelve consecutive costly show cancellations. What to do? In short order, Amoneeta was hired back, and, upon his return, so they say, the stars came out once again over the Mountainside Theatre. Amoneeta carried out his familiar ritual for years.

The stars shone, on clear nights of course, not only in the sky above the Mountainside Theatre, but also among the cast on the stage. There was Sam Owl, a quietly dignified elder of the tribe, standing tall and proud in his chieftain's robe, his very presence lending grace and gravitas to the whole enterprise. There was sweet Maybelle Ivy, with her own children gathered around her in the backstage darkness, ready to play her part on stage after walking a couple of miles through the woods bearing gifts of cornbread and homegrown squash for her friends in the company. There was the aging Ollie Jumper, face deeply lined, body bent from the weight of years, croaking out the words of "Amazing Grace" in Cherokee. I can hear it still.

Given the story they were telling, it seemed impossible to me that Ollie Jumper and the native Indian cast members could sing such words without irony. Perhaps they saw grace in the fact that despite the efforts of the white race to obliterate their presence in the lovely hills of western North Carolina, they were still there and remain there to this day, on land that is once more and forever their own.

Perhaps not. Perhaps they saw the singing of "Amazing Grace" as just something they were required to do to earn their weekly paycheck as members of the company of *Unto These Hills*. Either way, the irony of it was not lost on me, nor was the simple pathos of the melody sung out under the stars by a Cherokee grandmother with real tears flowing down the runnels of her face.

It was my privilege for a time to share the stage with Amoneeta and Ollie and Maybelle and all the rest of them. In August 1971, after spending the best part of the summer in Vancouver, British Columbia, I traveled back to North Carolina to spend the last week of the season with Jennifer in Cherokee. Jen was by now a seasoned veteran of the company, having spent several summers working there as a dancer and assistant choreographer, running brush up rehearsals and managing the dance corps during the run of the show. When I arrived at the company village ("the hill," as it was called), I was presented with a challenge that was to be, even in its fumbling execution, another of those tiny but subtly defining moments of my life.

Knowing little about me other than what he may or may not have heard from his assistant choreographer, Bill Hardy, the director of the show, invited me to play a small role for last week of the run—a humble Spanish soldier—with no spoken lines to learn and no difficult "stage business" to remember. How could I say no?

So here I was in late summer of 1971 standing in the forested backstage of the 3,000 seat Mountainside Theatre, costumed in faux metal breastplate and helmet, ready to march in military formation as part of Hernando de Soto's 16th-century expedition through the mountains of western North Carolina toward the great Mississippi River.

There had been no time for rehearsal. The requirements of the role, however, were simple. All I had to do was stay upright as I followed the footsteps of my fellow actors, similarly dressed, down a set of rocky stairs onto the sandy floor of the stage, crossing in a straight line from one side to the other. What could possibly go wrong?

Holding my fake long-handled halberd high above my helmet, I waited for my entrance. The lights came up. A startling brightness exploded through the tangle of trees. Fumbling my way toward the rocky steps, I began to sing with my fellow conquistadores: "Hombres vamonos in tierra nueva!"

Suddenly, I felt a fierce tug on the handle of my halberd. I was pulled backward and upwards, jerkily, like a fish on a line. With one foot floating in space, I looked up. The top of my axe was firmly wedged in the tangled branches of an overhanging scarlet oak tree. I tugged. There was a vigorous shaking of leafy branches. I tugged again, hard, and as my axe broke free in a shower of vegetation, my loose-fitting helmet fell forward over my face. In a flash, I felt as though I were trapped inside a mail box looking out through a tiny rectangle of unfocused light. I had no idea where I was going.

Conscious that all eyes were upon me, all three thousand pairs of them, I stumbled my way down the rocks like a kid in a game of blindman's bluff. With my halberd swinging vaguely in front of me, like a wet flag flying at half-mast, I limped across sixty feet of sand, ten wobbly steps behind the other actors. Seconds later—though it seemed an hour—I was received into the merciful dark of the backstage wings. "You OK?" one my fellow actors whispered. "Yeah, no," I whispered back. "I think I just failed my first test as a worthy soldier of Ferdinand and Isabella." It was further proof, if I needed it, that I was not going to be an actor.

In subsequent summers, I nevertheless played other roles, including the Reverend Sam Worcester, a steadfast advocate for justice for the Cherokee people, blew the dust off a piano accordion for five minutes of madness in a zany variety show, and worked backstage as a lowly assistant stagehand, raking the sandy floor before each performance and setting electrically charged flash pots for the spectacular battle scenes.

Humble as my position was in the company of actors and dancers, I was in the catbird seat to watch the drama unfold both onstage and off. To begin with, there was the *Unto These Hills* story itself, a fascinating and heartbreaking retelling of one of the darkest episodes in American history. Then there were the people—the actors, dancers, designers, technicians, and stage hands—who were telling it. They were, to say the least, a colorful crew.

A theatre company always has its share of memorable personalities and the drama at Cherokee was no exception. For me to spend the summers with the company of *Unto These Hills* in Cherokee was like stepping into the workshop of the Mad Hatter in *Alice in Wonderland*.

Like Alice after her tumble down the rabbit hole, I found myself in the rollicking company of wildly varied and often zany characters. There was the swaggering, fly-zipper-checking director, Bill Hardy, tapping the burnt contents of his tobacco pipe against the heel of his cowboy boots. There was his long-suffering wife, Martha Nell, a distinguished actress in the style of Maggie Smith or Angela Lansbury, greeting actors backstage as if throwing the robes of royalty over them, purring "Let me kiss the staaah." There was the crinkle-eyed Newton Neeley, spinning out puns and malapropisms and fake accents like Daniel Webster's firstborn son (Knoxville was "Knockersville," "dinner" was "dawner"). There was the outrageous Richard Pinkerton, whose foghorn laughter and crazy loquacity, not unlike Robin Williams's, tiptoed the border between genius and madness. There was the happy-go-lucky special effects whiz, Gene Echols, running a chess game between cues in the show. There was the grey-bearded technical director, George McKinney, presiding over a smoky late-night poker game in his studio on the hill and, in his spare time, creating an album of gorgeous photographic studies of Jennifer against the misty backdrop of the Smoky Mountains.

The list goes on. There was the urbane and super-cool Dallas Snyder, holding court in the costume shop, a nest of wicked humor and delicious gossip. There was the nonstop storyteller, Thom Jaros, otherwise known as "Trader Thom," who brought a benign New York peevishness to the management of the Cherokee Trader, a notable crafts and souvenir shop on the banks of the Oconaluftee River. There was the rollicking Trudie Marchbanks, who thought miles were longer in North Carolina than they were in Texas. And there was the actor's actor, the never-off-stage John Morrow, whose booming voice could be heard up and down the hillside company village calling for Rusty, his entirely out-of-control mixed-breed mutt. I can hear it now echoing off the surrounding hills: "Rusty! Rusty!! Rusty!!!"

Then there was the unforgettable Louis Nunnery. A former B-movie screen actor and one-time member of the Ballet Russe de Monte Carlo, Louis was a ballet master extraordinaire from Hickory, North Carolina, and artistic director of the Civic Ballet in Greensboro, where, for a couple of seasons in the 1960s, Jen danced in the corps de ballet. In Cherokee, he brought a weary off-handed energy to his various roles as choreographer, actor, and company clown. Attaching wacky, and sometimes wicked, nicknames to all and sundry—Jen was "Jenny Wren" and I was "Cowardy Custard"—he spun outrageous shaggy-dog stories while his listeners howled with gut-grabbing laughter. He cut a wide swath of wisecracking nonsense wherever he went. I have no doubt he'd have made a great Shakespearean fool or a fantastical Wizard of Oz.

One summer's night, so the story goes, after supervising pre-show preparations backstage, Louis took his customary walk up the terraced aisles to his seat in the Mountainside Theatre. He was always dressed to catch the eye, this time in a sweeping floor-length multicolored kaftan. As he neared the top row of seats, he became aware of an audience member pointing in his direction and saying, "There goes one of them damned hippies!" Raising one arm in the air like the magician of the enchanted isle, Louis called out, in nasalized tones that were a deliberate assault on the Queen's English: "Yeah! And a rich one, too!"

Louis Nunnery, costumed and enthroned

To get some sense of the eccentricity of Louis Nunnery, I need only list a few of his prized possessions: a historic log cabin adorned at the front with two-story Georgian columns, a bathroom draped in purple velvet with a "throne" to be stepped up to as necessary, a fleet of seventeen antique automobiles, including an ancient Rolls Royce named "Isabella Bigwad," and a pack of pampered white Russian wolfhounds who could, on cue, be induced to howl in surprising concert. He called them the "Mormonacle Dogs."

Every year, until his death in 2013, he sent us a handmade Christmas card that announced on the front cover: "Everyone needs something special for Christmas." Upon opening the card, we would be presented with a fine photograph of Louis in full costume and makeup, looking, as he would say, "geeooooorgeous"—like one of the over-the-top performers in one of his ballet extravaganzas. Something special, indeed.

Sometime in the mid 1960s, I am told, Louis invited the company of *Unto These Hills* to witness what he dubbed a "miracle" to be performed before their very eyes. He had prepared for the event by having the company's tech crew build a makeshift ramp just under the surface of the Oconaluftee River, whose dancing waters run in rills around scattered rocks toward the Indian Village of Cherokee.

The "miracle" was scheduled for very early one Sunday morning when the mists were still drifting over the water's surface. Company members gathered sleepily at the banks of the river, waiting in good humor for the conjurations to begin.

From out of the Smoky Mountains fog, Louis appears, dressed in a long white robe. He steps to the edge of the river, then out onto the ramp, hidden under the river's gently rippled surface. With great fanfare, Louis takes a few steps toward the other shore before turning to acknowledge the knowing, collaborative applause. He was, of course, "walking on water."

It was one of those moments—admittedly a touch silly and irreverent—when a theatre company could celebrate the make-believe miracles they and their rambunctious tribe have created from time immemorial on the stages of the world.

My days in Cherokee left made an indelible mark upon my consciousness. In the company of these spirited people, so creative, so passionate, and so free, I felt my heart opening to wide new vistas of experience and allowed more of the constraining walls of the past fall away.

By the end of my two years in Greensboro, with my Master's degree in hand, and knowing I was not going to be an actor, I began exploring other ways to become engaged in the vibrant enterprise of theatre.

With John Thompson's mentorship in mind, I decided I would learn everything I could about how actors use their voices to find and express subtleties of thought and emotion. I would also continue to explore the vast territory of the theatre's stories and find ways to share their life-giving bounty on other stages—the stages of lecture theaters and classrooms. My calling was to be a teacher.

So it was that I moved on to the University of Michigan for further training. This time my choice of place was not determined by a random search through college catalogs but by my desire to be near my soon-to-be wife. Jen was already immersed in her doctoral studies at Michigan to prepare for a career in theatrical choreography and teaching stage movement with a specialty in period styles, including her favorite, 17th-century Restoration comedy.

In the late summer of 1972, we moved to Ann Arbor, famous for its intimidating Big House (the football stadium seating 105,000 fans) and much less so for a sweet little house on Lawrence Street that became our home for the first two years of our life there. The two "houses"—one vast and intimidating and the other softly-furnished and welcoming—turned out to be emblematic of the two sides of my experience in this next phase of my life in America.

Driving our faithful little Buttercup into Ann Arbor, I sensed a quickening in the pace of life and a new level of intensity in the air. With its mix of contemporary and neoclassical architecture—the high glass facade of the Power Center, the great wide lawn of "the Diag," the cloistered quads of the law school—the place felt more East Coast than Midwest.

I was now in the heady company of world-class scholars and teachers, including "Doc" William P. Halstead, an encyclopedic theatre historian whose lanky, aristocratic bearing reminded me of my New Zealand mentor John Thomson. One of my most endearing professors was J. C. Catford, a renowned Scottish phonetician, speech and dialect consultant for the BBC, and bearer of some local fame for his amazing linguistic parlor tricks. To entertain his students or guests at a party, for example, he made a show of repeating the words of spoken sentences backward at conversational speed. I sat in on classes with J. L. Styan, author of numerous books on drama in performance, and once caught sight of playwright Arthur Miller browsing the shelves of the old Borders bookstore downtown. I took classes with the brilliant and always affable Bruce Gronbeck—who I would meet again in Iowa City—and the equally affable Howard H. Martin (yes, there were hilarious confusions), one of the most engaging teachers I ever met anywhere in the world.

Preeminent among my teachers in those years, though, was a professor of linguistics by the name of Kenneth Pike. I was richly blessed in meeting him.

Kenneth Pike

I had known Kenneth Pike by reputation for some time. One summer in the late 1960s, on little more than a whim, I sweated my way through a course in linguistics offered in Auckland by the Summer Institute of Linguistics (SIL), whose mission was to train linguists to map out grammars for previously unwritten languages.

Many SIL graduates went to on work with organizations like the Wycliffe Bible Translators. The linguistic methodology used in SIL and Wycliffe had been pioneered by Kenneth Pike.

The SIL course, led by the brilliant Darlene Bee, was my first introduction to the field of linguistics and also my first encounter with the concept of the "meme" so common in today's digital communications environment. I would soon learn that Pike was in fact one of the world's great linguists, author of groundbreaking theoretical works, and—with his linguist wife Evelyn—a tireless worker among native peoples around the world, creating alphabets and grammars for primal preliterate languages.

When he was appointed professor of linguistics at the University of Michigan in 1974, Pike was cited as a scholar whose "originality and energetic activity verge on the legendary." In honor of his pioneering efforts to rescue dying languages from almost certain oblivion (half the world's 7,000 languages were not expected to survive the 21st century), he was nominated by Illinois senator Alan J. Dixon for a Nobel Peace Prize.

One of the first decisions we made after arriving in Ann Arbor was to attend religious services at the University Reformed Church just a couple of blocks from our pretty ground-floor apartment on Lawrence Street. The pastor was Calvin Malefyt, dean of preachers in the Reformed Church of America, a man whose wide learning and deep wisdom were attractively contained in the chalice of a humble and loving heart. When Calvin learned of our interests in theatre and dance, he invited Jen and me to participate in the church's celebrations of worship.

At one such celebration I read the Biblical text for the day, a story from the Gospels as I recall, perhaps the one about Zaccheus, the little outsider in the sycamore tree. After the service was over, I heard a voice behind me, urgent and high pitched, say, "Interesting!" I turned.

There in front of me was a wiry bespectacled presence, dancing toe to toe like a bantamweight boxer, his eyes, flashing with bright intelligence, bearing in on me with an uncanny intensity. "Interesting," he repeated. "The way you interpreted that text. Take a look at this." He handed me a church bulletin with rapidly scratched notations in the margins. "This is my transcription of what you did with your voice when you read this morning."

He thrust the well-thumbed document toward me, the open spaces covered in rapidly scratched notations.

"See?" He pointed with his pencil. "You stressed this syllable here, and here…your pitch shifted upwards, and look…here you had a pause…about three beats…very effective. Also…right here…a change of key."

He paused a moment then asked, "You're an actor, right?"

"I cannot claim to be an actor," I demurred, "but I'm learning what I can about theatre and the actor's art."

"Look," he said. "I've been thinking for a long time about how actors do what they do. I've been trying for years to get theatre people interested in my work. Why don't you come see me some time?"

"That, sir, is absolutely fascinating," I said, finding my voice. "I'd love to talk to you about it."

"Do that," he said. He handed me his card and was gone.

The card read: Dr. Kenneth L. Pike, Department of Linguistics, The University of Michigan, Ann Arbor, MI 48109.

That, I suppose, is how you get to meet a legend.

A week later I was sitting in his office on campus. He was ready for me, like a fighter before the opening bell, every muscle tuned for action. He snapped on the lamp at his desk, adjusted a green eye-shade on his forehead, took a couple of moments to select a pencil from a his pencil box—it had to be exactly the right pencil—and, drawing a line on a sheet of clean white paper, said, "OK, now. Let's talk some more about what I heard last Sunday."

And so began a special relationship that lasted the best part of three years. We talked about actors and actors' voices and so much more: art, music, theatre, philosophy, theology, language, and well, life. We talked about divine calling. And family. During lunch one day—at home with his wife, Evelyn—he offered to create a course specifically for me on the intonation of American English, about which he had written a pioneering work. "All you have to do is recruit a couple of your actor friends to take it with you."

I twisted some arms. He taught the class. By the time it was over, I knew the direction I would take in my research and teaching, at least for the foreseeable future. The following summer we published an article together in *Language and Style* called, "Analysis of the Vocal Performance of a Poem: A Classification of Intonational Features." Graciously, Pike insisted that my name appear as first author. "You did all the writing," he said. "I just had some of the ideas." That was, of course, an understatement.

In subsequent years it was to be my privilege to pass on Kenneth Pike's ideas on intonation and voice quality to thousands of students and teachers in communication and theatre across the country, including many young actors in training at the University of Iowa and the University of Missouri–Kansas City. Some of these students became professors themselves, while others, like the lovingly creative couple Jody Hovlund and Ron Clark, became directors of their own theatre companies, and yet others went on to acting careers in major regional theaters companies, television dramas, and on Broadway. When Kenneth Pike died in 2000, I felt in the midst of my pangs of loss a sense of gratitude for the privilege of having walked a while in the company of a great American. Often when I think of him, I hear him say in that super-fast clip that so often reveals a megawatt intellect, "Finally got someone to listen. All right, now. What's next?"

The years in Ann Arbor were years of great highs and lows as I tried to balance the exhilaration of discovery with a lingering burden of grief at what I had left behind in my native land. I had no doubt that I was moving with the wind at my back and I continued to be exhilarated by the magnificent American landscapes, the dynamism of American culture, and the great cataract of ideas that tumbled from my new American teachers and fellow students. With Jen transforming our tiny apartment into a place of gracious hospitality, flowers and all, I felt sheltered in the company of new friends, some of whom remain part of our family circle to this day. Among these were Bruce and Judy Levitt, as artistically accomplished and full of life as any couple we have known, and Jim and Mary Wieland, whose loving presence and sense of fun have earned them a place among the truly "joyful ones" in our lives. Nevertheless, and despite all that serendipity, I felt in Ann Arbor an increasing heaviness in my heart.

It's no easy thing to leave a beloved country—especially a small one where every valley, every hill, every street corner seems to resonate with memory—and start again in a vast new land where nothing is familiar. It's not easy to be in a new place where so many accidental encounters—a crack in a sidewalk, a line of trees on a hillside, a whiff of salt air, the squawk of a seagull—take you back to where your soul was born.

Nor is it easy to leave a beloved people, whose existence you carry in every cell of your body, at a level beneath memory, and begin to feel at home where not a single person—not even your wife—knows who you were as a child. A refugee anywhere—even one who goes to a new country with dreams of another life—is essentially a lost soul, torn away from the silken strands of that other existence that once held them secure. As I wandered the world, with new horizons opening to me, I felt like Tom Wingfield in *The Glass Menagerie*, unable to let the beloved people of my childhood go. I was haunted by memories.

There were times in Ann Arbor when the sadness became more than I could contain. For long, dark weeks—especially in the depths of gloomy Michigan winters—melancholy brimmed within me like a dark flood. The howling dogs of depression snapped at my ankles, and there were days when I could barely keep them at bay. I remember one leaden morning standing on the stairs of our second-floor apartment on Lawrence Street, feeling such a weight pressing on me that I felt I could not move.

I had an 8 a.m. class to meet. The lecture I was scheduled to give seemed too much. The waiting class of intelligent, ambitious students seemed too much. Lacing up my heavy boots and zipping my jacket seemed too much. Walking through the snowy streets to the lecture hall seemed too much. It all seemed too much, and I gave in to the heaviness of its weight. In a gesture that seemed the opposite of prayer, but may actually have been the most honest prayer I ever prayed in my life, I collapsed with my arms folded between my knees and wept.

In those moments, the man became a child again, no more than an overwhelmed little boy from way down under, weeping for himself and for the whole messed-up world. He wept for his three stricken siblings, whose cries had haunted his childhood sleep. He wept for all the beloved people he had left behind, his mum and his dad, his brothers Bryan and Ian and Warwick and his sister Cecile, his neighbors and colleagues and friends. He wept for his gentle native land, for the smack of salt in the air, for the green hills dotted white with sheep, and for the sounds he would always hear as sounds of home—the tinkling bells of the tuis in the kauri forest, the rush of wind in the pohutukawa trees, the click-click of flax leaves along a fence line, the roar of geothermal steam in the volcanic heartland, and the thunder of surf crashing on the shiny black beaches of Piha, Karekare, and Muriwai. He wept for the memory of waters where he drifted without a care in a tiny white boat, for the melodies of songs such as "Yellow Bird" and "Pearly Shells" and "Po Kare Kare Ana," for punga ferns, and kōwhai flowers, and the white fringes of the toitoi grass. Perhaps more than anything else, he wept for the memory of his mother's voice calling him downstairs for a cup of tea and a peanut brownie by the fire.

I wept for it all, and the tears seemed to come from a place much deeper than I had ever known. I remained there in stillness for what seemed a long time. Then, wiping my eyes on my sleeves, I laced up my boots, shouldered my bag of books, and made my way through the dark snowy streets to class. With a watery sun rising in the eastern sky, I heard echoes of some familiar lines from Gerard Manley Hopkins's poem "Spring and Fall" and made them my own: "Now no matter, child, the name / Sorrow's springs are the same / It is the blight man was born for / It is Margaret you mourn for."

I found some comfort in the thought that my sorrow's springs were like those of every other human being who ever lived, including little Margaret, the original subject of Hopkins's poem. It was comforting to remember that I was not alone in my griefs, that others bore them, too. We bear our sorrows bravely for the most part and even in the midst of them look for the return of joy. It may well be that the experience of joy returning after times of great sadness can—if we so choose—prepare our hearts for the coming of the Great Joy beyond time. Our sorrow and our joy are both ways in which we are, as Abraham Heschel so beautifully put it, "in travail with God's dream."

There was always an end to Ann Arbor's dark winters. In April every year, the snows would melt and the blossoms of spring would appear: crabapple, dogwood, and cherry. The same was true in our next place of sojourn—Iowa City—where harsh winds of January gave way each spring to the gentle breezes and sunny blossoms of May.

Springtime in America is always a time of renewed hope for me, a time when its dark side begins to recede from my consciousness and its loveliness begins to reappear. In that sense, my years in Iowa were to be, for me, an American springtime.

CHAPTER 11.

Bright Fields of Iowa

" I have endeavoured to display the means
Whereby this infant sensibility,
Great birthright of our being, was in me
Augmented and sustained."
—*William Wordsworth,* The Prelude

In the late summer of 1975, Jennifer and I steered our brave little Buttercup south off Interstate 80 and took Dubuque Street into the heart of Iowa City, a verdant cultural oasis in the midst of the rolling cornfields of Iowa. Just the two of us and Buttercup, crammed to the gunwales with everything we owned, ready to begin a new life together.

We say goodbye to our brave little Buttercup, 1979

That we were there at all was the result of an unusual act of creativity on the part of the masterful Samuel Becker, chairman of the Department of Speech and Dramatic Arts at the University of Iowa. Dr. Beeker had initiated a search for an assistant professor to teach stage movement for actors, voice and speech, and performance studies (a field then known as "oral interpretation"). We applied for the job with a "two for the price of one" letter. Jen would teach the stage movement component; I would teach voice and speech and performance studies. Somehow, it worked.

Calling on the store of goodwill stockpiled over thirty distinguished years in academic scholarship and administration, Sam Becker created a single job for the two of us—a joint assistant professorship, the first in the history of the University and, at that time, one of the few anywhere in the country. This unique arrangement made it possible for us to live in the same place, teach our own specialties, and also—since we split the teaching load between us—take the time we needed to put the finishing touches on our dissertations.

So in September 1975, we met our first classes at Iowa.

There was always something magical about those first days of fall in the Midwest—the crispness in the air, the hint of gold in the morning light, the sense of new beginnings everywhere, the feeling of hopeful innocence that pervades the campus before the realities of assessment and evaluation set in.

Our first fall semester in this "little Paris of the plains" was no exception. It felt like a privilege to be there. Even when the shine of newness faded, as fall gave way to winter and year followed year, we found the university community in Iowa City a vibrant and life-affirming place to be.

Iowa City was in many ways the epitome of the Norman Rockwell America I had foreseen in my earliest dreams. Our home there was a pretty red-roofed cottage at 812 Melrose Avenue nestled under a green canopy of burr oak and pine. Across the street we could see red-brick porticos of Kinnick Stadium where on sunny fall afternoons we happily joined the crazy rituals of an American college football game, parking cars in our front yard with screaming college students clad in black and gold driving by in open convertibles. The yellow campus bus ("Cambus") stopped a hundred feet from our front door offering free rides to and from our faculty offices on the Pentacrest—a collection of historic buildings at the center of campus, including Iowa's Old Capitol built in 1842.

Our home in Iowa City, 1978–1983

Walking or riding eastward along the leafy streets, we could explore the coffee shops and bookstores of downtown or, taking a different turn, past cottage homes with variously tended lawns and gardens, could roam awhile among the busy lakeside picnic tables and the frisbees and leaping dogs in City Park.

Turning west on Melrose toward the cornfields, we could walk on Sundays to the nearby Presbyterian church—St. Andrew—where we were taken into the heart of a loving community and where we discovered friendships that were to last a lifetime.

I remember, for example, Dwayne and Becky Eckberg, who became kind of surrogate parents to us, welcoming us many a Sunday to join them and their three girls around a beautifully set table—white table cloth, cut crystal water glasses, freshly ironed napkins, and, at the center, an elegant arrangement of homegrown flowers. We felt such a nearness to them that after Barclay was born in 1978, we asked them to be his godparents. They accepted. It broke our hearts when they moved away to Virginia.

We felt a similar sense of closeness to Bob and Merrilee Beckman, so warm in their welcome, so adventurous in their thinking, so generous in their hospitality. In 1981, they became godparents to our newborn Alexander.

There was Alvin Desterhaft, esteemed pastor and forgiving tennis partner, whose laughing presence and thoughtful words gave eloquent witness to a wise and balanced world of faith.

There was Jason Chen, whose gentle companionship was a great comfort to me as together we wrestled with the meaning of our separate vocations in the world—mine to teach, his to ministry. In the words of Pat Conroy, Jason taught me the quiet words of kindness, showing me the wisdom of gentleness, urging me toward maturity of spirit, but "softly like an angel arranging clouds."

There was Phil Butin, the most gifted youth minister I ever met, who shared deep confidences with me in long late-night conversations and—after forty years of groundbreaking church leadership, including ten years as president of the San Francisco Theological Seminary—remains to this day a close companion of my heart.

There were so many more that the cup of our lives seemed filled to overflowing. There was a Paul Etre, an irresistibly vibrant presence in the Iowa City community, and Lois, his sweetheart of a wife. There was Carol Hindman, who opened herself to us in the liveliest of conversations and placed the kiss of loving care on the heads of our two little boys. There were Ed and Judy Allen, whose lightness of heart was so contagious we sometimes felt in their company as if we were floating on Iowa's silky summer clouds.

And then there were the Bakers—George and Marilyn—who have been for us the very embodiment of graciousness: gracious in physical bearing, gracious in conversation, gracious in gladness, gracious in sorrow, and gracious in hospitality. One of the high points of our year—for two decades—has been our return to their home in Snowmass Village, Colorado, where we have always felt deeply at home and at peace. Sitting with George and Marilyn in their high-vaulted living room, looking south toward Aspen Mountain and Buttermilk through a frame of shimmering aspen, Jen and I have often had a sense, deep in our bones, of being as near to paradise as we could be. Shadows only, of course, but shadows that are the shimmering evidence of something most deeply desired and most real.

With the Bakers in Snowmass, 2010

Much of the best of our days in Iowa City we saw though the eyes of our two young sons. With a five-year-old on hand and a two-year-old not far away, we looked with a different perspective on everything: the bridges spanning the river and the ducks swimming below, the cool blue swimming pool on the wooded hill above the park, the crowded aisles of the tiny grocery store across the railway bridge, the freight cars of the Rock Island Line thundering by a couple of times a day, the long-jump pit at the recreation center where two little boys built castles with their plastic buckets and spades, the bright orange pumpkins and the tiny goblins of Halloween, the flags and bands and fireworks on the Fourth of July, the fluffy rabbits and decorated eggs at Easter, the preschool art proudly affixed to the door of the pea-green refrigerator.

I rarely felt such joy as when I rode the shaded sidewalks with Barclay in his tan-colored seat at the back of my bike, both of us singing his favorite song from *Annie*: "The sun will come out tomorrow, bet your bottom dollar that tomorrow there'll be sun. Tomorrow, tomorrow, I love you tomorrow, it's only a day away."

Sometimes along the way, we'd stop for a "Joey Story." We'd sit in a cozy spot under a spreading oak and I'd repeat for him what he'd done so far that morning using the name Joey in place of his. "There once as a little boy named Joey," I would begin. "He was about four years old and he lived in a white house with a red roof. Joey loved Cheerios for breakfast. He enjoyed chasing them around the bowl with his spoon. If one of them was hard to catch, he'd say, 'Come here, fella,' and smile as he got it onto his spoon and popped it into his mouth. 'Mmmmm,' he would say. 'So good!' Barclay would listen to the story of his own early morning as if it were the original invention of the world's best storyteller.

In those days, Doozie was still too young to appreciate the clever conceit of the Joey story, and he preferred his own forms of

Two little boys

locomotion. He scampered around the house at lightning speed in the canvas saddle of a four-wheeled walker, babbling away in strings of his favorite new words: "naku" (milk), "apple-toss" (applesauce), "hoppitacoppa" (helicopter), "hot chockit" (hot chocolate), and "our Fred from feffen" (our bread from heaven).

One day, as he spun his walker around the screened-in porch, Doozie caught the edge of a fireplace brick and tumbled forward onto the concrete floor. There before the astonished eyes of the onlooking adults was an upturned aluminum cart, a screaming 20-month-old bleeding from his mouth, and a perfect baby's tooth lying on the floor like a tiny white bird's egg. Despite heroic efforts by his anxious mom and teary-eyed nana—and the staff at the nearby medical center—the bird's egg could not be returned to its nest in Doozie's upper jaw. And so, at the abrupt overturning of a baby carriage, our little boy's radiant smile changed into a charming impish grin. Even when his permanent teeth arrived some years later, that impish grin never went away. That may well by why his baby name "Doozie" has stayed with him for a lifetime.

Despite his missing tooth, Doozie smiles with Ariana Corrado, both age 3

It must be almost universally true that every man is in some way changed by becoming a dad. Without a doubt, I was too. I knew it the moment each of the boys was born and I first gazed into their liquid searching eyes, bearing the light of a thousand generations and beyond.

Why, in those moments—those moments of radical unveiling as new life comes into the world—did my own eyes start with tears? Why did I feel such contentment when, in the dark of the night, I cradled one or the other of them in my arms, and in the murmuring silence broken only by the squeak, squeak of the old wooden rocking chair, rocked them to sleep? The memories of those years still bring a touch of lightness to my heart that lifts me beyond time.

It was perhaps this stunning encounter with the miracle of birth that re-attuned my heart to the whispers of the Eternal that I had heard in those fleeting encounters with wonder as a child. I was soon to discover more about the significance of those whispers in the writings of a surprising new companion of my heart.

One crisp October day, after classes were over, I set off on a casual stroll around Iowa City's amiable streets—the best of America comes together in the cozy confines of its university towns—and soon found myself among the shelves of the iconic Prairie Lights bookstore.

In the spirituality and religion section, a favorite of mine, I picked up a book by an author I had not come across before. His name was Henri Nouwen.

The book was called *Reaching Out*. I leafed through its pages, then scanned the first few words of the introduction. How can I say it? I was astonished. The earth seemed to shift beneath my feet. It was as if the author had been peering into my soul for thirty years and was laying my deepest secrets open to the sky:

> "During the last few years, I have read many studies about spirituality and the spiritual life; I have listened to many lectures, spoken with many spiritual guides, and visited many religious communities. I have learned much, but the time has come to realize that neither parents nor teachers nor counselors can do more than offer a free and friendly place where one has to discover his own lonely way. Maybe my own deep-rooted fear to be on my own and alone kept me going from person to person, book to book and school to school, anxiously avoiding the pain of accepting the responsibility for my own life...The time seems to have come when I can no longer stand back with the remark, 'Some say...others say,' but have to respond to the question, 'What do you say?'"

I felt as if Nouwen's words had been written for me. I too had read many studies of the spiritual life. I had listened to many sermons, attended many conferences on religion, talked with numerous theologians, moved searchingly from person to person, and book to book, but had I really taken responsibility for my own inner life? Had I listened to the quiet voice at the core of my own being? Had I made my own honest response to the voice to be heard at the deepest places within me? For the most part, the answer was no.

For so many years, I had been little more than a mirror to the religious experience of others. I had allowed myself to be what I was not, spoken a language I had barely understood, behaved in ways that others expected of me rather than in honest openness to the whispers of the Eternal within. The roar of the external world had almost overwhelmed the mystery of my own inner being. It was time for a change. I bought the book.

In the days that followed, I let Nouwen's words sink deep into my heart, trying to absorb the meaning as well as the atmosphere of his writing. There was a freshness to his presence on the page, a whole new vocabulary, new words, new images. There was a radical honesty that I had rarely encountered before, a willingness to place faith in the context of existential doubt and despair. There was an almost miraculous immediacy in its echoes of my own thoughts and feelings. I felt as if the lights turned on in a room I'd known all my life but was, in this moment, seeing for the first time. The date inscribed on the inside cover of the book, written in my own hand, is October 1979. I was 38 years old.

Here are some of the insights I gained from my grateful meditations on Nouwen's life-giving words:

Insight #1: At some deep essential level we all feel—if we are honest—an aching aloneness. Even with loving people around us assuring us we are accepted, we are nevertheless on our own. Inside our skin, there is no one else but us. The world outside seems to hold secrets we do not share. It was going on without us before we were born; it will go on without us after we are gone. In the final analysis, it—the world, that is—doesn't care.

Insight #2: My sense of loneliness could be the ground out of which could grow a flower of quiet inner peace. At the very point of our aloneness, we can discover a place of rest deep within and, by an act of faith, surrender there to the presence of the Loving Source of life. It was a place that contemplatives over the centuries have called "solitude."

The distinction between loneliness and solitude now struck me with the force of a brick dropped by an angel from the open gates of heaven. My own solitude could be a return to the safe place I had glimpsed as a child, resting my head upon my mother's breast, dreaming on the woodpile, floating in the little white boat on the stillness of the lake.

Insight #3: A life of reassuring inwardness is not an end in itself; it is the starting point for a compassionate journey outward from myself toward the world. The purpose of finding a quiet center is not to isolate myself from the gritty realities of life, but rather to get the right perspective in the midst of them.

These and other insights from Nouwen's writing were life-changing for me. Through his courageous self-disclosures, I began to reclaim my own inner sense of trust in life. From that time on, religious faith was to be less and less a matter of struggling with concepts about God and more and more a matter of a return to the quiet rest in God I had known by deep intuition in my earliest years.

To a greater or lesser extent, the wisdom I stumbled upon in Nouwen's writing would set the course of the second half of my life. It was as if I had picked up a link in a daisy chain I had begun weaving many years before.

While Nouwen's writings were the catalyst to one great realization, that inner quiet was essential to hearing the callings of a loving God, the writings of someone quite different helped me come to another: that I needed to answer those callings in my own voice and not another's. The writer was Nikos Kazantzakis; the book *Zorba the Greek*. And at the burning heart of Kazantzakis's story, there was the character of Zorba himself.

I first met Zorba in the Academy Award-winning motion picture starring Anthony Quinn; I got to know him much better in many subsequent readings of the book. As this great shambling giant of a man came increasingly alive to me, my heart quickened with a desire to embrace life more and more as Zorba did. I loved the man's relentless curiosity. I loved his voracious appetite for the good things of life—music, dance, food, wine, work, and play. I loved his unabashed delight in the companionship of women. I loved the sheerness of his audacity. I loved the way he had released himself from the burden of living someone else's life and had found the freedom to be the man he was born to be. I loved the passion with which he embraced his own unique being—disappointments, paradoxes, and all.

In one of my favorite scenes, Zorba and his boss (the narrator of the story) are walking along the sandy shores of Crete, having just heard the news that Zorba's lover, Bouboulina, has died. Night has fallen, and the two men are in a somber, reflective mood. With his characteristic flair for the dramatic, Zorba waits in silence for a long time, holding in his hand a cage containing his pet parrot. He stares upward at the night sky in a sort of ecstasy as a constellation of stars detaches itself and falls away. "What can be happening up there?" he asks. "What can these things mean?" Then, as his thoughts drift back to his lost love, he asks in a trembling voice, "And above all, why do people die?"

There is a winning innocence to Zorba's questions, so childlike yet so profound. There is such sincerity here, such curiosity, such a desire to know. They are not the questions of a scientist or an amateur astronomer or a distracted tourist; they are the questions of a philosopher or a poet. They are the genuine expressions of a searching heart. They are original to Zorba not in the sense that they have never been asked before, but in the sense that, in this moment, they come unprompted and unrehearsed from within himself. They are not copycat questions but radically and originally his own.

Even before the questions, though, there is the silence. Sometimes, in the face of the mystery of the starry constellations on the night sky or the stark finality of death, the most original response we can make is to wait in silence. It is in the silence that wonder becomes fruitful. It is out of the silence that the truest words are born. It is out of the silence that the most important questions arise.

As I followed the story of Zorba and his boss in this scene and in so many others, I felt ice breaking around my heart and the shackles of reticence and fear begin to fall away. In the spirit of Zorba, I began, ever so gradually, to open myself up to the life-renewing power of my imagination, to honor my own true feelings about the world, to ask my own questions, to recognize my own passions, and to allow more time for the ecstasy of silent wonder.

After threading the insights evoked by Nouwen and Kazantzakis into the daisy chain of my inner life, it seemed to follow quite naturally that I should find myself crossing new thresholds and entering new worlds of experience. One such threshold led me into a place I had never before considered a place of welcome. The lives of the people I was to meet there seemed to be entirely of another order and they would offer me much to learn about my own.

CHAPTER 12.

Links in a Daisy Chain

"In truth each day is a universe in which
we are tangled in the light of stars."
—*Jim Harrison, "Horses"*

It was a warm Sunday morning in Iowa City. Late summer. Crickets chirped as I stepped out of the St. Andrew Presbyterian Church and fell into conversation with Mark Denison, one of my fellow churchgoers. Mark was a medical student at the university, a young man who approached his studies and just about everything else with curiosity in his mind and radiant expectancy in his eyes. We talked of this and that and began listing off some of the books on our night stands waiting to be read. I told him I'd made a start on another of Nouwen's books—his bravely personal *Genesee Diary*—and quoted a couple of fragments as best as I could recall them.

Catching the drift of my thought, Mark asked, "Have you been to New Melleray, Howard?"

"No," I said. "What's that?"

"It's a community of work and prayer not far from Dubuque," he answered. "A beautiful place of intentional quiet and reflection.

I think you would find it speaks to your heart. I know you'd be welcome there."

The more I thought about it, the more I sensed Mark was right. I checked the family calendar and booked a weekend stay.

From the moment I entered the courtyard of New Melleray, I felt a sense of homecoming, like I belonged somehow among these well-tended gardens and gracious greystone buildings. I felt a kind of kinship with the cheerful brothers, faithfully going about their day, offering silent witness to the presence of the Eternal. This is what I wrote in my journal, dated May 21, 1983:

> "The essence of this place is stillness, a quiet, engendering
> spirit of attentiveness and care. God's healing presence
> is in the stillness. Outside, I hear the sounds of water
> running and a scrubbing brush being applied vigorously
> to the concrete floor of the Abbey courtyard and cloisters.
> A monk is at work. Like his brothers, who have gone out
> to tend the animals, plough the soil, and mend the fences,
> he is busy exemplifying the relationship between work
> and prayer. I am thankful for him, and for this place."

My visit to New Melleray in 1983 turned out to be another link in the daisy chain that connected me back to the quiet but unmistakable experiences of wonder I had known as a child. With Jen's sweet encouragement (one time she packed handwritten blessings for me in my freshly laundered underwear), I returned several times.

My experience during such visits caused something to shift within me. I sensed I must follow a new path and consider my life in the light of new priorities. This did not, of course, mean any consideration of living in a monastery. While I was deeply influenced by the witness of the gentle human beings at the abbey—and the way of life they represented—I knew from the beginning that taking monastic vows would never be part of my calling. I lacked the discipline and the particular sense of vocation such a life would require of me. What is more, I was too attached to the colorful cavalcade of adventure that my present life offered me. Above all, I was already a married man, in love with my wife and young sons and committed to the health and well-being of my beloved family. The point of visiting the abbey had been not to stay there but to bring their spirit of quiet trust back home.

I began taking baby steps toward the kind of simplicity I had seen among the contemplative brothers. I decided, for example, that instead of going to church every Sunday as a matter of course, I would set aside one or more Sundays a month, preferably in a beautiful setting out of town, to listen to the whispers of the Eternal and write a journal. Somewhere among my things I still have the musings of those days collected in a broken-backed wine-colored notebook. I have no reason to believe I would find them particularly relevant to my life now—or even in any sense "useful." They are simply the record of what I was seeing and hearing thirty years ago in my intentional moments of solitude.

I chose to change my life in other ways as well. After five years as an assistant professor at the University of Iowa, I stepped away from the tenure track path, which would have required me to devote many hundreds of hours to research that increasingly seemed of secondary importance.

Major state universities like the University of Iowa have rigorous requirements for the granting of tenure—essentially a lifetime contract to publish and teach as a member of their academic faculties. To earn tenure, I would be expected to continue publishing widely in refereed academic journals, present more papers at conferences nationwide, serve as a consultant in my area of expertise, and accept multiple appointments to serve on departmental and university committees. I had by this time already accomplished some of these tasks. I had published a monograph and a few scholarly articles, presented papers at national conferences, led workshops around the country on the linguistics of spoken communication, and for a couple of terms had co-chaired the Department of Communication and Theatre Arts. The only problem was, my heart was not in it.

I responded quite differently, however, when in 1980, I was invited along with Jen to teach a course on creativity and spirituality at a theological college in Vancouver, British Columbia. Thoroughly fascinated by its possibilities, I set aside my scholarly research in linguistics and communication to focus instead on preparation for my three weeks in Canada. It turned out to be a decisive shift in priorities. My calling, it now seemed, was going to be something different. It began to take shape when Jen had a new calling of her own.

Sometime in early 1982, Jen received an invitation from Patricia McIlrath, a nationally recognized theatre director affectionately known as "Dr. Mac," to consider a job at the University of Missouri–Kansas City. She would be the Hall Family Foundation professor of theatre, teaching stage movement in the MFA acting program and working with the resident professional theatre company, the Missouri Repertory Theatre, as movement coach and choreographer.

Jen was thrilled at the prospect of working with this great lady of the American stage. She considered Dr. Mac a woman of sublime artistic vision. ("Keep in your souls," she once said, "some images of magnificence.") After a weekend visit to Kansas City, where she saw a sparkling six-hour production of *Nicholas Nickleby* directed by Leon Rubin, Jen was more than ready to join Dr. Mac's team in the "City of Fountains" and be a part of the vibrant theatre community there.

We made the final decision together over hamburgers and fries at one of Kansas City's institutions, Winstead's on the Plaza. Between sips of a frosty lemonade served with a cherry on top, Jen said, "I think I'd like to do it. I feel it's time to move on and be a part of the life of the big city." Reassured that new opportunities would open up for me in Kansas City as well, and ready to step away from academic obligations that were less and less captivating to my heart, I answered, "I'm ready to go, too."

It was time to move on from the America of cozy college towns to the America of country clubs and slums, the America of urban freeways and professional sports, the America of Jean Harlow, Fred Harvey, Tom Pendergast, Thomas Hart Benton, J.C. Nichols, William Rockhill Nelson, Harry Truman, Charlie Parker, Buck O'Neill, and Walt Disney.

Six months later, our days in Iowa City were over. We rented a truck and moved south to the place where the Kansas and Missouri rivers meet and where we would come face to face with disturbing new realities, and where new beloved people would come into our lives. Wide new horizons, like the great plains sprawling out to the west, were opening up before us.

Though we felt a weight of sadness over what we left behind in Iowa, we nevertheless got off to a good start in Kansas City. Through the kindly graces of Stan and Ann Nelson—our hosts on a previous visit—we found a home in the community of Westwood Hills, sweetly nestled on the Kansas side of the Kansas-Missouri state line.

It was a tiny city-within-a-city, graced by curved streets, stone bridges, flowering street entrances, and cottage homes nestled under canopies of towering oaks, sycamores, and sugar maples. Our own grey stucco cottage, with its welcoming white chimney, peeped shyly from under the balletic limbs of a 100-year-old ash tree. The local folks had designated Westwood Hills "the most beautiful little city in Kansas." To us, it seemed like the most beautiful little city in the world. It still does.

We didn't have long to appreciate the serenity of it. The fall semester of 1983 was soon upon us. Dressed as always in a black full-body leotard colorfully sashed at the waist, Jen launched herself energetically into full days of teaching stage movement and period styles followed by long late nights of rehearsal for both the university and professional theatre companies. I took up new responsibilities as director of education and community outreach for the Missouri Repertory Theatre and as adjunct professor in the departments of Theatre and Communication.

We were busy, especially with the preparation of new courses, but for me, the demands were not the same as they had been before. With the weight of tenure-track obligations lifted from my shoulders, I now had more time to do what seemed to me of greater value: to enter more consciously into the economy of grace, to spend more time with my growing boys, to teach with more freedom and creativity, and to become more actively involved in the neighborhood and the wider community.

It's essential to my story that I make clear what—or rather, who—made this shift in priorities possible for me, and economically feasible for our family. It had everything to do with the woman I married. No man was ever more blessed in a wife, and, if I may say so, no sons more blessed in a mother.

As I stepped away from the formal professional responsibilities of academia, Jen was more than ready to take them up. Over the next thirty-five years or so, with characteristic grace, discipline, and imagination, she carved out a brilliant career as a professor of theatre, specializing in period styles of dance and movement; choreographing scores of shows from *West Side Story* to *The Way of the World* to *A*

Christmas Carol; serving on half a dozen committees, including the departmental promotion and tenure committee, presenting papers on her groundbreaking work at conferences all over the world, and travelling nationwide as advisor to young faculty in her field.

On the strength of her long list of accomplishments and her national reputation, Jen was promoted in 1997 to full professor, and in 1999 she was given the Outstanding Service Award by the National Association of Theatre Movement Education. Even in retirement, she has chosen to be creatively engaged in teaching master classes and in professional consultation. Adapting her expertise in movement training for actors to other ends, she has created a new career teaching nonverbal communication skills to professionals in courtrooms, hospital operating rooms, and clinical consulting practices.

In all of this, Jen has remained a lovely presence in our home— elegant, thoughtful, undemanding, emotionally balanced, kind, and incomparably well-organized. Her ability to anticipate what was needed at any given time was, and is, a wonder to me. It is simply not possible for me to overstate the importance of her professional accomplishments and her forgiving heart to the overall welfare of our family and to my own search for the kind of simplicity that seems to have been necessary for my life. Excuse the cliché, but I could not have found my true path without her.

The quest for that path continued amidst the excitement and the challenges of finding our sense of place in a new community. The distance from Iowa City to Kansas City is about 300 miles, but the chain of daisies I had been threading during my days in Iowa easily stretched that far. I continued exploring the fragile border between time and what is beyond time. I had questions.

Where, I wondered, were the other places of reflection like New Melleray? Who were the other writers of contemplative insight and imagination who might accompany me on my search? I found the answer to both questions in a place called Assumption Abbey, set in the sensuous folds of the Ozark Mountains of Southern Missouri. It was here, not far from the small town of Ava, that I met another of the great soul companions of my life. His name was Cyprian. Just that.

Father Cyprian, an ordained priest, was a monk of the abbey, and, in the way of the Trappists, a wise and humble man. Trappists are men and women who live in communities of work, prayer, and hospitality, taking vows that include intentional daily hours of silence. Their order is named after the town of La Trappe in France where it was founded in 1664. Formed by such a life, the best of them, like Cyprian, are human beings of gentle presence on the earth, sweetly attuned to the contours of another country, a reality beyond time.

Fr. Cyprian at Assumption Abbey. Photo by Jennifer Moore for the Springfield News-Leader.

During my first day at the abbey, Cyprian showed me around the grounds and agreed to become my soul companion on subsequent visits. My walks with him were a revelation. It was as if I had somehow been joined by an unusual fellow pilgrim on the road to Canterbury Cathedral in medieval England or on the contemporary Camino de Santiago in Spain. The purpose of each journey was the journey itself.

We'd set off each day on a path through the extensive woods surrounding the abbey. Time seemed to stand still as we wandered under great spreading white oaks and shortleaf pines, through the traceries of flowering dogwood, alongside trickling streams, past fields of wildflowers, and under rocky crags. Now and then, Cyprian would reach his gnarled hands to touch, with great tenderness, a blue violet or white aster or creamy orchid and say, "Beautiful, is it not?" Sometimes we would simply walk in silence, Cyprian delighting in each new thing as if seeing it for the first time.

At some point, a wider conversation would begin, flowing naturally and easily from where we were in the moment. He never had an agenda. There was never anything he needed to say. Everything sprang from being present to the whispers of God in the air, in the light, in the water, in the trees and flowers, and in our stories, freshly remembered as we walked. "How are you, Howard?" he would ask at some point. "How's Jennifer? And the boys?" I would open my heart to him and the forgiving presence of the Eternal Beloved would fall on me like a benediction.

In Cyprian's gentle, reassuring presence, I became aware as never before of the way religion works in an integrated life. I saw that religion becomes effectual not through complex discourse or burdensome efforts to prove the superiority of one proposition over another, but by a condition of the heart that, in faithful recognition of the transcendent order of our being, naturally overflows in wonder, gratefulness, humility, kindness, and care.

As we wandered the forestlands around the abbey, I became especially conscious of Cyprian's unaffected humility. Wearing the simplest of clothes, heavy brown work boots poking out incongruously below his black monk's habit, a knitted wool cap perched on his close-shaven head, he spoke in soft, easy tones, his sentences sprinkled with laughter. He would spin folksy stories about his brothers in the monastery, about his own birth family scattered around the world, about the birds and animals that shared the forests around him, about his work in the kitchen where he helped mix ingredients for the abbey's famous holiday fruitcakes.

He would ask questions as if he himself were seeking answers, waiting for new insights. After an hour or so, he would guide me back to the monastic compound, where he would gently take his leave, ready to do the laundry for folks like me who were guests of the community. He was a man at peace, having chosen one thing: a life of surrender to the rhythms of the Eternal.

My visits to Assumption Abbey continued for several years, and each one brought me back to a place of simple trust while new thoughts fed the springs of my deepest inner life. Each time I was there, I felt what English satirist Tony Hendra felt in the company of his beloved Father Joe as they wandered the ancient grounds of Quarr Abbey on Guernsey Island: "a down-to-earth saintliness," a sense that "a loving eternal presence was but a breath, or a touch, away."

After one of our walks around the abbey grounds, I stopped by the community library and browsed awhile. I had no idea that contemplatives like Cyprian had produced so much good writing over the centuries—or so much good poetry. I scanned the shelves. Quite by chance, I laid my hands on a well-worn copy of Thomas Merton's 1961 book *New Seeds of Contemplation*. I stood there turning its pages for a long, long time. It was not an easy book, but even on first reading, I found myself opening to a world of fresh insight.

As I later learned from reading his 1948 autobiography, *The Seven Story Mountain*, Merton's life had been nourished by a convergence of widely diverse experiences. Born in 1915 to a New Zealand artist father and an American Quaker mother, in the town of Prades in the

French Pyrenees, he'd spent his childhood years in Flushing, New York, and later for a while in Bermuda. As a young man, under the influence of great teachers at Cambridge, England and Columbia in New York City, he'd read widely in poetry, fiction, philosophy, theology, and the classics. Such influences stimulated his imagination, made poetry of his writing, and fed into the stream of his thoughts on the most delicate of relationships—the relationship between the human soul and God.

Not long into my first reading of *New Seeds of Contemplation*, I came across a few lines, so deep in meaning, so lovely in expression, I felt they came from another place to reach me in my very depths:

> It is the love of God that warms me in the sun and God's love that sends the cold rain. It is God's love that feeds me in the bread I eat and God that feeds me also by hunger and fasting. It is the love of God that sends the winter days when I am cold and sick, and the hot summer when I labor and my clothes are full of sweat: but it is God Who breathes on me with light winds off the river and in the breezes out of the wood. His love spreads the shade of the sycamore over my head and sends the water-boy along the edge of the wheat field with a bucket from the spring, while the laborers are resting and the mules stand under the tree. It is God's love that speaks to me in the birds and streams; but also behind the clamor of the city God speaks to me in his judgments, and all these things are seeds sent to me from His will.

To this day, I find this affirmation unspeakably beautiful. As I reflected on these ideas, there in the library of Assumption Abbey, I felt my heart ever so slightly but unmistakably surrender to the Love I could actually feel in the warmth round me. I felt its brittle shell soften to the tenderness I could actually see in the humble presence of Cyprian and in the undeniable loveliness of the world surrounding the abbey. It was like my experience of beauty when I was a child, but different. Now I could place it another context, more inclined, as the poet Jim Harrison put it, to see each day as "a universe in which we are tangled in the light of stars."

The idea that the seeds of God's will were potentially present in the light as well as the darkness, in the extraordinary and the mundane, shifted the way I looked at everything. Given the possibility that anything at any moment could carry within it the seeds of the Eternal, I began to look around me with a new alertness and would occasionally be rewarded by a gift of wonder or insight from which new life could grow. The source of such grace, as Mary Oliver suggests in her poem "Praying," did not have to be something beautiful; it could be something very ordinary indeed:

> It doesn't have to be
> the blue iris, it could be
> weeds in a vacant lot, or a few
> small stones; just
> pay attention, then patch
>
> a few words together and don't try
> to make them elaborate, this isn't
> a contest but the doorway
>
> into thanks, and a silence in which
> another voice may speak.

Weeds in a parking lot? A few small stones? Is it possible to see even these as little revelations? As tiny whispers from the heart of the One who is the source of beauty? If so, what was I to make of self-evidently beautiful things, like enduring works of art or self-sacrificing acts of human tenderness?

And so it was that I began to shift my focus from an anxious search in the forest of religion to a more restful surrender in the glade of simple trust. It was a shift of focus, not an attainment. I began to know a little of what it meant to rest in the grace of the world and breathe free. I was taken back to the whispers of the divine in the beauties of the natural world, the lives of kind and humble human beings, and to the miraculous stories of homeward return—like that of the prodigal son—I had heard in my earliest days. I was to be significantly helped in this by the time I spent with the Quakers.

For a couple of years, I met with a small group of Quaker Friends in the Hyde Park neighborhood of Kansas City. I was joined on Sunday mornings by my writing companion, Grant Mallett, a man of unique gifts and a pilgrim heart, a true original who has developed the skill of making and nurturing friends into a high art. On Sunday mornings, in the simplest of spaces, Grant and I rested for a while in the quiet, sinking gratefully into the mystery of the Eternal and listening for God in the evocative silence of gathered friends.

For a time, I felt surpassing moments of freedom from my habitual struggle with words and ideas, unconstrained for a while by the effort to get things conceptually "right." I was in a sweetly generous place where I could sense the democracy of grace, each person in the room equally accepted into the embrace of the Beloved. In the gathered silence, we were as one. There was no preference for eloquent words or wide theological knowledge or age or race or gender or social position or dress or body type. We were all equally, as George Fox once wrote, "still and cool for a time in our own minds and hearts."

I've often wondered why more folk have not found their way to the trustful quiet of Quaker communities. I have similarly wondered why, in the busy rush of the 21st century, more of us have not found sanctuary in the kind of prayerful life practiced by the humble people in the community at Taizé. Let me explain.

In the spring of 1993, Jen and I decided it was time to introduce our sons to the wider world beyond the shores of the United States. The old-world wonders of Europe were calling. We each chose something we most wanted to see and planned our trip accordingly.

Jen wanted to see Maggie Smith play Lady Bracknell in *The Importance of Being Ernest*, so we began in London. Doozie wanted to see the courts of the All England Lawn Tennis Club, so we took the train to Wimbledon where he was able to stand, racquet in hand, on the famous Centre Court. Barclay wanted to watch the peloton of the Tour de France riding into Paris, so we found a spot on the curb of the Champs-Élysées as Miguel Induráin raced by in his coveted yellow jersey. What I most wanted to do was visit the small village of Taizé in Burgundy. So, after our time in London and Paris, we drove into the bucolic wine regions of east central France and headed for Taizé.

The town of Taizé is not itself the reason for visiting there. The actual town has little to appeal to curious travelers, a village of undistinguished stone structures in the hills not far from the ancient monastic abbey at Cluny. What began in Taizé nearly eighty years ago is a different matter. The Taizé I wanted to visit was a community that has grown up on the wide meadows adjacent to the village.

Founded in 1940 as a sanctuary for people fleeing the Nazi terrors, this unusual commonwealth has become widely known as a place of pilgrimage for young people seeking a new vision of what religion can be at its most sublime. At the heart of its life is a beautiful hour of music and prayer—held three times daily in the summer months—elements of which have been included in the liturgies of religious communities all over the world.

We arrived in Taizé on an early morning in May 1993. We soon found ourselves in the company of hundreds of fellow pilgrims, most in their teens and early twenties. Under the shelter of a plain wooden structure called the Church of Reconciliation, we joined them in a thoughtfully crafted liturgy: the sweetest songs of meditation, periods of expectant silence, and spoken prayers in multiple languages. No pulpit. No sermon. No appeal for funds. No impressive personalities. No TV monitors. No sense of us versus them. The white-robed brothers—full-time residents of the community—sat humbly among the other worshippers from what seemed every nation on earth. As candles flickered, we sat together in the loveliness of simple beauty, united in the harmonies of uncomplicated faith.

At the end of the hour, there were a few moments of exultant stillness. Then, as if a soft wind was passing among us, the singing began again. Half an hour later, we were still there, softly intoning one of the tenderest hymns of contemporary religious culture: "Ubi caritas, et amor, Deus ibi est." "Wherever there is kindness, wherever there is love, there, too, is God."

These words and the heartbreaking melody on which they floated summed up the spirit of Taizé and perhaps explains why one religious leader called Taizé "that little springtime." To this day, Taizé is a reminder to me of religion at its best. Beautiful. Fresh. Inclusive. Hopeful. A kind of religion honored as much by silence as by the spoken word. As Brother Roger, the community's co-founder, once wrote, "God understands our words and our silences, too. So often silence is all there is to prayer."

So it was that by slow degrees the wisdom of restful silence became apparent to me, not simply as the indispensable ground of my own religious life, but also as the wellspring of religious brother- and sisterhood. I was now in search of a sense of inner quiet that gave rise to nurturing words and compassionate presence.

At the same time, I found myself more and more in the kindly presence of yet other companions of my heart, poets and religious philosophers, whose work seemed to come from a place of engendering silence. Old and new, they were for me the poets of transcendent life. They included, among others: Martin Buber, Abraham Heschel, Wendell Berry, David Steindl-Rast, Frederick Buechner, and John O'Donohue. While I heard their voices only in the pages of their books, they helped open new vistas of imagination to me. Even when they were not being overtly religious in their subject matter, their writings were suffused with transcendence. I remain forever grateful to them for the gentleness with which they approached the mystery of divine life and the courtesy they have shown when speaking of God and the soul.

Spurred gently onward by my encounters with the humble Trappist monk, the visionary brothers of Taize, and the poets of sacred life, I began to feel a greater clarity in my sense of calling in the world, and saw new opportunities on the path that lay ahead. I began to look differently on my vocation as a teacher and revise some of the content of my classes. I became more aware of the extraordinary gift of friendship and more intentionally grateful for the beloved people in my life. I undertook new projects as a way of giving back to the world some of what I had been so mercifully given. Before I speak of those, however, I turn to what emerged as my life's primary calling—indeed, the luminous background to all the others: becoming the best dad I could be to our two young sons.

CHAPTER 13.

Under the Stars

"The sun will sometimes melt a field of sorrow
that seemed hard frozen; may it happen for you."
—Sheena Pugh, "Sometimes"

Life for all of us, I think, is a kind of wandering. It's never a straight line from cradle to grave. At any one moment there are options to consider and choices to be made, and each choice for good or ill moves us on from where we have been to places we have never been before.

One of the choices I made after settling into our life in Kansas City was to spend part of my summer with my young sons exploring the vast and varied landscapes of the United States and Canada. Jen was more than willing to let us go on these adventures. She chose to spend her own summers teaching in New York City at the Loyd Williamson Actors Movement Studio and enjoying the artistic and culinary delights always so close at hand. It was a bargain we were both delighted to make.

And so, for fifteen consecutive years, the boys and I set off in our well-travelled van loaded with backpacks, camping gear, and the most basic of food supplies: Frosted Flakes, Dinty Moore stew, hot dogs,

ketchup, mustard, bread, peanut butter, and jam. Starting each trip with "One World (Not Three)" by the Police cranked up high on the audio system, we followed our hearts in a new direction every year: straight west to the Rockies and on to Utah and Nevada; southwest to Arizona, New Mexico, and California; northwest to Wyoming, Montana, Idaho, Washington, and Oregon; north to the Great Lakes and British Columbia, northeast to New York, New Hampshire, Vermont, Maine, and Nova Scotia, south to Arkansas through the Deep South to New Orleans, and southeast to North Carolina, Georgia, and Florida.

We drove by day and camped at night, staying at any one location no more than two or three nights, finding at each turn in the road new vistas to wonder at and places that presented boundless opportunities for adventure.

We hacky-sacked with my brother Bryn in a spectacular setting east of Provo, Utah, our tents spiked down at the foot of a sheer 1,000-foot mountain face. We emerged like well-boiled lobsters from the rustic hot pools in Saratoga Springs, Wyoming. We woke up with snow on the ground (in July) on top of Grand Mesa, Colorado.

We canoed to an island on Vermilion Lake, Minnesota, where we shared the night with family of bears snorting and huffing around our campsite. We got up at dawn to play in the pristine valleys and folds of Sand Dunes National Park. We swam in the cool aqua-blue waters of northwestern Florida and baked in the summer sun on the startling white sands of Destin and Panama City.

Canoeing on Lake Vermillion

Sunning on the white sands of northwest Florida

And that's only the half of it. We got soaked in heavy rain alongside the thundering river in Poudre Canyon. We abandoned our wrecked tents after a microburst in the national forest near Jackson

Hole, and sank our inflatable rafts in the Merced River in Yosemite Valley. We beat off swarms of stinging flies on Michigan's Upper Peninsula and ran out of food at Long Lake, so that our camping buddy, Reid Peryam, was reduced to eating Coco Roos on Wonder Bread for breakfast. We clambered along the knife edge of the Black Canyon of the Gunnison in Colorado and, after our hike, enjoyed the juiciest hamburgers in the world in one of Gunnison's rustic cafes. We chomped on hot dogs at a folksy minor league baseball game in Thunder Bay, Ontario, shot nine holes of golf on a perfect late afternoon in Bayswater, Wisconsin, and sailed flat-hulled boats into whiplash winds near Halifax, Nova Scotia. We also met two of the most remarkable human beings it was our privilege to meet in all of our travels. They appeared to us like angels in a tiny town called Encampment, Wyoming (population: 450).

Our camping expeditions to the high plains around Encampment had come about because of our friendship with a unique pilgrim soul named Reid Peryam, one of Doozie's classmates from primary school days. Reid's family had been early pioneers in the Encampment River Valley and longtime keepers of the John Peryam Ranch, a lovely acreage just off Wyoming State Highway 230. With Reid as our host, we often visited the Ranch, where members of the wider Peryam clan—including Reid's dad, Alan, his uncle Andy and Aunt Susan, and his uncle Steve—gathered around us as if we were long-lost members of the family. They offered the best of High Plains hospitality: warm dry beds (and showers) in the century-old ranch house, hearty breakfast cookouts in the spectacular countryside, and sizzling steak dinners with all the sauces, fixins, and beverages our hearts could desire. No one, we concluded, welcomes guests from the flatlands with greater generosity of spirit than the Peryams of Wyoming, and to this day we say, "God bless 'em all."

"Country boys"
on the Peryam
Ranch

During one of our stays in the rustic luxury of the Peryam Ranch, we were introduced to a lovely Korean-American woman named Sunny Behonek, a friend of the Peryam family. Over the years she became our friend as well. Incandescent with the joy of life, Sunny had turned her unadorned High Plains cottage into a place of serene spiritual grace and hospitality. People often came by to talk with her or to meditate in her "quiet place"—a tiny wooden structure she built on one side of her home, attractively decorated with handmade paper lotus blossoms. Once a year, a high-ranking chaplain of the United States Navy flew out from Annapolis, Maryland, to spend a few days in restful reflection with her, meditating daily in the simple beauty of her sacred space. One summer, the boys and I also joined her there for a time, sitting comfortably on pillowy cushions while candles flickered on the altar before us. Barclay and Doozie sat there almost miraculously still while I rested gratefully in the bountiful silence that enveloped us all.

Looking back on those days, I sense that Sunny was a kind of gentle messenger from beyond time. She was, in her absolute simplicity, all joy and pure generosity. The handmade sign on her unlocked door read: "If you think you need anything in my home more than I do, go ahead and take it." In her enchanting company, we could see no clouds in the sky, no threat anywhere of stormy weather.

As if that were not serendipity enough, there was a second angel waiting for us in tiny Encampment. Her name was Mabel Peryam, Reid's great aunt. Through an amazing set of coincidences, beginning with her invitation to join her for a tasty farm-fresh breakfast in her home, Mabel became a kind of soul-friend to my own mother Rene, far away in New Zealand. The beauty in the soul of one was echoed in the soul of the other. They wrote letters and cards to each other for several years until first one then the other passed away. To mark the loveliness of their friendship, we laid a memorial of white, sea-smoothed quartz, carried from New Zealand's Bruce Bay, on Mabel's sandy grave above the town.

Howard and Bryn beside the memorial stone in Encampment, Wyoming

I leave my sons to remember the rest—all those dreamlike summer days, accompanied by our favorite soundtracks: *Best of Roger Miller*, Sting's *Bring on the Night*, *American Graffiti*, Paul Simon's *Hearts and Bones*, and *Kings of Comedy*. We played them over and over again, singing along at full voice, anticipating the comedic punchlines, enveloped in our own tiny carnival of melody and laughter, the vibrations as good as they get.

Upon reflection, I can remember few pleasures in my life greater than a smooth ride at seventy miles an hour on one of the broad, undulating interstates of the American West—say Interstate 90 in Montana, between Bozeman and Billings—my exhilarated self at the wheel of the swooping Econoline, the dry air redolent of last night's smoky campfire, the music turned up loud, and my two young sons riding snugly alongside, singing their hearts out. To have just one of those rides back, set on a continuous loop, would be like stepping backward into paradise.

On these summer escapades I felt moments of exaltation that reminded me of the persistence of *joy* and the thousand small ways life's possibilities can be made manifest. I was often reminded how throughout life I have experienced moments—as we all have, I hope—when the best we had hoped for actually comes true, when the worst that we had expected does not, and when little unexpected serendipities occur without any conscious intention or planning on our part. At such times I have been blessed with the comedy of the ordinary as glimpsed in Sheenagh Pugh's poem:

> Sometimes things don't go, after all,
> from bad to worse. Some years, muscadel
> faces down frost; green thrives; the crops don't fail,
> sometimes a man aims high, and all goes well.
>
> A people sometimes will step back from war;
> elect an honest man, decide they care
> enough, that they can't leave some stranger poor.
> Some men become what they were born for.

Sometimes our best efforts do not go
amiss, sometimes we do as we meant to.
The sun will sometimes melt a field of sorrow
that seemed hard frozen: may it happen for you.

Like the speaker in the poem, I have had my share of times when best efforts did not go amiss. I have experienced small miracles in the midst of very ordinary days. I have seen small wonders that we might dismiss as purest fiction if we didn't know they were real. One such wonder connected me in an unusual way with a beautiful little town high in the Colorado Rockies.

The story begins in the summer of 1991. Our annual camping trip had taken us to the great bold panoramas of southern Colorado. We had first traveled west by way of the sensuous folds of Sand Dunes National Park and Durango's spectacular Vallecito Lake, had turned homeward past the Black Canyon of the Gunnison, the Grand Mesa National Forest, and had camped a night perched on a cliff's edge overlooking the Colorado River at Glenwood Springs.

Before driving on to Denver and the great eastward plains, we had pulled off I-70 for lunch and gas in a place the Chamber of Commerce had dubbed "Colorado's Main Street"—Frisco, in Summit County (The town had been named in 1875 from a combination of letters in the St. Louis-San Francisco Railway Company.)

I remember standing by the pump at the Loaf 'N Jug on Main Street filling our aging Dodge Caravan with gasoline and feeling mildly irritated at the price—$.79 per gallon. Aggravation turned quickly to something more like wonder, though, as I looked up at Mount Royal rising spectacularly above the town's Old West shops and its log cabin restaurants. In an instant, I felt strangely drawn to this particular place.

There is no doubt that it's a pretty town—on one highly subjective list "one of the coolest small towns in America"—but there are a lot of pretty small towns in America. Indeed, we have our share even in the wide open spaces of Kansas—Westwood Hills, Cottonwood Falls, Council Grove, Abilene, Lindsborg. But this was different.

It was a kind of deja vu in reverse, as if I was recognizing it as a place I already knew in the future. I dismissed it as a silly fantasy. After all, I reasoned, dreaming like this is just part of the DNA of a kid descended from immigrant grandparents. But I remember a special sense of wistfulness as we drove east out of Summit County past Lake Dillon, dotted with white sails, and on toward our lives back in Kansas City.

By the time we had passed through the tunnel at the Continental Divide, I had the distinct feeling that I was leaving behind something that would somehow come back into my life. There was, at my core, a quiet sense of destiny.

Fast-forward 21 years. After two years working his way around the South Pacific and East Asia, Doozie had returned home to Kansas City ready, with renewed focus, to explore the next stage in his life's journey. Inspired by the beauty of the parks and forest lands we had seen on our camping trips, and by the loveliness of urban parks he had seen in cities around the world, he had begun to think about the wisdom of preserving such natural environments and the careful planning required to make them accessible to visitors like him.

He'd been particularly struck by the beauty of the trails around The Rocks and Royal Botanical Gardens in downtown Sydney, Australia. Standing on a boardwalk above the golden crescent of Bondi Beach, he had felt grateful that, even in the midst of the vast urban infrastructure of a world-class city, he found himself in a beautifully cultivated natural sanctuary. The first hints of a possible life calling began to gather in his mind. What kind of profession might bring him close to such places and enable him to preserve their beauty for others?

Energized by a new sense of purpose, he set off for graduate school at the University of Missouri at Columbia, where he completed his master's degree in Parks, Recreation and Tourism, with a thesis applying Mihaly Csikszentmihalyi's theory of flow to the enhanced enjoyment of park trails and forest walks. Then, in 2012, it was time to look for a job.

What is the formula for connecting calling and place? Common wisdom on this varies. Some have argued that it's best to find a job first, then choose a place to live. Others have argued, by contrast, that it's best to pick a place first and find the job where you want to live. Doozie chose the latter. On numerous visits to Summit County, west of Denver, he had come to feel this was a place he'd like to be, not so much for the skiing and snowboarding, which draws most people there, but for the natural beauty, casual lifestyle, and the constant promise of adventure. When a friend, Adam Still—the most radiantly charismatic bartender in Colorado—offered him a place to stay in his condominium in Wildernest, nestled at 9,000 feet under the great bulk of Buffalo Mountain, he made his move into the high Rockies.

Eighteen months later, in the late summer of 2014, Doozie began his job as programs manager for the Friends of Dillon Ranger District, (FDRD) whose stated mission is "to promote stewardship of the White River National Forest in Summit County through partnerships, volunteer service, education, and support." With its combination of indoor and outdoor settings and its mix of creative brain work and physical labor, the job was well-matched to his gifts and experience. It was what he had been looking for.

Doozie at work

All this was serendipity enough. But there was more. After a search around Summit County for a suitable place to call home, Doozie finally decided on a condo—in Frisco, Colorado.

Doozie's condo was a snug little place of basic mountain design that, his realtor admitted, "needed a lot of tender, loving care." No matter. It was his, and soon dear friends like Steve and Adam Wessell would drive into the mountains to help him give it the upgrades it needed. Frisco would be his home. And because of his presence there, it would, in a sense, be my home, too. My dream and his had converged. Once more I had seen that, sometimes, things don't go from bad to worse but from good to better. Sometimes a person aims high and all goes well. Sometimes green thrives. Sometimes sunlight breaks through the clouds. Sometimes we are graced by the happy endings of the human comedy.

Looking back now from the perspective of seventy-plus years of life, it is good for me to remember the times when my best efforts did not go amiss, where the sun melted the hard frozen field of sorrow, where everyday conversations opened up pathways to serendipity and lightness of heart, where in the simple play of words I could celebrate the pure dance of life.

That is perhaps a very complicated way of explaining why I so often found delight playing games with words, just exploring, for its own sake, the fun of language. Especially on camping trips, when my spirit felt unusually free, I indulged myself and "entertained" the boys with a stream of meaningless verbal gags. I offered them, and they offered back, a steady flow of malapropisms: ("I seem to have lost my glockenspielen" (socks), "Let's stop for a hammy burglar" (hamburger), "It's coldilocks and the seven wharfies" (It's cold), "It's tooth hurty" (It's 2:30). To this inconsequential nonsense I added spoonerisms like "Steakback Outhouse" for "Outback Steakhouse," "Eel cut stoats" for "steel cut oats," or "celastic purgery" for "plastic surgery"). With the boys chiming in, I offered verbal fragments like "parthel for Thelia!" or "Who cutttee your hair likee dat?" Also on the menu were verbal outliers like "Ronnie's coming" for "It's going to rain."

There are, I should add, family stories connected to many of these verbal gags. The phrase "Parthel for Thelia!" came from the lips of a little girl named Celia, an impish five-year-old with Down syndrome who in the 1950s was Jeffie's classmate in a special preschool for children with disabilities. Two mornings a week, they traveled to school together in a taxi. One morning, as Jeffie hopped into the car, Celia noticed he was carrying a shoe box-sized package neatly wrapped in brown paper. She assumed, wrongly, that the "parcel" was intended for her and exclaimed in a toothy lisp: "Parthel for Thelia!" To this day, when we give or receive a gift, small or large, the Martin family of Westwood Hills repeats little Celia's phrase. It's an honored family tradition. When I hand the first copy of this book to Barclay and Doozie, I hope I have the presence of mind to say: "Parthel for Thelia." If I do, I have no doubt they will know what I'm talking about.

"Who cuttee your hair likee dat?" was a phrase my father often repeated from a childhood memory. His dad sometimes gave little

Torrey a rough haircut using a pair of shears. One morning, after such a shearing, the two of them walked into the local greengrocer's shop. The shopkeeper peered at tiny Torrey's oddly butchered thatch and asked, "Who cuttee your hair likee dat?" For the rest of his life, Dad used the question to express his surprise at anything that struck him as odd. If he saw someone with his tie draped at an odd angle or his hat slightly askew, he'd say in mouth-cupping confidentiality: "Who cuttee your hair likee dat?"

The phrase "Ronnie's coming" was a slightly obtuse way of saying "It's going to rain." The German world for rain is "Regen." President Reagan's first name was "Ronnie." Hence, if one of us said "Ronnie's coming," we meant "It's going to rain." The boys and I were perfectly sure we were the only ones in the world who knew what we were talking about when proffering this gem. We felt mildly triumphant about it.

Playing games with language expressed the lightness of our spirits in those days of freedom on the road and, speaking for myself, helped celebrate the laughter to be found beyond time's horizon.

Sometimes, as I have said, bad things don't happen. Sometimes, of course, they do. Even on those memorable camping trips, things didn't always work out as we had dreamed. I think, for example, of our brief emergency situation on the road at 11,000 feet in the Rocky Mountains.

In the searing heat of July 1989, the boys and I were heading west on a trip through Colorado and Utah to the Sierras of California. We were in great spirits. The van's engine purred as we sped on dry roads across the wide Kansas prairie, through the cat's cradle of Denver, and up the I-70 ramp into the foothills of the Rocky Mountains. We had Roger Miller on the tape deck with the sound turned up loud. As we approached the Eisenhower Tunnel about an hour out of the city, we were singing heartily along with Roger: "I'm a man of means by no means, king of the road." We were high on a cocktail of speed, comfort, togetherness and the sheer thrill of adventure on the open highway. We were just moving on out. Privileged royalty of the road.

Then, like a pretty dream interrupted by a fire alarm, everything changed. We were halfway through the 1.6-mile tunnel when the van's engine coughed, refired momentarily, then died. We coasted to a stop. I checked the fuel gauge. Plenty of gas. Not a sound from the engine, not a note from the tape player, not a word from us. Silence. A red X flashed above warning all traffic that our westbound lane was closed. We heard an eerie metallic voice: "Stay where you are. Emergency assistance is on the way. Do not get out of your vehicle. *DO NOT GET OUT OF YOUR VEHICLE.*"

Other cars swished by as we sat in helpless bewilderment. Stranded in a vast howling cylinder, I tried the engine again. Nothing. I waited another 30 seconds and tried again. Nothing. And again. This time— the engine sputtered uncertainly and kicked back into life. A couple more coughs, a jackrabbit or two, and we were on our way once more. The music came back on. Roger Miller again. With humbler voices, less confident now, we joined in: "I'm a man of means, by no means, king of the road."

The engine never shut down like that again—nor did we at any other point pass through a tunnel so high above sea level—but for the rest of our trip we were never quite so sure. We laughed about it, of course, but our jests and jokes were chastened by the thought that things could so easily have turned out otherwise. Whenever I hear the song "King of the Road"—itself an irony about the helplessness of financial destitution—I think of the irony of any claims we can ever make to "kingship," to outright control, of anything. Even in our moments of greatest triumph, we are utterly contingent creatures of the earth. There is a necessary tension between our vitality for life and our vulnerability within it. Vitality and contingency: one of life's great paradoxes.

Few things have presented the irreconcilable polarities of life more starkly to me that the experience of being a dad. The safe arrival of Barclay and Alexander into the world, and their flourishing into resourceful, tenderhearted young men, was—and is—a blessing beyond words to express, to say nothing of the ways they so exquisitely reflect the grace and loveliness of their mother.

As every parent can attest, though, I have held the gift of our sons in trembling hands. While I was thankful for their healthy birth, I was frightened by the potential for a catastrophe of the kind my own parents experienced. I was visited often by haunting daydreams. While I was happy to see my little boys running enthusiastically to school with their backpacks bobbing behind them, I was troubled by thoughts of unforeseen disasters on the way. In my overactive imagination, for example, I would "see" the flash of a car at the intersection of Rainbow and 50th Street, oblivious of the red light and the crossing guard, careening into a handful of chattering children, and tossing them aside like arching rag dolls. I would "see" one of my own young sons among them, inert on the pavement, and would "hear" myself screaming invectives in breathless fury at the imagined perpetrator of the crime.

Coming back to reality and realizing that, in all likelihood, both boys were just fine, safely at school, working their math puzzles or drawing their colorful butterflies, I would simply offer them up to the Other Father in a cautious inarticulate prayer of hope. When they got home safely on such days, blithely unaware of the storms that had erupted in their father's nervous brain, I would wrap them in my arms, giving them an extra squeeze of welcome at the doorstep.

Off to school

I was to offer that extra squeeze of welcome another time when something happened that remains in my memory like a knife jammed into my skull. It was on another of our annual camping trips, somewhere near the "four corners" where the state lines of Colorado, New Mexico, Utah, and Arizona converge. Driving north toward Wyoming on a two-lane highway beyond the magnificent Mesa Verde National Park, battling hard winds for a couple of hours, I decided to check the gear we had roped to the top of the van. I pulled off onto the wide gravelly verge, stepped out, and closed the door behind me.

The two boys were strapped in their seats at the back, playing contentedly with their furry animal hand-puppets—Chippy the chipmunk and Ricky the raccoon—the windows open to the hot desert winds blowing through the cabin. Cars and trucks roared by at high speed, their wind-wakes rocking the van: *whomp…whomp…whomp.*

Then, in one terrifying instant, I saw a rear door fling open and felt a violent rush of air. In the madness of the moment, I heard a little boy's high pitched wail: "Chippyyyyyy!!!!!!" The buffeting winds had snatched Barclay's furry chipmunk out of his hands and sent it flying across the highway. I watched in horror as an oblivious little boy exploded out of his seat and with no thought of the howling dangers left and right, dashed heedlessly across the blacktop into the sagebrush wilderness, his tiny ragged companion flipping end-over-end like tumbleweed.

Screaming his name, I sprinted in his direction and caught him up in my arms. He was clutching his mangled puppet to his chest, murmuring "Chippyyyyy." I held my young son close to my heart as if I could never let him go. Fifty feet away, a massive fourteen-wheeler screamed by on the straight dry road. Even now, when I think about it, I feel a jolt of terror deep in my bones. What if the worst had actually happened? It remains unthinkable.

Our days together on the byways of America were days of new beginnings for me, and new beginnings always suggested new possibilities. The wonder I felt at the unfolding landscapes of snowy headlands or high flat-topped mesas—on the colorful streets of cozy small towns with their art galleries, ice cream shops, and farmers markets, among the wildflowers of previously unseen mountain meadows, in the golden halo of aspen groves we had never camped in before—brought fresh awareness of life's invitation to newness. Our travels were a constant reminder that I am, as are we all, a creature of hope. As musician Paul Simon put it: "Everybody loves the sound of a train in the distance / everybody thinks it's true." All new horizons tremble with expectancy.

Eventually, of course, there came a time when our annual camping trips were over. While I had delighted in the physical and emotional emergence of our two boys through each stage of life, I had rushes of sadness in realizing that each innocent childhood day was a once-only affair, a unique moment that I would never get back, and there would be a time when I had to let them go. While I sang my way through the adventure of visiting colleges they might attend and driving them to their chosen campuses for their freshman years—Barclay at Hope College in Holland, Michigan, Doozie at Kansas University 50 miles away—there was no such song for the accumulating miles between us as I drove back home. My return journeys from Holland and Lawrence were tearful odysseys, with overtones of another, final, goodbye. Nevertheless, my love for my sons, then and now, has given me a fresh understanding of what it means to think of God as the Beloved. Let me explain.

Toward the conclusion of *The Weight of Glory*, C. S. Lewis wrote, "To be loved by God, not merely pitied but delighted in as an artist delights in his work, or a father in a son—it seems impossible, a weight or burden of glory which our thoughts can hardly sustain. But so it is."

I had read these words when I was a college student, but I had not yet been ready to receive them as true for myself. I had over the years heard many wordy discourses on the topic of God's love, crammed with eloquent phrases and stately affirmations such as "God's love is infinite and never-ending, wider than the ocean, deeper than the sea." But I had never felt in my heart the kindly weight of God's love expressed as a sort of delight, a luminous joy, like that of an artist in her work or a father in his child. On reading Lewis's words again, however, not long after my bittersweet journeys to pack the boys off to college, I felt a quickening of my heart. I now heard that magnificent affirmation "So it is" in a different key. I sensed a "yes!" arise from deep within.

Having known the inexplicably sweet agony of being a dad, I was now better prepared to imagine the nearness of a Loving One beyond time and space. My heart leaped up at the thought that the Eternal Beloved, so dimly perceived in youthful apprehensions, took delight in me as I did in my own boys. "What if God's love is actually like that?" I asked myself. *"What if it really is so?"*

Now that they are grown and gone, Barclay with his wife, Ali, among the ancient narrow lanes and flowering plazas of Barcelona, Doozie with his faithful Boston Terrier mix, Titus, at the foot of Mt. Royal and the spectacular Ten Mile Range of Colorado, I dearly miss the sweet riot of two small boys giggling and tumbling around the house. There is still a lingering grace, though, in knowing they are but a phone call away.

Even as I write this, I take comfort in the thought that, however far away my sons may be, they'll be happy to see my name pop up on their tiny screens. Indeed, I just heard a reassuring ping on my phone. It's Barclay. He's calling from his home in El Born in the historic heart of Barcelona. I feel blessed beyond words.

CHAPTER 14.

The Grace of Great Things

"What's lost is nothing to what's found
and all the death that ever was
would scarcely full a cup."
—Frederick Buechner

There are moments from childhood we remember outright; others we recall only because they've been reported to us by others. The following is one of the latter.

It's 1944. I'm sitting in my highchair in our Bayswater kitchen watching as my father buttons on his overcoat, hugs my mother, and steps out the front door on his way to his work as a salesman at the Farmers Trading Company. My mother gathers me up in her arms and asks, "Where's Daddy going?" I answer, "Daddy bang a penny." It was, I am told, my way of saying, "Daddy's going to bring some money home." And so "banging a penny" entered the family vocabulary as a way of talking about work.

The idea of work as "banging a penny"—of exchanging my time and labor for money—lay dormant in my consciousness for most of my early life. I became a teacher in the first place because I needed a job. After graduating from Auckland Teacher's College in Epsom, I was appointed at the age of 19 to a class of 42 twelve-year-olds at the Normal Intermediate school (the equivalent of junior high).

It was a rough start to say the least. Though well-prepared in theory, with a fat pile of handwritten syllabi and lesson plans stuffed in my clean leather satchel, I was not ready for the small battles to be won by a teacher in any classroom anywhere in the world. There is first of all the critical battle for "control."

Before anything good can happen in a classroom, a teacher has to secure the learning environment, just as the curator of an art gallery has to secure the space so that a rich and appropriate exchange can take place between the art and the patrons. It's a delicate balance. Make a classroom too restrictive and you take away the joy of learning. Make it too lax and learning is almost invariably swallowed up in chaos.

I was too young and too naive to strike the right balance. In the summer of 1960, there were mighty events unfolding on the world stage—the call of American forces to join the furious fighting in Vietnam, an American spy plane shot down in Soviet airspace. While all this was taking place elsewhere, I was preoccupied with tiny engagements of my own: keeping the lid on a boiling pot of preteen energy while trying to actually teach something. I barely made it through.

Looking back on it now, I realize that the children in my class at the Normal School were actually, for the most part, the fresh budding flowers of a young and vigorous country, nearly four dozen healthy young New Zealanders with ruddy windswept faces and vitality enough make the walls around me burn. There were just too many of them in one place. I lacked the mental toughness and social confidence to secure the learning environment for good things to happen. I had been placed there too soon. It would be many years before I stepped into a classroom with the vision and experience necessary for me to feel the profession of teaching worthy of my whole heart.

Even in the earliest years of my teaching career, though, I occasionally caught glimpses of the joy and fun of teaching at its best. I certainly met my share of unforgettable characters.

One of the most memorable of them was a young apprentice carpenter who appeared in one of my classes at the Auckland Technical Institute (now the Auckland University of Technology). He was by any measure a genuinely funny guy, a class clown without disruptive intent or hint of malice. His name was William Pairama. My job, in the second term of 1969, was to teach him and his peers the English language skills required for certification in their various trades: carpentry, electrics, and plumbing.

In a reading for one such class, with William mischievously occupying a seat in the back row, we came across the word "dense." I asked: "What does the word 'dense' mean when used to describe building materials?"

Someone called out, "very hard."

"Good," I said. "How about a single word?"

"Impenetrable," suggested another.

"Yes!" I said. "Now, how do you spell it?"

William's hand shot up. With slightly bemused deliberation, he spelled it out. "I-m-p-e-n-e-t-r-a-b-l-e."

"You've got it, William," I responded. "Well done!"

Looking at me in comic disbelief, he asked: "Really?"

"Yes, sir," I said. "Absolutely 100 percent correct."

Grinning with delight, William leaned back in his chair, placed his thumbs under his armpits, stuck out his chest, and in an exultation of genuine pride and self-knowing irony, called out, "Professor. William. Pairama!" Then, collapsing in a pile of giggles, he buried his face in his arms and vigorously slapped his hands on his professorial desk.

To this day any reference to Professor Pairama in our family conversation is greeted with gestures of knowing delight. It's one of our inside jokes. If I come up with an unexpected solution to a household problem (like successfully re-plumbing the toilet) I become, momentarily, "Professor Pairama." If I offer an acceptable variation on my standard recipe for cheese toast, I earn the tongue-in-cheek honorific of "Chef Pairama." Any evidence of surprising expertise, no matter how simple or complex the task, earns for the doer of the deed the honorific of "Pairama." I wish William Pairama—wherever he is after all these years—knew how long I have remembered him and how famous he has become in our little part of the world.

Over the course of the next ten years—in Auckland, North Carolina, Michigan, and Iowa—my desire to teach was kept alive by the appearance in my classrooms of other bright spirits like William. Each of the new students in my classrooms had their own stories to tell and their own dreams to realize; each had something to contribute to my own evolving story. My desire to become a teacher was also quickened by my continued fascination with the possibilities of the storytelling arts of theatre and film—the wisdom revealed in their narratives and the techniques used to create their magic.

My imagination seemed to be growing apace with every new theatrical production I saw. In a cramped bohemian theatre just off campus at the University of Auckland, I watched a disturbing portrait of the poet Dylan Thomas, brilliantly acted, drinking himself to death in his boathouse in Laugharne. There was a stunning black-and-white staging of Chekhov's *Cherry Orchard* at the Vivian Beaumont Theater in New York. There were memorable productions of Shakespeare's *The Tempest* and Berthold Brecht's *Mother Courage* at the University of Michigan. There were haunting explorations of desperate souls in Tennessee Williams's *The Glass Menagerie* and Arthur Miller's *Death of a Salesman* at the University of Iowa. Also at Iowa there were a couple of musicals that shimmered with light, *West Side Story* and *Carousel*, choreographed with crackling energy by my own Jennifer Martin.

These, and so many more, evoked a kind of first wonder in me, a new awareness of the limitless possibilities of theatrical storytelling and a fresh curiosity about the cavalcade of human experience they represented. Even as I continued to teach voice and speech for the actor using the methodologies I had adapted from Thompson and Pike, I was increasingly aware of what a university class in theatre could be at its best—a place where students could behold wonders and their imaginations set free.

Wonder often leads to wonder, imagination to imagination, inspiration to inspiration. As I became increasingly open to new ways of seeing the world through theatre, I became more consciously susceptible to the seductions of the other arts as well—poetry, music, dance, and visual art—and to the "dearest freshness" of the natural world around me.

With gentle nudges from my contemplative companions, including Brother David Steindl-Rast, whose little book *Gratefulness* was a revelation to me—I also began seeing works of art as bearing within them the whispers of the Eternal. Was this why I had been so drawn to theatre in the first place? Was it this that persuaded me at last that teaching could become a calling worthy of my life?

I got my answer to both questions when Jen and I were invited to teach at Regent College in Vancouver, British Columbia. Over three summers in that jewel of city, between 1980 and 1988, we freely explored the borderlands of creativity and spirituality, building the content of our classes on the belief that all creation is an expression of the Love beyond all love, the Play beyond all play, the Dance beyond all dance.

From this point of view, any creative act in service of the good is, at some level, a reflection of an inexhaustible Creator at work in the world. By paying humble attention to instances of such things—including the wonders of the natural world—we hear at times the whispered call of the Eternal. By answering that call with our whole hearts, whether tending a garden, nurturing a safe and happy home, acting in kindness toward a neighbor, writing a poem, staging a play, or teaching a class, we become participants, consciously or not, in divine life.

With Jen by my side, leading dance meditations at the beginning of each class, I talked about God as Creator and all of creation as the product of inconceivably vast and complex imagination. We saw works of art as web-like antennae tuned to the vibrations of the Eternal. We saw creative acts as ways of participating in the work of a Divine Artist in renewing and healing the earth. We considered art as prayer and prayer as art. We danced. We sang. We improvised dramatic scenes. We walked in prayerful silence in the forest. We shared the delights of music, poems, plays, and works of visual art. We gathered shells and stones and seaweeds and—again in the prayerful silence—created mandalas in the sand on one of Vancouver's beautiful beaches. We sat in silence in the presence of the Eternal manifest in the beauties of nature and art and, as the great story tells us, in the companionship of the one called Christ.

We tried in each class to open ourselves to the whispers of God in the world around us and craft our own responses of gratitude and praise. We ourselves felt blessed in this endeavor, and we had affirming indications that our students felt the same.

One of the participants in the class, for example, sent us a suite of nine short poems, inspired by thoughts from our lectures, and attached the following postscript: "So here they are: my poems. The time with you and Jennifer this past summer was one of the most fulfilling periods of my life. Thank you. E. M."

Other affirming responses came in, too. A young Canadian presented us with a "thank-you" card featuring a battered rowboat tied up on the slick, dark rocks of a misty cove in Nova Scotia. Inside she wrote: "I've recently been feeling a bit like the old boat in this photograph, deserted and beached on the rocks. From the first day of your class, I began feeling alive, animated, energized again, in touch with the whispers of the divine within me."

I had reached another turning point in my life. After three summers teaching in Vancouver, I felt I had found the key components of my life's calling. It was now clear what the subject matter of my teaching should be: to introduce my students to the grace of great things. Also clear to me was why I so deeply desired to teach it: to help students see works of art as possible ways of opening to life in its deeply desirable wholeness. I wanted them to see the creative process itself—in art and elsewhere—as a way of acquiring habits of the heart essential to living life in its fullness.

The task before me was to translate what I had learned while teaching at a theological college into subject matter appropriate to the curriculum of a state university and to the lives of men and women in a diverse secular society. One of the outcomes of that process of translation was the creation of a project called the Jellybean Conspiracy.

The Jellybean Conspiracy, which we dubbed "the theatre of kindness," was both a theatre show and a movement. Through it, I wanted to send out a call for a more thoughtful inclusion of kids with intellectual disabilities—kids like my own siblings Olive, Jeffie, and Alison—into the cultural and social life of American high schools.

The first act of the Show was an anthology of short pieces—monologues, sketches, mimes, poems, songs—featuring the voices of young people with intellectual disabilities and their parents, siblings, and friends. The pieces were staged as they would be in a variety show. Performers with intellectual disabilities (called "Jellybeans") were coached by, and worked together with, their typically developing peers.

Program cover, Jellybean Conspiracy Show

In the Jellybean Conspiracy Show we came to see everyone as a "jellybean," because we share a common humanity. Though we are all different by the accidents of genetic inheritance, we are all alike in one crucial respect: we are all, without exception, creatures of mysterious sacred origin and possess an unquestionable right to be here in this world. At the silent core of our beings, we all carry passports from that as yet "undiscovered country."

One of the pieces in the first act included a short poem by Scottish poet John Burns called "Dancer: A Poem for My Autistic Daughter." The poet speaks of his own daughter, diagnosed with a form of autism, who had been able to find her own hidden grace as she danced upon the windswept grasslands (the Skeabost) on the Isle of Skye.

While the audiences watched the dance, I watched the audience. I could see so many among them make the hoped-for connection: the dancing girl was not just a girl with autism, but a vibrant presence in the world, a graceful part of nature, connected somehow to a deeper joy. Her presence was a gift.

In second act of the Show, students with and without intellectual disabilities performed a one-act play called *Dance with Me*, adapted from Linda Dougherty's prizewinning play, *Bless Cricket, Crest Toothpaste, and Tommy Tune*. The key to the success of the Show was that the role of Tom was always played by an actor with Down syndrome or similar disability. This character was renamed Tam when a young woman was chosen for the part.

The Show touched hearts in extraordinary ways. Parents, siblings, teachers, administrators, kids with disabilities, and kids without disabilities were all caught up in a common spirit of tender joyfulness. A dad from St. Louis, eyes trembling with tears, caught up with me one night in the theatre's lobby, and said, "I never thought I'd see the day when my kid would be the star of the school play. Jellybean made it happen, and I'm the proudest dad in the world."

Kids from the special education classes gladly claimed their due as members of the cast and crew. The typically developing theatre kids hugged their fellow Jellybeans as though they were part of an extended family. There was laughter. There were tears. There were spontaneous bursts of song. Jubilant company members asked one another to sign their playbills. Spontaneous dancing broke out on stage after the final curtain. Sometimes it seemed as if the sense of kindly belonging would last a lifetime.

Words of gratitude poured in. A student actor from Kansas City wrote, "The Jellybean Conspiracy was so remarkable to me and to everyone who saw it. The monologues were just the most touching things I've ever seen. I played a girl who had a brother with a disability, but in reality I play that part every day. The Conspiracy opened my eyes to things I had not seen before."

A special education student from Missouri asked her dad to write for her: "Jellybean gave me that feeling of inclusion and love that I never thought I would find. I found a place where I belong, a place where I feel needed and important."

The first Jellybean Show was produced in 2004 at Richmond High School, Missouri, under the skilled direction of theatre teacher Jill Jones. Because of the vision and talent of the many fine teachers like her, the secrets that were locked away in the hearts of my own disabled siblings were shared with the hearts of uncounted others. Over a period of ten years, the Show was performed hundreds of times in high schools all over the United States, reaching an estimated combined audience of 200,000. They continue to this day.

It has been said that good ideas attract good people and great ideas attract great people. The Jellybean idea attracted the very best. There was Kaye Bomgaars, who readily volunteered to organize our earliest fundraising events and did so with irresistible creative flair and ladylike grace. There was Doug Conlan, who with the whole-hearted support of his loving wife, Mary, served as the sunniest and most effective volunteer coordinator and board member any nonprofit agency could ask for. There was Andyla Holman, an almost angelic presence whose compassionate heart and unmatched attention to detail ensured the spectacular success of our later fundraising events. There was Dr. Michele Kilo, one of Kansas City's finest advocates for the welfare of children with disabilities, who brought first-rate professional expertise and a fun-loving heart to her many years of service as chair of the Jellybean Board. And then, among so many others, there was our choreographer and goodwill ambassador, Gabriella Muñoz Lucas, known to her friends and family as Gaby.

Gaby exploded into the Jellybean family like a ball of fire. As choreographer of numerous Jellybean Shows, in Kansas City and in rural Missouri and Kansas, she coaxed the most reluctant of feet to tap and two-step with hers and encouraged hundreds of young men and women—indeed, all of us privileged to work with her—to join in the very dance of life. With her megawatt smile, her big inclusive heart, and her irresistibly welcoming embrace, she embodied, as no one else could, the very spirit of the Jellybean movement. Everyone she met, especially children who struggled with acceptance among their peers, felt they were, in some inexplicable way, a gift to her life and uniquely beloved.

Gaby Lucas with two of her Jellybeans

The photograph of Gaby I have included among these pages reveals, far better than words can ever do, the unearthly joy that drew so many into her circle of belonging. She was—and is—"la curadora de corazones," the healer of hearts. Her parents, Armando and Lulu Muñoz, so far away in Coatzacoalcos, Mexico, need to know that, through this truly special one of theirs, a light came into the world that will never be dimmed.

The sense of calling that lay underneath my work with the Jellybean Conspiracy also surged through my preparations for an introductory course in theatre that I was to teach for over twenty years, beginning in 1994 at the University of Missouri at Kansas City. I named the course "How Theatre Can Change Your Life."

The title was not hyperbole. To this day I believe that, when approached in a way that nurtures insight and imagination, the theatre and other arts possess the power to crack open the hard shell of habit-bound lives like my own and admit the entrance of a liberating light.

I'd now like to offer some of the ideas I shared with my students in the exhilarating years I was privileged to be their teacher. In doing so, I'll try to reveal why I felt my teaching in those years had become charged with purpose and, in my mind at least, had become so much more than a way to "bang a penny." Teaching this course was a project—like Jellybean—that seemed worthy of my best self. I offered it my whole heart.

CHAPTER 15.

How Theatre Can Change
Your Life

*"The light that puts out our eyes is darkness to us.
Only that day dawns to which we are awake."*
—*Henry David Thoreau*, Walden

I t's the fall of 2005. I'm in a lecture theatre in Royall Hall on the
garden-like campus of the University of Missouri–Kansas City.
Looking up at the rows of bright young faces, eighty or so in all, I
run through the usual preliminaries. I introduce myself, welcome my
teaching assistant, distribute an outline of lecture topics, and spell out
requirements for successful completion of the course.

Perching myself on a high wooden stool (I always preferred to
teach from a stool; it was, I felt, a good place from which to begin
a conversation), I check my notes, take a deep breath to calm the
butterflies, and begin with Lecture 1. Supplemented by spur-of-the-
moment improvisations, which are always among the creative joys of
teaching, the opening of the lecture went something like this:

Ladies and gentlemen, this is a course about how theatre can change your life. I borrowed the title from a book by Alain de Botton called How Proust Can Change Your Life. *In the first chapter, de Botton tells the story of the editor of a French newspaper in the 1920s who invited local celebrities to offer their answers to this question: If you knew the world was coming to an end the day after tomorrow, how would you change your life?*

One respondent said he would take the opportunity to climb a mountain he had never climbed before, another said she'd try to kiss as many men as she could, a third said he'd just keep playing tennis or golf until the final bell was rung. The most intriguing response, however, came from a famous Parisian named Marcel Proust. "If I knew my life were coming to an end," he wrote, "I would choose to do nothing out of the ordinary at all, because every moment would seem like a precious gift."

It was a point of view that Proust had already explored in the novel that had made him famous: "In Search of Lost Time." As de Botton puts it, Proust's seven-volume book, whose title is sometimes translated as Remembrance of Things Past, *is "a practical, universally applicable story about how to stop wasting time and start to appreciate life."*

This potentially life-changing idea, this alternative way of seeing the world, has been universally affirmed by philosophers, contemplatives, poets, and artists throughout human history. It is the essence of what we might call the economy of grace. When we become aware of how time passes, we become more gratefully aware of the gifts contained in each moment of experience, as Denise Levertov does in her poem entitled "Living":

> The fire in leaf and grass
> so green it seems
> each summer the last summer.

The wind blowing, the leaves
shivering in the sun,
each day the last day.

A red salamander
so cold and so
easy to catch, dreamily

moves his delicate feet
and long tail. I hold
my hand open for him to go.

Each minute the last minute.

In the fifteen weeks of this semester, we'll see how our encounters with theatre—and other arts—can cause us to stop in the midst of life's distractions and become more fully aware of life's fleeting gifts. We'll also see how such awareness can provide the fuel for the fires of creativity within us, awakening us to the graces of life, moving us to reflect upon them, and kindling a desire to transform them into new gifts to be offered back to the world.

From this beginning, we entered the heart of the class. We watched plays on stage and on film. We read the work of theatre artists, drama critics, philosophers, novelists, and poets. We invited playwrights, directors, actors, and designers to take us inside their own personal creative processes. We talked about ideas that had come as personal revelations to me as I had explored the entrancing worlds of theatre. In one lecture, for example, I offered reflections on theatre and what might be called "the great paradox" of human existence. In another, I introduced the three types of story told in the theatre: comedy, tragedy, and tragicomedy—and explored how each offers a unique vantage point from which to view our own lives.

In the last lecture of the course, I tried to answer the question that had been implicit in all our preceding conversations: Is the theatre—and all the other pictorial, acoustic, and storytelling arts—somehow really important to the health of our lives? Is it in some sense essential to our humanity? Here's how I ended my reflections in the final lecture:

In The Knowledge of Man, *philosopher Martin Buber writes, the following: "In the course of becoming human there appear, incomprehensible in their origin, two constituent elements of the person: dissatisfaction with being limited to needs, and longing for perfected relationship."*

What Buber is saying here is essentially this: In our quest for meaning and identity, we must satisfy two great desires. We must first satisfy a deep and original desire to transcend our mere physicality—to do more than what our bodies alone can do and find fulfillment in the realms of thought, feeling, imagination, and spirit. Secondly, Buber is saying we must also satisfy an equally primal desire to do better in our relationships with other human beings and with the wider world.

In the course of our fifteen weeks together this semester, we have directly and indirectly explored the idea that, at its best, the theatre can be a like great cafeteria of the soul, offering food to nourish the mind, quicken the emotions, and stimulate the creative imagination. It does this in part by posing—and searching for answers to—the great questions of existence, the questions that arise in the darkness as well as the light and in the flickering shadows between.

In its tragedies—like King Lear *or* Death of a Salesman, *for example—the theatre poses the questions that arise when we are in the darkness: Why do we suffer and die? Why does evil so often prosper? And why is goodness so often such a fragile, vulnerable thing? Why is happiness so short-lived?*

In its comedies—like Midsummer Night's Dream *or* Fiddler on the Roof—*the theatre poses the questions that arise in the sunshine of our days: What makes for a good life? What is the secret of joy? How do we find love? How do we sustain the love we have found?*

In its tragicomedies—like Waiting for Godot, *for example, or* Our Town —*the theatre poses the questions that arise in the twilight: Where shall we go for guidance when we feel lost? How can we live at peace in the midst of ambiguity and uncertainty? Why is there not a clearer path through the intimidating complexity of mortal existence? Is it immoral to seek happiness in a world not yet redeemed from cruelty and injustice?*

Over these past weeks, we have also explored ways the theatre can shed a revealing light on the nature of our relationships with one another—how we seek to perfect them and why we so often fail. The theatre's stories, offer us a vast array of dos and don'ts in our primal quest to live more harmoniously with our fellow human beings. They offer tales, both cautionary and inspiring, about how we have struggled since the beginning of time to deal with lovers, parents, children, friends, neighbors, colleagues, fools, geniuses, and all the rest, even the powers beyond time and space.

Thus it is that the stories of the theatre, like the vibrant illusions of all the arts, can offer us gifts of great value to the human spirit. Through these stories it's possible to enter a state of mind in which the burdens of life can seem lighter and our sense of life infinitely richer.

So go out and enjoy the theatre. You'll find it flourishing everywhere. And remember that, if you approach its stories with a humble mind and a willing heart, it can change your life."

And so the class ended. There were times during each semester when I felt a quiet sense of affirmation that the class has been worthy of my best efforts. From some, I received the gift every teacher cherishes— seeing eyes light up with the recognition at the birth of some fresh insight. From others I received the gift of kind words of appreciation that remain with me even now as I enjoy the harvest years of retirement.

There were days like this when the classroom became a privileged moment of meeting between a gift offered and a gift received. I tried to offer my students a gift of story and insight bound with ribbons of affection and passion. They offered back their own gifts of expressed delight and surprise. To realize that I had touched a single life, let alone many, in such transformative ways has been the source of greatest satisfaction to me.

I cannot of course claim that there were no difficult days in the classroom. There were times when I myself was dull and uninspired, and I knew my students knew it. There were cold winter days when I didn't feel well enough to give them my best. There were days when my best efforts seemed to come to nothing and I was disappointed by the glazed-over, unresponsive looks that signaled the ideas that meant the world to me had failed to catch fire in minds of others.

Even on days when I was not at my best, however, there were occasions when the students themselves brought unusual insight into the classroom along with a sprinkling of lightness and laughter.

There was the professional football player—a member of the Kansas City Chiefs—whose innocent bewilderment in class stood in marked contrast to his disciplined ferocity on the field.

There was the veteran of the Iraq War, still dressed in army fatigues, who, after being plunged for a year in the brutal clarities of war—clear chains of command, clear contrasts between friends and enemies, clear and measurable objectives—struggled with the benign fuzziness and naked subjectivity of the stories told in the theatre.

There was the young woman, single mother of three, working two jobs, keeping her household together, taking six hours of coursework toward the eventual goal of a university degree and a new career, who found new courage for life through hearing the stories of other courageous lives, like those of M'Lynn, Shelby, and Truvy in *Steel Magnolias*.

There was the intelligent young man struggling with drug addiction who, with searching eyes and probing questions, seeking perhaps an insight that might help him escape the prison of addiction and pain in which he seemed to be trapped.

There was the student of urban planning who found connections between the work of an urban architect and that of a theatre designer, seeing in ways I had not how each facilitates the movement of people in space to create both easy flow and meaningful convergence. After class was over, he left me a book that I still prize as a remembrance of the deep soul connection that is sometimes possible between a professor and a student.

There was the lovely and well-read student of social sciences, headed for a career in gerontology, who brought to the class a wealth of experience in American roots music and jazz, and often joined me for vigorous coffee conversations about the stories being lived out in her own original and adventurous life.

There were so many others. And so, as years went by, I realized that when students stepped into a class in theatre like mine, they were stepping into a different world—away from the demanding abstractions of science, economics, business, and law and into the playful paradoxes of theatre. They found it to be a world where they were invited to push aside the curtains of one domain of experience— the domain of facts, systems, and competitive advantage—and to open another: a domain of spontaneity, wonder, and appreciation. They were free to explore the widening horizons of their imaginations.

It was here, in this world, that students experienced a new context of delight, a less competitive and more playful universe, where thoughts could flow easily from one point of mutual interest to another. In one hour together, for example, we might consider the dehumanizing consequences of blind ambition, the complex affections of a parent for a dysfunctional child, the bleak inner landscape of a blasted marriage, the diminishment of powers in people as they age, and so much more.

In such exchanges, students seemed to intuit a new sense of freedom and delight and bore witness to it in all manner of ways. Increasingly I came to think of my work in the classroom as a privileged means of introducing students not just to the stories of theatre, but also to a much bigger world I have characterized as "the economy of grace."

In the fruitful days of my retirement, I have been thinking about the economy of grace, finding some of my most reliable guides to that alternative realm of experience among treasured friends and increasingly so among the poets. In the next chapter, I offer a few reflections on what I have discovered about that alternative economy, that other way of responding to the material gifts of the world, indispensable to every life but so often hidden from conscious reflection and excluded from intentional nurture.

CHAPTER 16.

The Economy of Grace

*"The fundamental task in life is to give life to others.
We receive life, we transform life, we give life away."*
—*Jean Vanier*

I f I ever entertained any doubt that Jen and I had found in Westwood
Hills, Kansas, the right place to live the second half of our lives, I
would reassure myself by remembering the blessing of a friendship that
was born there. In the heart of that tiny city of 170 homes, just one
curved leafy street from our own, I was invited into the trust of a man
who lived as few others I have known—with genuine humanity and
grace. It was through him that I remembered, as an existential reality,
the qualities at the heart of a life well-lived—wonder, humor, humility,
and kindness. His name was Stan Nelson.

What can I say about Stan Nelson that begins to represent all
he came to mean to me? He was an American original. Farmer's
son. Air Force pilot. Korean War veteran. Neurosurgeon. Clinical
researcher. Medical school department chair. Ham radio enthusiast.
Husband. Dad. Uncle. Grandpa. Soccer coach. Piano player. PVC
pipe flute maker. Composer and arranger. Bird-watcher. Nature

lover. Adventurer. Hiker. Long-distance cyclist. Inventor. Tinkerer. Storyteller. Playwright. But that's just resumé material. The substance of the man was so much more.

At some point in the late 2000s, perhaps 2008 or 2009, Stan and I started taking morning walks together. With our mutual friend, Tom Magstadt, we would leave the cozy confines of Westwood Hills, and make our way across Rainbow Boulevard into Westwood. We'd walk past the old radio tower on 50th Street, around the Old Mission Junior High School and the ballfields of Bishop Miege High School, then head off down Canterbury Street where Fred Torrance lived in his modest prairie bungalow, occasionally stopping at Fred's house for coffee and donuts. We'd go on through the grounds of St. Agnes Catholic Church past the welcoming neocolonial facades of the Fairway Shops and Rainy Day Books, across the playing fields of

Stan and Ann Nelson

Westwood View Elementary School, and, before heading home, felt on our faces the refreshing spray of the stone-circle fountain in Joe Dennis Park.

These were walks like no others I can remember in my life. The conversation flowed with easy grace. Questions turned to reflection and reflections to laughter, fancy taking flight from remembered and misremembered fact. We opened each other up, often whimsically, to a wide range of topics: astronomy, biology, ham radio, politics, history, geography, mythology, religion, sociology, art, music, novels, poetry, theatre, dance, and film. Our words became the sacraments of a communion whose essence was beyond words. More significant than the topics we discussed or the conclusions we never reached was the spirit that seemed to animate every exchange—a feeling of connectedness and welcome, a shared sense of the richness of life, the fun at the heart of things.

Sometime in 2012, we became aware that Stan's time was shorter than we had reason to hope. He had been diagnosed with a return of Acute Myelomonocytic Leukemia (AMML) and needed to undergo a series of drastic treatments at the nearby University of Kansas Medical Center. Our conversations now became richer, more filled with significance, than ever before. Time was palpably more precious, our companionship tinged with hints of mortality. We began stopping almost every day at First Watch in Fairway for coffee and a pancake and would wrestle for hours with the questions and issues tumbling urgently through our brains.

One morning after our customary walk, Stan asked us to join him at home for breakfast. We were welcomed at the door by Ann, his bonny bride of 60 years, and there before us was an old-fashioned South Dakota breakfast, laid out like a small feast in a cozy corner of heaven: sunny grapefruit rounds already cut in segments, boiled eggs perched invitingly on porcelain egg cups, strips of crispy bacon, coffee, toast, and—my heart skipped a beat—orange marmalade.

As we shared the uncomplicated bounty of that dear table, I asked myself: How much better does life get than this? Cherished companions, lively conversation, and toast with orange marmalade. It must have been something like this that William Kittredge had in mind when he wrote, "Paradise is life lived in the presence of that which is most loved." I felt in those moments that we were as close as you can get.

One companionable morning, as we wandered the shaded streets of Westwood, Stan stopped as he often did to pick up a small object lying on the side of the road. It was a round metal washer, about two inches in diameter, like a skinny hockey puck with a hole in the middle. Stan looked at to for a few moments and began to speculate. How did it get here? What was it made of? What part did it play in some complex system? What possible devices might require a part like this? Stan put the washer in his pocket and we walked on. One of us asked if there was anything he could do with his tiny found object. "I don't know yet," he replied. "But I'll think of something."

Knowing the contraptions and devices Stan had come up with over the years—the pine-cone Jayhawks, the PVC pipe flutes, the newspaper trash bags, the magnet and paper-clip motors, the crystal-based radio sets, the motion-activated cameras, the small-engine bikes and carts—we had no doubt he would come up with something improvised from a skinny hockey puck with a hole in the middle.

Martin Buber once said, "The garland of the everlasting is woven from the blessings of the moment." When Stan Nelson picked up a washer on the road, or stood in wonder at a blossoming dogwood, or hushed to the song of a Carolina Wren in the branches of a Bradford pear tree, he was offering us an irreplaceable gift. He was weaving a garland of the everlasting before our eyes and placing it lightly over our shoulders.

Stan Nelson was many things in his life, but, for me, none was more important than this: He was truly, deeply, naturally humble and kind. When he walked alongside us, he told us stories from a rich harvest of memory, embellishing each tale with sound effects and gestures unmistakably his own. When asking questions, he asked with genuine curiosity and listened as if it mattered what we had to say. When he explained difficult ideas—the theory of relativity, the workings of a cyclotron, the making of the atomic bomb, the relationship of brain and consciousness—he did so with infinite patience and, out of courtesy for less nimble minds, rarely disclosed all he knew. When he talked about his sons Pete, Ted, and Reid— one the head of the department of prostate cancer research at a major cancer research center, another a specialist dental surgeon, the third a quick-as-a-whip courtroom lawyer—he rarely spoke of their professional accomplishments. He told stories instead of what made them endearingly human, their quirky ways, their latest "disasters," the funny things their kids were up to. There was no need in Stan to make himself look good on the resumés of his offspring. He was anchored securely inside his own skin. And as far as I knew, the well of his kindness never ran dry.

At some point during his final months, just before going back into hospital for treatment, Stan slipped a piece of paper into my hand. It contained a quote from one of his favorite philosophers, Unitarian minister Raymond Bragg. It read, "When there is a better chance for manhood and womanhood, a freer air, a grander openness, a fuller personal initiative; when there is more laughter, and freedom, and fine, spontaneous humanity, then, indeed, there will be priceless gain." In knowing Stan, I had indeed breathed a freer air, discovered more laughter, and known in the flesh a more spontaneous humanity. In his company there was indeed priceless gain, and folded in that mystery there lay, for me, a reassuring hint of the eternal.

One of the places Stan and I often met was the Roasterie Factory Cafe on Southwest Boulevard. We chose it partly because of its aviational theme—the antique aircraft poised above the roof, the tarmac-like polished concrete floors, the ticket-counter coffee bar, the jet-engine-case information desk, images of a WWII DC-3 everywhere, on mugs, posters, shirts, caps, coffee makers and video screens. In the "terminal," facing east, we would sit underneath a gleaming forty-foot image of a DC-3 poised like a great butterfly on a sun-kissed tarmac. For an ace pilot from the early years of jet flight, it was the perfect place to feel once more the exhilaration of elegant machines thrusting into the adventure and danger of the open skies. It was the perfect place to spend an hour or more with a veteran airman to remember and to reflect.

One day, on a whim, I bought a pressed-metal poster of the Roasterie's DC-3 and gave it to Stan as a memento of our conversations in this place. Realizing that our days together like this were numbered, I asked him to do me a favor. "I'll be flying with you as far as I can," I said. "At some point, though, you must fly where I cannot yet go. When you get settled into your flight path, I want you to look over your right shoulder. I'll be there alongside, taking my lead from you."

He smiled. "I'll do it," he said. "I'll do it."

After Stan died, Ann invited me to stop by the house. She had something for me from my friend. It was the metal poster of the DC-3 I had given him earlier. He wanted me to have it. And on the back, there was a message, copied by another hand, but in his own reassuring words. It was as if he were looking back over his shoulder, calling to me from somewhere Beyond. The note read:

To Howard,
We are flying the DC-3 at 5,000 feet.
The oil pressures are in the green,
As are the fuel and hydraulic pressures.
So we are flying happily
Into the sun on a beautiful morning.
I turn to the right and
There you are, my wingman,
Covering for me.
Our visibility is unlimited.
From Stan
24 May, 2013.

To be called "wingman" to this great soul was one of the great privileges of my life. In more than one sense, he was my beloved companion of the stars. I still feel I am taking my lead from him.

What is a friendship worth? A true friendship—like that I found with my companion of the stars—is literally without price. It exists, like song and laughter, kindness and beauty, in a realm where monetary values do not apply. At its best, it is a free exchange of selves with no motive other than mutual openness and receptivity, accompanied by a pervasive sense of gratitude. It is, in short, an excursion into an alternative economy of life—what I have chosen to call the economy of grace.

To live in the economy of grace is to live in the light of the manifest generosity of the universe. It is to appreciate the gifts we have been given simply by virtue of being alive, to celebrate the abundance of life's free offerings, and in a spirit of gratitude offer our own gifts back to the world. It is to encourage in ourselves a spirit of freedom, spontaneity, innocent laughter, and deep joy—and to nurture in our relationships an openhearted generosity of exchange, heart for heart, mind for mind, blessing for blessing. It is also, in my story, to acknowledge that where there is a gift, there is a Giver; to live in the economy of grace is to live in silent gratitude to the Eternal Source of beauty and goodness.

In modern Western culture, we are not typically socialized to see the true value of our exchanges in the economy of grace. We are more likely, instead, to be educated for interactions in the economy of trade where we look for advantage in the possession of life's gifts and think of them as means to other ends. In the economy of trade, we relegate the various beauties of the world, including the precious individuality of other human beings, to the background of our consciousness while we pursue other ends. Our loss is incalculable.

The point is beautifully made in the opening paragraphs of Tolstoy's novel *Resurrection*, where the citizens of Count Nekhlyudov's town seem not so blissfully unaware of what really matters to their lives:

> It was not the spring morning which they considered
> sacred and important, not the beauty of God's world,
> given to all creatures to enjoy—a beauty which inclines
> the heart to peace, to harmony, and to love. No, what
> they considered sacred and important were their own
> devices for wielding power over each other.

The good people of Nekhlyudov's town, like the vast majority of us who are citizens of the world, are so preoccupied with the insistent demands of the economy of trade that we are barely aware, if at all, of the existence of the realm of grace. In doing so, we are missing out on much that makes life ultimately worth living. It is, of course, entirely natural and appropriate for us to focus a portion of our attention to living in the economy of trade and developing the aptitudes we need to succeed in it. We have an obligation to provide nourishment and shelter for ourselves and our families; indeed, it would be irresponsible not to do so. But, as Tolstoy points out, it is a mistake to fix our attention *only* there. Joining in the chorus of contemplatives and poets of the ages, the great Russian novelist reminds us that there is a voice within us that cries out for fulfillment in that other realm, the realm of grace, where we catch sight of the beauty that "inclines the heart to peace, to harmony, and to love."

On a recent Saturday morning, I was sitting at breakfast with my longtime companion of the breakfast cafes, sidewalks, and parks of Kansas City: David Howard. We entered, as we had many times before, into an economy of grace, where the pleasures of conversation and presence are enjoyed for their own sake and for no other. Every question a gift. Every family story a gift. Every moment of laughter a gift. Every attempt to listen, understand, and reassure, no matter how inarticulate, a gift.

If, at any point in our conversation, one or the other of us were to shift the conversation to matters of getting and spending—how, for example, the other might be useful in widening the other's professional network or improving an investment portfolio—we would be moving ever so slightly into the economy of trade, where different rules apply. If we were to allow this to happen too often, the graced nature of our friendship would begin to fade.

While teaching at the University of Iowa in Iowa City, I remember being disappointed when a young man I had known for some time—and considered a friend—unexpectedly turned a coffee shop conversation into an opportunity to sell me life insurance. It was for me a small betrayal of the conditions of friendship, a sad diminishment of the purely gifted nature of the exchange between friends. My disappointment lay not in the young man's legitimate desire to grow his business and provide for his family. I respected that. It arose rather from a confusion of realms of experience. I had expected the freedoms implied by the economy of grace and was drawn instead into the obligations of the economy of trade.

On Christmas Eve in 2014, one among many such evenings over the years, I remember being so deeply immersed in the economy of grace that I felt my heart would break from the wonder of it. There, beside a blazing fire, I was warmly surrounded by the dearest ones on earth: Jennifer, my beloved of forty-some years, and our two grown and as yet unmarried sons. We talked. We laughed. We sang. We read the Christmas stories of childhood—*Bialosky's Christmas, The Gnome from Nome, The Little Blue Tea Set, The Runaway Sleigh Ride, The Best Christmas Pageant Ever.* We sipped our tea and shared thick slices of Jen's orange cranberry nut bread and offered up our stories of Christmases past. We remembered days of sadness and disappointment, and sat silently for a moment in memory of a kindly neighbor whose life had recently been cut short by the aggressive return of cancer. We were together in our joy and sorrows, successes and failures, and were held for a time at the very heart of the economy of grace. It was paradise.

In a world of commerce and trade, where mortgages have to be paid and obligations must be met, it's sometimes hard to make the case for assigning value to the economy of grace. How does Edvard Grieg's Piano Concerto in A minor help pay my health insurance? How does a casual breakfast conversation with a friend advance my career? How does reading *Bialosky's Christmas* around the fire increase the likelihood of my getting a headline in *The Kansas City Star* or *Time* magazine? Clearly it does not. On the other hand, why is it that the unrelenting pursuit of some career advancement or public recognition seems so often to leave something deep and essential out of my life?

One of the recurring themes of contemplative wisdom is that success in the economy of trade does not easily translate into fulfillment in the economy of grace, nor does it ultimately satisfy the deepest hungers of the heart. There is no dollar value we can assign to experiences such as love, friendship, family, and respect, yet we value them highly all the same. Their worth can no more be properly assessed in the world of trade than a sunbeam can be captured in a bottle and placed on the shelves of a five and dime.

The same may be said of our experiences of wonder and perplexity, those moments when we are surprised by the delicate miracles of existence or plunged into its dark, inexplicable mysteries. Such moments seem to appear whenever our powers of reasoning end, when in our encounters with the plausible, practical world, we hear echoes of a yet undiscovered country, a vast realm of the eternal trembling on the edges of experience. Heschel calls it "the ineffable." "The search for reason," he writes, "ends at the known; on the immense expanse beyond it only the sense of the ineffable can glide. They (the knowable and the ineffable) are as far from and as close to each as time and calendar, violin and melody, as life and what lies beyond that last breath."

I found myself once more on the shores of the ineffable when a few nights ago I read a report that scientists now believe the universe to be ten times larger than we'd previously thought. The vast reaches of space are the spectacular home to as many as one trillion galaxies like our own Milky Way, a swirling panorama of stars which is itself 100,000 light-years across. Reflecting on a dance of such amplitude—a world of imagination so vast—my mind reaches a point where it can go no further. All that's left is wonder.

But the mystery of space is perhaps too obvious a case in point. As the poets from time immemorial have reminded us, there are occasions of wonder everywhere, in flower-bedecked hillsides, in the natural grace of little children, in the loveliness of beautiful women, in the courage of compassionate men, in the gestures of kindness to be found in most unexpected places.

As I write this, I'm sitting in one of my favorite coffee shops— Crows—near the campus of the UMKC campus. A tsunami of impressions fills my senses, mixed with the delicious agony of memories flooding back from my years of teaching in lecture halls and classrooms not far away. The information flowing into my consciousness—to say nothing of my unconscious—is almost infinite in its extent and variety. A bright-eyed barista with tattooed arms passes a 20-ounce coffee to a tall, spindly customer in black stovepipe jeans and grey canvas sneakers. At a nearby table, a woman in a tartan jacket like-talks her way through a job interview ("I have, like, tons of experience with, like, proofing and copyediting"). On a construction site across the street, white helmets bob above the line of a green safety fence. Birds flutter among telephone wires stitching together a bouquet of oak leaves turning yellow. A grey-suited businessman strides purposefully through the door, slim MacBook Air under his arm, black cords dangling at his waist. A tearful young woman, sitting not ten feet away, processes unwelcome news about the loss of her job. Moment by moment, a starburst of impressions—some of them flooded with light, others darkened by shadow.

It's literally too much to take in. I cannot attend to it all. If I remain fixed in the economy of trade, my own default position, I may think of all such routine encounters of life as mere distractions, as irrelevant background noise to the tasks of trade and accomplishment I have set myself. But if I give myself permission to be engaged, if I step away from the flow of undifferentiated information to really see what's going on, if I look with eyes of curiosity and kindness on what is there to be seen, I may be able to claim some of these little encounters as gifts offered to enrich my life, as invitations to step into the light and shadows of the meadows of grace.

Poets are good at this. They are first of all seers who are deeply engaged with what they experience. They peer at the world with expectations of surprise. They look at things that most of us would ignore and find in them small treasures of surpassing value. They find *some* thing in what, for lack of attention, would otherwise be *no* thing.

In the course of our many companionable hours in the coffee shops of Kansas City, my late friend Harris Rayl and I often marveled how poets find significance in experiences others so easily overlook. In our regular poets society of two, we would read poems that celebrate, for example the radiance of the thorns on a rosebush (Billy Collins), the weeds in a vacant lot (Mary Oliver), the persistent curiosity of a dying cat (Ann Iverson), the laughter of old men in a restaurant (Athena Kildegaard), and the sound of a lead slug dropped in a lead plate (Thomas Lux).

In the economy of grace, it turns out that everything is in some way worthy of remark. It is the quality of the experiencing that makes the difference. Because of the quality of my experience of shared insight and mutual vulnerability in Harris's company, I feel a heavy weight of loss at his recent passing at the age of 66. He was taken from all of us, especially from his beloved Betsy, too, too soon.

The quality of experiencing—its openness, depth, and patience—is the key to the sensibility of all artists, including those who would be artists of living. By their openness to visual experience, painters see what others do not see. By their depth of listening, musicians hear sounds others do not hear. By their patience in observing the beauty of a world in motion, dancers feel in their bodies what others do not feel. By their attentiveness to the subtleties of human relationships, playwrights, directors, and actors imagine stories others do not imagine. By keeping their hearts in quiet humble awareness of the undulating edge between finite and eternal, contemplative poets, pick up gleanings from a realm that others often overlook. Wendell Berry's poem "The Lilies" is a perfect example:

> Hunting them, a man must sweat, bear
> the whine of a mosquito in his ear,
> grow thirsty, tired, despair perhaps
> of ever finding them, walk a long way.
> He must give himself over to chance,
> for they live beyond prediction...
> Found, unfound, they breathe their light
> into the mind, year after year.

This is a delightful record of the quality of experiencing that can mark our lives when we enter the economy of grace. It is an intentional search for the surprising gifts of life, in this case a kind of treasure hunt for a certain wild beauty on a long walk among the hills. What the speaker is looking for is neither more nor less than the sight of a pair of lilies in bloom, "at ease in the air as souls in bliss." Just that. Their loveliness is sufficient.

And here is Berry's point: Even if the lilies are *not* found, their loveliness persists because they remain vividly present in his memories of past encounters. Found or unfound, they are manifestations of grace. One way or another, they are, like so much that is beautiful in nature, a source of revelation and a cause for gratitude.

I love waterfalls. My early favorite was Huka Falls in the volcanic heart of New Zealand's North Island. On our regular excursions to Lake Taupo in the 1950s, we'd pull off the main south road onto a scenic overlook and watch transfixed as the great waters of the Waikato River thrashed through Aratiatia's rocky channel and thundered downward in a raging arc of turquoise and white. As the ground shuddered beneath me and the air roared, I would feel a mixture of exhilaration and awe. How beautiful the form and colors of these great waters! How terrible to be caught in those powerful currents, trapped beyond enduring in the churning foam in their depths! It was all grace.

Many years later, in 2001, I stood beneath the tumbling tresses of Dry Falls, on the Cullasaja River near Highlands, North Carolina, my face damp with the drifting spray, and felt a return of that same sense of wonder and awe. As the waters poured out over an overhanging bluff so we could walk under its hissing crystalline arc, I felt within me an exultation of praise. With Jen by my side, I went back many times to that lovely natural cathedral, almost invariably falling into an attitude of wordless prayer. It was an unforgettable delight to me to be drawn by those graceful leaping waters into presence of the ineffable, to sense divinity there, and to dwell for a while in the exuberant generosity of the natural world.

Dry Falls

I would, if I could, say much more about the beauties of the natural world and their power to tug me into wonder, but others have done this far better than I. To read the works of John Muir, Edward Abbey, Thomas Berry, Wendell Berry, Annie Dillard, Robert Macfarlane, or any one of a thousand poets, is to recognize that this is so. For now, it is enough for me to be grateful that the economy of grace is potentially present in any place and in any life encounter.

I'm writing these words in Kaneohe, Hawaii, where I have just witnessed an act of unexpected kindness. In a local McDonald's notable for the tiny invasion of eager chickens scratching in the well-manicured parking lot outside, I watch as an elderly woman—a Hawaiian native—slowly counts out her nickels and dimes to pay for breakfast. The numbers just do not seem to be adding up. With withered arthritic fingers, she moves her coins like chess pieces from one side of the counter to the other. She pauses and looks up. A sales assistant bends down close beside her and says, "Ma'am, you don't have to find any money. The people across the way (she points to a young couple on the other side of the restaurant) have already paid for you."

The old woman's face lights up and she clutches her dry flaxen bag close to her chest. "Thank you," she beams, turning in the direction of her kind benefactors, smiling from across the way. "Thank you." If it is true that kindness is beauty in action, then I have just been present to a moment of touching beauty, a treasured moment in the economy of grace.

Just days ago, Ann Nelson told me the story of another such treasured moment of her own. It was 6 o'clock on Christmas morning, 2017. Ann was on her customary run in the snowy dark in the direction of the KU Medical Center where her late husband had been an esteemed researcher and teacher. As she approached the campus on Rainbow Boulevard, she stopped briefly to admire the cheery holiday lights on a tree in front of one of the older red brick buildings. Within seconds a police car drew alongside and an officer stepped out.

"Are you doing OK?" he asked.

"Yes officer, I'm fine," Ann replied, somewhat startled.

"Sorry, ma'am. Not you," he said. Pointing toward the base of the tree, he added, "him."

Ann looked behind her. There, under the tree with the lights, she saw a grimy face and a wild head of hair emerging from under an oily coat. She watched as the officer knelt beside the homeless man and handed him a breakfast sandwich from a nearby restaurant and a steaming cup of coffee.

"Merry Christmas, buddy," he said. "Now, let's see if we can find you some place warm to spend the day."

It was an exemplary instance of two human beings at home for a while in the economy of grace.

Any moment in time or place in the world can provide a point of entry into the realm of grace. This has been especially true of my encounters with various works of art, whose very existence begins in wonder and whose very end is the evocation of yet another kind of wonder.

A significant part of the story I have told in these pages is a record of my gradual discovery of theatre and poetry and music and storytelling as offering privileged invitations into the economy of grace. From the day many years ago when I sat transfixed as a raggedy group of actors lit up my imagination with comedic scenes from Shakespeare, from that day to now, I have increasingly come to see the vibrant illusions of the arts—when they are in service to the good—as portals into other domains of being as essential to my life as the warmth of the sun.

The surprises of artistic beauty are everywhere. They are there in the delightful outdoor sculptures of Kansas City's Country Club Plaza and in the exquisite floral plantings along the state highways of western North Carolina. They are, of course, notably on display in galleries, concert halls, theatres, gardens, restaurants, and libraries, almost anywhere in the world. Such beauties and such places are all serendipitous reminders of that alternative economy that is essential to the health of a human life. As novelist Joseph Conrad once said, "the artist appeals to that part of our being that is gift and not an acquisition and therefore is more permanently enduring."

I have spoken thus far of how I have found my way into the economy of grace through the varieties of beauty in the world and the miracles of human kindness. Such experiences lie at the core of my trust in the ultimate goodness of things and my hope for the fulfillment of being outside of time and space.

But—and this is a very important "but"—there are those other experiences of life that I must also take into account. In any reflection on the economy of grace, I have no choice but to consider the darker realities of human existence: violence, suffering, injustice, diminishment, and death. These realities remain present in my consciousness like an unhealed wound and continue to trouble my dreams, as they did when I was a child. What am I to make of them in the light of the economy of grace?

The more I have seen of the suffering of the world, including the heartache of my parents and their three disastrously impaired little ones, the ravages of diminishment and disease in the dearest of siblings and friends, and the bravely hidden despair of America's poor, the more I have recognized that there is much about life on this earth I do not know and never will understand.

Suffering is a problem as insoluble as the vastness of space and the enigma of time. I have wrestled endlessly—as we all have—with the problem of pain and the manifest injustices that have corrupted human societies since the dawn of time.

It's impossible to reconcile the pervasive existence of self-sacrificial human kindness with the incomprehensible unfairness of the accidents of birth. It's impossible to reconcile the grace of the world with its overwhelming burden of cruelty and suffering. It's all but impossible to reconcile the God who is present in the good and beautiful and the God who seems absent from what is horribly disfigured and outright evil. All I can do is offer some thoughts that have come to mind as I have reflected back on the way my parents bore their own griefs and as in more recent years I have tried—within the relatively safe limits of my own native timidity—to walk alongside some of the most disadvantaged of God's children here in my adopted homeland.

It has been said the fate of the poor in America is worse than anywhere else on earth. From one point of view, it's an absurd notion. Even the poorest Americans have access to some kind of shelter and some kind of medical care, and many own TVs, cellphones, and broken-down cars. But poverty is not just a matter of material possessions; it's also a matter of the spirit.

The poor in America are surely among the most dispirited on the planet. In this big, brash, dynamic nation, to be poor is to feel small, and angry, and perpetually exhausted. Worse still, it is to feel crushed by a sense of failure. Everyone in America—including the poorest of the poor—has access to the unblinking commercialism of popular culture. Everyone is incessantly confronted by images of happy twenty-somethings running up huge tabs at sumptuous bars, gorgeous couples running free on white sandy beaches or lounging on hammocks beside horizonless pools, unblemished families driving luxury SUVs though lush manicured neighborhoods and multi-million dollar estates for sale in privileged urban enclaves.

The hidden assumption behind such images is that privileges like these are somehow accessible to all Americans and that the attainment of this exalted American dream is merely a matter of personal ambition, hard work, and the passage of time. Thus, at least at a subliminal level, the poor in America feel responsible for their own fate; they see themselves as failures in a system where the race goes only to the swift, the prizes only to the winners, and where the last will always be last. This enervating sense of desperation lies at the heart of my friend Debbie Maguire's difficult life in the city of Hallmark Cards, sprawling white-bunkered country clubs, and billion-dollar sports franchises.

I remember the first day I met her. She was sitting on the front stoop of a ramshackle red-brick quadruplex on Independence Avenue in Kansas City's northeast side, a strong three-month-old baby wriggling in her arms. I was there as a volunteer with the Good Neighbor Program, a nonprofit organization that served families who'd fallen between the cracks in America's bewildering social welfare apparatus. I said "hello" and asked her how she was doing. She answered: "Pretty good." I asked her the name of her baby and how he was doing and she answered, "This is Mikey. He's pretty good." The phrase "pretty good" turned out to be her practiced way of presenting her own brave face to a world of troubles. No matter what, things were always "pretty good."

Abandoned by her husband before the birth of her second child, she moved from place to place in search of cheaper rents and kindlier landlords, picking up jobs where she could—in-home childcare for needy neighbors and minimum-wage shifts at nursing homes. After a heavy fall in a city bus (getting to work) she suffered injuries that resulted in long-term disability, and life now required her to raise her two boys on an allowance of $850 a month supplemented by food stamps and church-based food pantries.

She had a succession of men in her life, none as reliable as they pretended to be, most of them practiced freeloaders, some mentally

unstable, others needy, manipulative, and abusive. More than once
she was forced to seek shelter from violent and potentially murderous
partners, one of whom—we'll call him Lucky—was jailed for setting
fire to her apartment. I received numerous calls from Lucky in jail trying
to sweet-talk his way back into Debbie's good graces. I felt it safer for
Debbie—and me—that he remain behind bars. In the long run, Lucky
was not so lucky. He was murdered in a fight with a fellow inmate.

Thirty years later, her sons grown and gone, Debbie is fifty-plus
years old, living alone in a rent-controlled apartment ($250 per month)
on Kansas City's East Side—and increasingly dependent on Medicaid
for the treatment of her chronic health conditions. She calls on the
Salvation Army and a welcoming religious community in Independence,
Missouri—bless them—for social support and religious consolation.

For three decades I have done what I could to be a good neighbor to
Debbie—taking her grocery shopping, celebrating birthdays, arranging
picnics in the park, funding a weight-loss program, visiting her in
the hospital, acting as a legal reference, picking her up on dangerous
streets with oblivious Americans swishing by in their air-conditioned
SUVs—but still she is essentially alone, still at the mercy of an economic
system that so cruelly favors those who already have enough and works
erratically at best for those living on the vulnerable edge of destitution.

During my years of trying to be Debbie's "neighbor," I have learned
a great deal about the desolations of poverty in America. It means
having the heat cut off in the winter because you can't afford the gas
bill. It means desperate phone calls for help from city services only
to get the beep-beep of unanswered lines. It means waiting for hours
in unfriendly hospital emergency rooms and finding no one waiting
for you when you arrive back home. It means being stranded by the
roadside because you literally do not have the cash to buy a few gallons
of gas. It means driving cars in constant need of repair and losing jobs

when they break down. It means accumulating hand-me-downs and leftovers in musty, cockroach-infested apartments, using whatever means you can find to take the edge off the pain. It means all these things and more. Just ask Barbara Ehrenreich, who wrote so movingly about it in her bestselling exposé, *Nickel and Dimed*. And now, as I write this, the political climate is such that the agony of the poor in America seems only to be getting worse.

The plight of the poor in America is, of course, a fate shared by the economically deprived everywhere. It is, for me, one of the insoluble perplexities of existence. How am I to make sense of suffering in any consideration of the economy of grace? Where is the grace in lives wracked by injustice and shattered by violence? Where is the grace in abused children, battered wives, rat-infested apartments? Where is the grace in the misery of the bewildered refugees camping out on the borderlands of Mexico and the United States or caught in the crossfires of civil wars around the world, in Yemen, in Syria, in Sudan?

The only way I can begin to answer these agonizing questions is to consider the possibility that there is, perhaps, some grace in the persistence of hope. I have from time to time seen a little light in the dogged daily persistence of people like Debbie (she talked often of what she would do someday when she was "back on her feet") and in my own flickering sense of trust that the travails of the oppressed are not the ultimate end of their story. Is there some redemptive grace in the power of great suffering to rescue us from easy presumption in the face of inexplicable mystery? Is there grace in the call to compassion that lies implicit in the shadows of anguish and misery?

Maybe it is so. In my darkest moments I try to take comfort from the witness of others who have known great suffering and yet out of the harshest of soil have allowed the loveliest blossoms of kindness and humility to grow. "A great anguish may do the work of years," writes

George Eliot in *Adam Bede*. "And we may come out from that baptism of fire with a soul full of new awe and new pity."

With that tiny flame of faith and hope burning at the silent center of my being, I have, with some difficulty, found it possible to live more or less gratefully even in the midst of the world's anguish. It's not that I am grateful for the darkness itself but that even in the darkness I can occasionally see some light, like C. S. Lewis's "promise of sunrise resting immovably on the mountains." I try to follow the wisdom of the contemplatives, like Brother David Steindl-Rast, who suggested that, while we cannot be thankful *for* everything, we can nevertheless try to be thankful *in* everything. It's a high ideal, but I see the wisdom in it.

And so, therefore, I go on searching for reasons to be thankful. I continue to find consolation in the companionship of poets like the gloomy old Welshman, R. S. Thomas, who once in a while sees a brightness breaking through the bleakness of his life's landscape, as in his poem, "The Bright Field":

> I have seen the sun break through
> to illuminate a small field
> for a while, and gone my way
> and forgotten it. But that was the pearl
> of great price, the one field that had
> treasure in it. I realize now
> that I must give all I have
> to possess it. Life is not hurrying
>
> on to a receding future, nor hankering after
> an imagined past. It is the turning
> aside like Moses to the miracle
> of the lit bush, to a brightness

that seemed as transitory as your youth
once, but is the eternity that awaits you.

As I write this chapter at the beginning of a new year (2019), my faltering words are a kind of pledge to live more intentionally in the economy of grace I have tried to describe. My task in the days I have left is to live gratefully and generously in the bounty of life's gifts, both the light and the dark, following in the footsteps of beloved mentors and friends, including the one called Christ. Offering myself in kindness to others where I can, I am seeking to prepare myself for a Time beyond time when I step from the shadows into the Light beyond all light, the Love beyond all love. I would like to be counted among those who, in the words of William Blake, are "put on earth a little space, / That we may learn to bear the beams of love." I have only little space left to me on this earth and, oh, so far yet to go.

Progress Report

Young
I pronounced you. Older
I still do, but seldomer
now, leaning far out
over an immense depth, letting
your name go and waiting,
somewhere between faith and doubt,
for the echoes of its arrival.
—R. S. Thomas, "Waiting"

Sometime in early 2018, when I was in the final stages of writing my story, I came across a poem by Anne Porter called "Music." The poet begins by asking why it is that, hearing the sounds of beautiful music, we sense "a shy yet solemn glory"? Perhaps, she suggests, we are hearing the echoes of a country where our souls were born, a lost native country whose fields and transparent streams we dimly remember. And perhaps we are vaguely recalling at the shining heart of that country the presence of a dearly beloved Someone:

> The One who waits for us
> Who will always wait for us
> In those radiant meadows

Yet also came to live with us
And wanders where we wander.

As I read these words, I felt I was looking at fragments of my life reflected back from the rippled surface of a lake. Images flashed to mind of moments when I, too, had felt that mysterious sorrow in the heart of beautiful music and, indeed, of every kind of beauty.

I thought of my young mother's voice sounding sweet and pure in the raw darkness of a winter morning. I could hear my father singing his songs of impossible hope beside the bed of his dying Olive, her dewy fresh-faced loveliness now forever gone. I could hear Vera Duncan's voice greeting us at our Crescent Road door with her symphony of laughter and good cheer. I could hear the adagios of Grieg's Piano Concerto wafting from Gerry Lee's battered record player in a long-ago grammar school music class. I could hear the slap of waves against the prow of a little white boat on the safe waters of Two Mile Bay. I could hear the songs we sang for Joe Kennedy as the tears ran down his craggy granite face. I could hear the music of light and the spoken word in a rag-tag production of *A Midsummer Night's Dream,* and in the lovely chants of the community of Taizé in the hills of Burgundy, where the chants and the silence seemed to bring back memories of my own lost native country.

Anne Porter's poem seemed to offer in summary the essence of my own soul's story. It seems that the central quest of my life had been to discover the source and significance of that mysterious sorrow. Could I interpret the shocks of beauty I had known in natural world—"the fields / Their fragrant windswept clover / the birdsongs in the orchards / the wild white violets in the moss / by the transparent streams"—as lingering echoes of things I had not yet seen? Could I hear them as whispers overheard from "some far-off / And half-forgotten country," a place to which I ultimately belong and for which my heart is bound like a migrating bird returning to its summer home. At some point in my life I had felt free to answer that question with the simple affirmation: Yes. I could.

That affirmation has made all the difference. At some level of my being, I felt a return to the sense of safety I had experienced in the floating shell of the little white boat on the lake. Just as my existence on this planet is as real as the table on which I write these words, wrapped in the crystal light of the coffee shop at the Nelson-Atkins Museum of Art, so it is, at the same time, a shadow—an intimation—of what is Ultimately Real. As I thought about the possible relationship of the real in time and the Real beyond time, I went back in memory to my first experience of falling in love.

I first saw her among a group of family friends picnicking on the beach at Taupo's Acacia Bay. It was the summer of 1957. I was fifteen, she perhaps a year older. One glance at her radiant young face, her blue eyes and golden hair, and I was lost to my accustomed self. My whole being came into focus around her and the sounds of the rest of the world—the roar of the motorboats, the hiss and thump of the waves, the laughter of children playing in the coarse grey sand—faded into the background, to the far reaches of my consciousness. From that moment on—for a year or more—I was obsessed with the image of this willowy creature who seemed to me the very flower of loveliness. I remember riding the train through her home town late one night, thinking how blessed was every house and every street to have been seen by her eyes and touched by her feet.

Yet in my shyness and insecurity, I never told her of my love. I wanted to tell every little star and every rippling brook—as Jerome Kern's popular song puts it—but I did not tell her. Ah! the pathetic irony of grieving for things we never had. One year after I first saw her on that sunny beach, I heard news that she given her heart away to someone else. Sadly, hopelessly, I had to let her go even though she had never been mine. To this day, whenever I pass through that small town in central New Zealand, or even hear its name, my heart jumps a little in my chest.

Here is my point: The exquisite agonies of that first summer love also brought faint intimations of another kind of love. It was a foretaste of the kind of love that would drop slowly into the very core of my identity and rest there through all the seasons of life, radiant summer, green spring, golden fall, and dark, cold winter. It was a foreshadowing of the kind of love that would find two souls together, touching, as they gaze into the innocent faces of their newborn sons or as they say their last goodbyes. The burning desire of that teenage boy was undoubtedly real, but it also contained within it an echo of something ultimately more real—the love of trusting companionship, the love of vows fulfilled and promises kept.

The experience of love, I have come to believe, is the existential foundation of every human life and is the indispensable starting point for recognizing the possibility of transcendence and the real existence of the inwardness we call the soul. Everyone, please God, has their own deep heart's home. Everyone, please God, has a primal sense of belonging that flows in part from our earliest childhood sense of trust in existence. Some have called it our "precious inwardness," "an inner radiance," or "the hidden beauty within." Abraham Heschel, whose wisdom I have long admired, calls it "something transcendent in disguise." We learn to recognize it through the sense of wonder—and safety—we feel in the presence of lovingkindness and beauty.

Do we, indeed, all of us, have the experience of being loved somewhere at the core of our being? Are there fragments of the Eternal buried in each life, no matter how bruised and stricken and in despair? Did my own younger siblings, gasping for air in their fragile bodies, still know at some level that something in them was eternal? Is it possible that at the heart of all our experiences of beauty lies a personal presence—"the longed-for beauty / Of the One who waits for us / Who will always wait for us / In those radiant meadows?" I choose to believe it is so.

It is no doubt difficult for some to accept this way of characterizing the presence of the Eternal within the boundaries of time and space. The identity of this "One who waits for us" is probably different in the experience of everyone who ever lived, but for reasons particular to my own story, that One is most purely reflected in the kind and compassionate Jesus who walked in leather sandals among the dusty hills of Palestine and who walks with us now, in memory and in every instance of kindness and beauty, as Christ the companionable beloved.

The story of my own inner life resembles, in its own stumbling way, that of Frederick Buechner as told in his memoir *Now and Then*. "Through a series of events from childhood on," he writes, "I was moved, for the most part without an inkling of it, closer to the Mystery out of which (religion) arose in the first place until, finally, the Mystery itself came to have a face for me, and the face it came to have for me was the face of Christ."

How was it that the face I saw in the world's beauty was that particular face? I can only say that it was in large part a gift bestowed by my serenely beautiful mother, by my courageously cheerful father, and—despite the unfortunate disguise in which it was presented—by the core affirmations of my religious culture of origin. It is true, as I said at the beginning of my story, that my youthful spirit was all but overwhelmed by the austerity and verbal excess of that culture, but it is also true that certain of its essential verities remained buried deep within me like seeds waiting for the warmth of the springtime sun.

One of my favorite things to do as a child was to dig up potatoes in the family garden. I saw it as an adventure akin to hunting for Easter eggs. While my dad preferred to dig his lovingly tended harvest for himself—as well as selecting his own prize beefsteak tomatoes—he sometimes let me do it.

Under his watchful eye, I'd press deep into the dark, mounded earth, both feet on the shoulders of the gardening fork, and, with a strong push on the handle, lever out a heavy tangle of dirt, green-brown stalks, stringy white roots, and little nuggets of potato gold. Holding the stalks, I'd shake the tangle until the sweet fresh tubers, some of them still heavy with moist loam, tumbled free to be gathered up in a tin bucket, or "billy." One dig might yield a disappointing potato or two or maybe nothing at all, the next a satisfying multitude—six, or eight, or even ten. I would count them as if they were treasures of incomparable worth. With my mouth watering at the prospect of fresh boiled potatoes smothered in butter, I would set aside the tangle of earth and stalks and roots, once the wormy nexus of engendering, and take my small harvest indoors.

The rediscovery of the usefulness of my inherited religious tradition was a bit like forking up those potatoes. It was the end result of a lifetime of search, sometimes disappointing and depressing, sometimes liberating, yielding secrets that set my spirit soaring. I spent many hours digging up the tangled mass of my heritage—including of course my own inevitably childish misapprehensions of it—and shaking it until its life-giving nuggets fell free and I could take them into the vessel of my heart. Sometimes the only way to get what I was searching for was to turn my family's religion upside-down, to cast off what was no longer essential, and claim the very gifts for which the garden had been planted in the first place.

And so, by a process of turning over and shaking out, nudged along by wise intuitions from poets and contemplatives, I was able to lay open what was essential for my own life. I began to discern the deeper callings that lay implicit in my early experience of transcendence and was able to take a whole new look at the religious story I had heard, essentially without comprehension, in my childhood years.

With the perspective of the years, I can now see that the religion of my childhood offered me a story that gave meaning and context to the intuitions of the Eternal I had already, in some sense, "known."

My astonishment at the dance of the clouds in the sky had nurtured in me a readiness to hear the story of the Eternal coming near in the child of Bethlehem.

My amazement at the cockabullies in the glittering stillness of the lake had prepared my heart for the story of Divine love present in the beauties of creation.

The sense of safety I had felt in the little white boat had prepared my heart to choose the safety I could find in the story of One who even in the anguish of his suffering knew he was not alone.

The serene tenderness of my mother's love had prepared me to accept the possibility of a God of supremely tender love.

The persistence of song in my father's breaking heart had made it possible for me to finally accept the astounding story of resurrection, of life reawakening with sweet surprise, as Robert Shaw put it, like the seed of a flower blossoming into life out of the moist darkness of the earth.

The choice I made to rest in such improbable certainties was made in the freedom of my imagination and accordance with the intuitions of my heart. I made it not by turning my face from the abyss of suffering but from out of its very depths. I have chosen Joy, as Wendell Berry once wrote, "even though I have considered all the facts."

Whether I find myself in valleys of darkness or on the ridges of light, I have learned it is best for me to come back to the quiet inner place of trust where, at the deepest level of being, I feel so deeply at home.

To feel at home in the psychological sense is to feel anchored in a place of welcome no matter where I am in the world. I feel that sense of welcome in the presence of the loving people in my life: caring family, faithful friends, and kindly neighbors. I think especially of how it feels to spend a quiet evening with my earthly beloved, Jennifer, the one I married in Greensboro, North Carolina, the best part of five decades ago.

It will soon be Jennifer's birthday. For a couple of hours, I have stepped away from our Tudoresque stucco cottage in Westwood Hills into the cozy surrounds of the Roasterie Coffee shop in Westwood, Kansas, to add a few lines to my story. As I sit here, wrestling with words, happily distracted by people coming and going, I feel a merciful contentment in knowing that my beloved waits for me. She may not be in the house at the moment of my arrival, but years of faithful love have taught me that wherever I am, she is waiting. For me.

And in our quiet evenings together, the house is alive with her presence. We talk some, but not a lot, responding rather to intuitions and subliminal cues, exchanging wordless glances and touches, reaching consensus over many things through a kind of harmonic convergence rather than a complex exchange of spoken words. The rest is silence. It's a silence, though, that has a richness to it, a fullness comprised of a thousand shared memories and uncounted acts of forgiveness.

It was that kind of love I had in mind when, to my surpassing joy, I presided over the wedding ceremony of my elder son Barclay and his beloved Ali. Joining with Ali's parents, Alan and Linda Ebright, Jennifer and I offered these words as a benediction upon them as we stood together—now a wider, more fulsome family—within the great hall of Kansas City's Union Station: "What greater thing is there for two human souls than to feel they are joined for life—to strengthen each in all labor, to rest on each other in all sorrow, to minister to each other in

all pain, to be one with the other in silent, unspeakable moments—at
the moment of new birth and at the moment of last parting?" In that
particular instance, I could indeed think of nothing greater. Except to
add this: that as beautiful Alison Ebright became Alison Martin, I could
not help but imagine another equally radiant young woman, also named
Alison Martin—the one who'd been taken from us so long ago—
slipping in beside us. It was as if our own little Ali, wholly restored
in body and mind, had broken gently back to us through the mists
of time.

*Barclay and
Ali's wedding,
June 2017*

Why should not such thoughts arise when I think of my relationship
with the Eternal Beloved? Why should I not find rest in the thought
that the One who loved all Creation into life, and sustains my very
existence even now, is waiting for me in the secret chambers of my heart?

Why should I not find in the presence of natural things—the
faithfulness of the rising sun and the beauty of still waters—a reassuring
reminder of the faithfulness and beauty of the One who made them all
and who wanders where I wander?

Why should I not find comfort in the thought that sometimes new
life bursts in beauty out of the old?

To accept such things as true for me requires, of course, that I choose to believe in a miracle—and probably more than one. But as a mortal creature faced with the vast unknowns beyond time and space, surrounded on all sides by the inexplicable mystery of life and presented daily—especially as I get older—with thudding inevitability of death, what better choice do I have?

The immortal part of me craves rescue from the limitations of mere physical existence and most deeply desires rescue from the abyss. For that reason, nothing short of a miracle will do. In the following lines, W. H. Auden speaks for me and, I think, for many of us who live for the time being within the boundaries of a finite number of days, a fixed number of beats of our flickering hearts:

> How could the Eternal do a temporal act,
> The Infinite become a finite fact?
> Nothing can save us that is possible.
> We who must die demand a miracle.

Since, as Auden says, nothing can save us that is possible, we must find our ultimate destiny in what is not. Our religions are the stories of the miracles that save us. The story of the One spoken of in the gospels is all miracle, from his arrival our planet as the embodiment of the Creator, to his life of sacrificial compassion, to his coming back to fresh new life after death, which is the most unthinkable—yet necessary—miracle of them all. I have chosen to believe that story as true even though, as Wendell Berry once wrote, "I have considered all the facts." This is not to say I considered all the facts that were possible for me to know, but rather all the facts that were given to me to know.

I have tried to live my days in the light of the glories of immortal being that I have glimpsed from time to time, following as nearly as

I can the example of the infinitely loving One whose home is both heaven and earth. I have failed in this more than I have succeeded, but the journey has been an exhilarating one and I offer these reflections as a way of expressing my gratitude to all those who have accompanied me along the way.

In memory, I can still see myself as a kid floating in the safety of the little white boat. I see a time when I drifted in stillness on the glassy surface of the lake, the beauty around me mirrored in a Beauty within. I see a time when the waters seemed to rise up against me and, even with my brave little brother alongside, I felt vulnerable and afraid. I see a time when a great launch, regal in its trim of polished wood and brass, slowed down its heavy engines and smoothed the angry waves before me. And, as I follow in the wake of this Majestic Apparition, I see—even now—the sun-drenched shores of Home glowing on the farther shore.

Selected Writings that Helped

Beckett, Samuel. *Waiting for Godot* (1955).

Berry, Thomas. *The Great Work* (1999).

Berry, Wendell. *Collected Poems* 1957-1982, *Re-collected Essays* (1965-1980).

Buber, Martin. *The Way of Man* (1966), *Now and Then* (1983), *The Knowledge of Man* (1988).

Buechner, Frederick. *Sacred Journey* (1991).

de Botton, Alain. *How Proust Can Change Your Life* (1998), *Status Anxiety* (2005).

Edson, Margaret. *Wit* (1999).

Fraser, George MacDonald. *The Steel Bonnets* (2001).

Hendra, Tony. *Father Joe* (2005).

Herbert, George. *The Works of George Herbert* (1994).

Heschel, Abraham. *I Asked for Wonder* (1983), *Man is Not Alone* (1951).

Jerome, Jerome K. *Three Men in a Boat* (1889).

Karr, Mary. *Sinners Welcome: Poems* (2006), *Lit* (2009).

Kazantzakis, Nikos. *Zorba the Greek* (1965).

Keillor, Garrison. *Good Poems* (2002), which includes quoted poems by Jane Kenyon, Wendell Berry, Howard Moss, Robert Hayden, Thomas Lux, William Stafford, Mary Oliver, Sheena Pugh, Denise Levertov, and Richard Jones.

Lewis, C. S. "The Weight of Glory" in *Screwtape Proposes a Toast* (1965), *The Great Divorce* (1976).

Merton, Thomas. *New Seeds of Contemplation* (1972).

Miller, Arthur. *Death of a Salesman* (1949).

Mitchell, Stephen. *A Book of Psalms* (1993).

Nelson, Gertrud Mueller. *To Dance with God* (1986).

Nicholson, William. *Shadowlands* (1993).

Nouwen, Henri. *Reaching Out: The Three Movements of the Spiritual Life* (1975).

O'Donohue, John. *Anam Cara* (1997).

Oliver, Mary. *New and Selected Poems* (2004).

Porter, Anne. *Living Things* (2006).

Shaw, Robert (trans. libretto) *Haydn: The Creation* (1992)

Steindl-Rast, David. *Gratefulness: The Heart of Prayer* (1984).

Thomas, R. S. *Collected Poems: 1945-1990.*

Tolstoy, Leo. *Resurrection* (1966).

Vanier, Jean. *Becoming Human* (2008).

Wilder, Thornton. *Our Town* (1938).

Williams, Tennessee. *The Glass Menagerie* (1944).

Acknowledgements

Many thanks to my readers and memory consultants: Cecile Alexander, John Alexander, Phil Butin, Jason Chen, Mark Clark, David Howard, Tom Magstadt, Grant Mallett, Barclay Martin, Doozie Martin, Jennifer Martin, Ian Martin, Warwick Martin, Chad Milton, Rosemary Helen Reece Morgan, Ann Nelson, George Pagels, Reid Peryam, Michael Price, Elizabeth Rackley, Harris Rayl, Harvey Rees-Thomas, Gary Ripple, David Austin Sawyer, Margaret Thomas, and Ondra Williams. Thanks, too, to my editorial and publishing consultant, Lucas Wetzel, who believed in the value of what I was doing from the start and devoted many valuable hours to helping me bring the project to completion. To Kevin Kotur, for his helpful editorial suggestions and keen eye in proofreading and fact-checking the text. And to Spencer Williams for his skill and expertise in designing this book.

I am deeply grateful to them all.

torment of income disparity

Cover painting by Brian Cameron

Printed in the United States of America
Shady Orchard Press
Westwood Hills, Kansas

ISBN: 978-0-578-91731-3